ADVANCED

WordPerfect®:
FEATURES & TECHNIQUES

Version 4.2

Eric Alderman
and
Lawrence J. Magid

Osborne **McGraw-Hill**
Berkeley, California

Osborne **McGraw-Hill**
2600 Tenth Street
Berkeley, California 94710
U.S.A.

For information on translations and book distributors outside of the U.S.A.,
write to Osborne **McGraw-Hill** at the above address.

A complete list of trademarks appears on page 311.

ADVANCED WORDPERFECT®: FEATURES & TECHNIQUES

234567890   DODO   8987

ISBN 0-07-881271-2

To Rachelle, my love and inspiration
—*E.A.*

To Patti & Katherine, for their love and patience
—*L.M.*

CONTENTS

ACKNOWLEDGMENTS

Although many people contributed to this project, no one deserves more credit than Gail Todd, our technical editor. Her guidance and assistance helped immeasurably, providing needed organization and clarity.

Also, we want to thank Jeff Acerson and Layne Cannon of WordPerfect Corporation for keeping us up to date and accurate.

In addition to thanking those who helped us as a team, we each would like to express our gratitude:

To Arthur Naiman, for being an invaluable, accessible veteran.

To David Barry, John Boeschen, and Paul Hoffman, for sage advice at the beginning of this long process.

To Steve Michel and Dale Coleman, for advice and encouragement throughout.

To the many people who purchased WordPerfect from ComputerLand of Albany while I was technical support manager there — my unwitting instructors during a three-year WordPerfect training session.

Lastly, to Rachelle DeStephens, who provided (and continues to provide) stability, comfort, and undying encouragement. Her example of strength, perseverance, and chutzpah has helped me reach for opportunities that may otherwise have passed me by.

Eric Alderman
Berkeley, California

To Peter Ivory of the Magus Design Group, for first convincing me to try WordPerfect.

To my colleagues at Know How, for helping to define what computer learning is all about and for putting up with my idiosyncracies.

To Martha Groves, Martin Baron, John Lawrence, and others at the *Los Angles Times,* for providing a forum where I could voice my reactions to WordPerfect and other programs.

To Burt Alperson, who, despite his undying loyalty to Microsoft Word, helped me through some of the more interesting challenges that found their way into macros and other tips in the book.

To my wife, Patti, and my daughter, Katherine, for their patience, understanding, and companionship.

And finally, to Andrew Fluegelman (1943-1985), my friend and collaborator, who helped teach me the meaning of excellence.

Lawrence J. Magid
San Francisco, California

INTRODUCTION

This book is meant primarily for the WordPerfect user who, after using the program's basic functions for some period of time, has decided to explore some of its more advanced ones. While the book's main emphasis is on WordPerfect's macro programming ability and merge facility, the book discusses each of the program's "high-powered" functions.

If you have just purchased WordPerfect, the first thing you should read is Appendix A, "Installation." In fact, even if you are already using the program, you might still read through this appendix to learn the best way to install the program to meet your own needs.

After you have properly installed WordPerfect for your system, you should consider going through the TUTOR program provided with WordPerfect. This book is intended for those who have used WordPerfect for some period of time or who are already somewhat computer literate. The tutorial, on the other hand, is especially helpful for those new to computers in general.

Another source of information is available with WordPerfect's Help key (F3), which leads you to the program's Help screens. If you need more help with a particular subject, refer to the appropriate section in Chapter 1, "Basics Refresher." While this chapter does not cover all of WordPerfect's basic functions, it does give a detailed description of the most important ones. It also provides some general rules and guidelines that every WordPerfect user should follow.

At the end of the book is a chapter entitled "Macro Library." This chapter contains over 20 complete, documented macro applications in such areas as document translation and office automation. One of the most important things it will teach you is how a complete macro application is constructed—for example, how several macros can be used in conjunction to form a macro routine.

Before you use the applications found in "Macro Library," you should understand the general process of naming, defining, and invoking a macro. If you need help, refer to Chapter 2, "Macros." The advanced concepts described there (such as the Pause for Input function, looping, and branching) are put into practice in the "Macro Library."

If you plan to use macros with even moderate frequency, consider purchasing the WordPerfect Library, from the makers of WordPerfect (see Appendix D, "WordPerfect Library"). This package contains, among other useful programs, a macro editing program called M-Edit. Without this program, creating long macros can be tedious, and editing (changing) them *in any way* is simply impossible. For short, simple macros, this limitation does not normally cause a problem since you could quickly reenter the steps of the macro that you wanted to modify. However, for creating and editing more complex macros like the ones listed in "Macro Library," M-Edit is invaluable.

WordPerfect has been a unique product in that it has attracted both beginners and advanced users. While not overwhelming for the first-time user, it has provided an ever-increasing number of professional features. These features remain in the background until needed—this book will help you lure them into the open.

NOTATIONAL CONVENTIONS

The following conventions are used throughout this book:

	Example
User input is shown in **boldface**	Type **letter.mac**
WordPerfect keys (which are identified on the keyboard template) are enclosed in <angle brackets>	Press the <Bold> key
Standard PC keys are shown in SMALL UPPERCASE LETTERS	TAB
Keys that are struck together (you hold down the first and then press the second) are separated by a plus sign	CTRL+ENTER
Keys that are pressed in succession are separated by a comma	HOME, HOME, UP ARROW
WordPerfect keys are followed by the keys you actually press the first time they are mentioned in a section	Press the <Center> key (SHFT+F6)

The SHIFT key is indicated by SHFT, the CONTROL key by CTRL, and the ALT key by ALT.

WORDPERFECT RELEASES

WordPerfect Corporation releases updates to WordPerfect every few months. These updates fix problems with previous releases and sometimes add minor features. Each is identified by the date it was released. To determine the release date of your copy of WordPerfect, start the program and then press the <Help> key (F3). In the upper right-hand corner of the screen will be the release date.

This book is as accurate as possible through the 11/18/86 release of Version 4.2.

ORDERING A DISK

To receive a disk containing all of the macro routines found in Chapter 10, "Macro Library," several merge examples, the Macro Menu Generation Routine that creates menus like the one in Chapter 3, the Automatic Document Reload procedure described in Appendix C, and other useful WordPerfect tidbits, send a check for $19.95 to

Alderman/Magid
48 Shattuck Square, Suite 13
Berkeley, CA 94704-1140

You can also use the order form at the end of the book.

Disk Order Form

You can order a disk that contains all of the macros, procedures, and BASIC programs found in this book. The disk contains:

1. **All macros listed in Chapter 10, "Macro Library"**
   Each of these macros can be used immediately as-is, or customized using M-Edit, Satellite Software's macro editing program. The "Making WordPerfect Like WordStar" key macros are also included for both ProKey and DesqView.

2. **The macro menu system in Chapter 3, "Merge"**
   An example of a macro menu system (like the one shown in Chapter 3), along with on-disk documentation.

3. **The Automatic Document Reload procedure in Appendix C**
   Both the BASIC program WPRUN.BAS and the required batch file WPRUN.BAT.

4. **Primary Merge document examples**
   A variety of Merge document examples for letters, labels, and reports.

5. **The Line Feed Strip program in Chapter 8, "Integration With Other Products"**
   The Line Feed Strip BASIC program listed in the "Dealing With ASCII Files" section of Chapter 8. This program removes line feeds from a Text file so that it can be edited on a system like the Apple Macintosh.

To receive the disk, complete this form, and send it with a check for $19.95 to:

Alderman/Magid
48 Shattuck Square, Suite 13
Berkeley, CA 94704-1140

WordPerfect Disk Order Form

Name: _____

Street: _____

City: _____

State: _____ Zip: _____

1 BASICS REFRESHER

This book is a guide to WordPerfect's advanced features, most notably macros and merging. However, Chapter 1 will provide a refresher for those familiar with the product as well as an accelerated tutorial for experienced computer users who are new to WordPerfect.

This chapter is not meant to be used as an introductory tutorial on WordPerfect. If you are new to computers, work through the TUTOR program included with the program. This self-paced tutorial takes a basic, step-by-step approach to learning WordPerfect.

Throughout the remaining chapters of this book, we will assume that you have mastered the basic editing skills discussed in this chapter. If you are currently a WordPerfect user, reading this chapter may help you to understand some aspects and basic concepts of the program that you have overlooked. In this chapter, as well as throughout the rest of the book, we have included references to Chapter 10, "Macro Library," where you can find out how macros can make many tasks simpler.

THE EVOLUTION

In the beginning there was the cursor. Soon there were columns and rows, letters and symbols. Then menus and prompts appeared, followed closely by hidden codes and keyboard templates. In the end, there were macros and merge, columns and math, indexes and tables of contents.

As the program has evolved, many of its features have been improved with added capability and increased speed. There have also been a dramatic number of features added to the program since its birth. Its most basic editing concepts, however, have remained the same — a tribute to their popularity.

THE CONCEPTS

The key to fully mastering WordPerfect lies neither in memorizing the location of the function keys nor in trying to learn what they all do. Rather, mastery requires an understanding of the three basic concepts that underlie the program's operation. If you learn WordPerfect with these concepts in mind, you will ultimately have both an appreciation of the program's power and the ability to use this power efficiently.

The "Clean Screen" Concept

As a modern writer, you recognize the benefits of using a word processing program. You are prepared to dive headlong into the world of *block moves* and *line formats*. You accept that you will be spending some time operating the word processing program instead of actually writing.

But when the time comes to put thought to screen, what do you want to be looking at? Do you want a cluttered screen with a program menu at the top? Do you want control characters and other unintelligible squiggles intermixed with your text? Do you want two-letter codes indicating an indented paragraph or a change in line spacing? Or would you rather see *your writing*—underlines where you have underlined, emphasis where you have emphasized, and indents where you have chosen to indent?

WordPerfect provides a "Clean Screen": only the text you enter is displayed, with a single line of document information at the bottom. Some formatting commands, such as boldfacing and margin changes, are immediately reflected on the screen. Others, such as page formatting and printer controls, are inserted with a *hidden code* that you can't see unless you need to.

The result is a pleasant environment for writing, one that shows only what you want to see: your words.

The "Unnamed Document" Concept

When you start WordPerfect you are presented with a blank editing screen. From this screen you enter new text or retrieve any document and then save the document with any name. This flexibility, which means that you are not "locked in" to any one file name as you are with many other programs, provides a number of advantages.

Saving (or Not) After Editing

Every WordPerfect document that you create will be saved on disk under a *file name*. However, when you begin writing a document, you don't always know what its file name should be. WordPerfect allows you first to write your document and then to name it when you save it. That way you don't have to think of a name before the document is written.

There will also be times when you want to create a document that will never be saved. For example, if you are writing a quick personal letter or memo, you will probably want to print the document without saving it to disk. With WordPerfect, you can just clear the screen when you're through printing, and you'll be ready for the next document.

A Document by Any Other Name

In WordPerfect, you can save a document with any name, at any time. You might want to use this ability to maintain some standard documents or formats. For example, you could retrieve a document as a standard form, fill it in appropriately, and then save it with a different name. Or you might be modifying a document when you realize that you want to keep the original version intact. You can save the revised version with a different file name. Both of these tasks require lengthy procedures with many other word processing programs.

Clearing and Retrieving

When you retrieve a document in WordPerfect, it appears on the screen at the current cursor position. If the screen is clear, this is of no consequence. If, however, you are already editing a document, the text of the retrieved file will be inserted in the text of the current file, at the current cursor position.

This can initially cause confusion, especially if you are used to programs like WordStar or Lotus 1-2-3, which automatically clear the screen when a new file is loaded. With a little practice, however, you will learn to use this handy WordPerfect feature to combine documents easily. If you forget that documents are *combined* when the screen isn't cleared before retrieving a file, your documents will seem to be mysteriously increasing in size. Therefore, if you do not mean to combine two documents when you retrieve a new one, always remember to *clear the screen* first.

To clear the screen, press the <Exit> key (F7), type **N** for "No Save" or **Y** for "Yes Save" (whichever is appropriate), and then type **N** for "No Don't Exit WordPerfect."

The "Hidden Codes" Concept

When you use one of the WordPerfect function keys to modify your text in some way, or when you press either the TAB or the ENTER key, the program automatically inserts a hidden code in your text. To see these hidden codes, you press the <Reveal Codes> key (ALT+F3). The lower half of the screen is then altered to display your text intermixed with strange abbreviations that represent all of the various codes that were previously invisible.

If you are a first-time WordPerfect user, this can be a frightening experience, but don't let it scare you away. Once you understand what is going on, you will see why it is important to use the <Reveal Codes> key frequently.

For many of the formatting features, the code specifies a particular style that will remain in effect until another such code is entered. For instance, when you use the <Line Format> key (SHFT+F8) to change your margins to 20 left and 54 right, the program inserts a code that looks like this:

```
[Margin Set:20,54]
```

Why don't you see that information on your screen? The reason is that it is a *hidden code,* so it is visible only when you use the <Reveal Codes> key. These margins will remain in effect until you make another margin change.

It's important to keep in mind that every time you make a format change, another hidden code is generated. If, for instance, you indecisively change the margins four times in a row before you start to type, four codes are generated in succession. The first three are superfluous, since only the last will actually affect any text. It is important to use Reveal Codes to delete unnecessary codes. A document with unnecessary codes is a messy document.

The Reveal Codes function is discussed in more detail later in this chapter.

THE CARDINAL RULES

There are three cardinal rules that you should always keep in mind when using WordPerfect. They are

- *Always exit WordPerfect with the* <*Exit*> *key (F7) before turning off the computer or restarting it with the CTRL+ALT+DEL key sequence.* After exiting, you should see the DOS prompt, which is usually A>, B>, or C>.

- *Always make sure the screen is clear before retrieving a new document.* To clear the screen press the <Exit> key, and then type **Y** to save the current document if you haven't yet done so or type **N** if you don't want to save it. Then answer **N** to the prompt "Exit WP (Y/N)?" and the screen will clear.

- *If the printer doesn't print when you tell it to, don't tell it to print again.* There is most likely some problem that needs to be corrected. Refer to the section on maintaining the print queue in this chapter.

USING HELP

Software companies expend a lot of energy (and spend a lot of money) designing and building comprehensive on-line Help facilities for their programs. Manuals and books are good ways to learn about a product since they can go into depth about its various features, but they can never be as convenient as a good Help facility for jogging the memory. Many people, though, use a program's Help facility only occasionally or not at all. Instead they riffle through a book, trying to find the right chapter, or they just give up and call the local computer store.

WordPerfect's Help has been continually expanded and improved since the program's introduction. Although not what is classically considered "context-sensitive" (that is, the program knows what you are trying to do when you ask for help), it is nonetheless an excellent Help system. Every WordPerfect user should use Help.

To use the Help system, press the <Help> key (F3) anytime WordPerfect is displaying the normal document editing screen. If you are using a floppy-based computer system, you may have to insert the Learning Disk in one of the disk drives and then tell WordPerfect where to find the Help file by pressing the drive letter. (See Appendix A, "Installation," for a discussion on disk swapping.) When you press the <Help> key, you will see a message explaining how to use the Help function.

CURSOR CONTROL

WordPerfect has many commands that let you move the cursor around the screen and through your document. It can be overwhelming to look at a complete list of them. However, you should learn the most important ones as soon as possible, since they will probably be the most used of WordPerfect's functions. No matter which of the program's features you intend to use, you will *always* need to use the cursor positioning controls to move quickly through your text.

Rigidity or Freedom?

There are essentially two types of word processing programs: *rigid* and *free-form*. Rigid programs limit movement of the cursor to areas that already contain text. Free-form programs allow the cursor to be positioned anywhere on the screen.

WordPerfect is a rigid program. It will only allow you to move the cursor to a part of the screen containing text, spaces, tabs, or other text positioning codes. As you move the cursor through your text (as described in the following sections), you will see the cursor jump to the end of a short line, rather than move out into the "void."

If you want a centered title in the middle of a blank screen, you must generate the correct codes to get there. You cannot simply move the cursor to where you want the title to appear and start typing. You have to press the ENTER key several times to move to the middle of the screen and then press the <Center> key to move to the center of the line.

Short Trips

The four arrow keys on the keyboard generally move the cursor one character or line in the direction shown by the arrow. If the cursor jumps to a different column position when you move it to a short or blank line, it will return to its original column position when you move onto a line that is long enough.

When used in combination with the CTRL key, the RIGHT ARROW and LEFT ARROW keys move the cursor by whole words instead of by individual characters. This is a useful way to move quickly through a line.

The gray − (minus) key on the far right side of the IBM keyboard is the <Screen Up> key, and the gray + (plus) key is the <Screen Down> key. These keys position the cursor at the top or bottom of the screen the first time they're pressed, and then they scroll the text in screenfuls (24 lines at a time). This is the best way to scroll the document when you want to read the text on the screen.

The HOME key serves many purposes, but only in combination with other keys. By itself, it does nothing. Pressing the HOME key once puts WordPerfect into a "Short Cursor Trip" mode. The next key that you press determines where the cursor will go. After you press HOME,

- The LEFT ARROW key moves the cursor to the beginning of the line, or if you're using wide margins, to the left edge of the screen.

- The RIGHT ARROW key moves the cursor to the end of the line, or if you're using wide margins, to the right edge of the screen. (If you're using normal margins, pressing the END key performs the same function as pressing the HOME, RIGHT ARROW key sequence.)

- The UP ARROW and DOWN ARROW keys move the cursor to the top and bottom of the screen, respectively. (Pressing the <Screen Up> or <Screen Down> keys performs the same function as the HOME, UP ARROW or HOME, DOWN ARROW key sequence.)

Long-Distance Trips

While the <Screen Up> and <Screen Down> keys move the cursor by *screenfuls,* the PGUP and PGDN keys move by *pagefuls.* PGDN moves the cursor to the top of the following page, and PGUP moves it to the top of the previous page. This is a good method of scrolling when you want to move in bigger jumps than a screenful at a time.

Pressing the HOME key twice puts WordPerfect into a "Long-Distance Trip" mode. Pressing the UP ARROW key next moves the cursor to the top of the document; the DOWN ARROW key moves it to the bottom of the document.

The CTRL+HOME key sequence performs the "Goto" command. As with the HOME key, the action this sequence initiates depends on the next key you press, as follows:

- To move to a particular page, press <Goto> (CTRL+HOME), type the page number, and press ENTER.

- To move the cursor to wherever it was before the last cursor movement command, press the <Goto>,<Goto> key sequence (CTRL+HOME, CTRL+HOME).

This sequence is convenient when you are cutting or copying blocks of text. For example, let's say you are somewhere in the middle of a document and you want to copy a paragraph to page 23. After copying it, doing a <Goto> page 23, and pasting the text, you can use the <Goto>, <Goto> sequence to return the cursor to its original position.

- To position the cursor at the beginning of your most recent block (even if the block is no longer highlighted), press the <Goto> key (CTRL+HOME) followed by the <Block> key (ALT+F4).

This sequence is useful if you want to perform more than one procedure on the same block of text. Since most of WordPerfect's block commands automatically turn Block mode off, the text will no longer be highlighted. To rehighlight a block after issuing a block command, press the <Block> key, followed by the <Goto>,<Block> sequence.

TEXT EDITING

WordPerfect's basic editing procedures are very simple. When you see the program's "Clean Screen," you simply begin typing. The program will wrap your text at the default right margin. You end paragraphs by pressing the ENTER key. You can also generate blank lines with the ENTER key.

The key marked INS on the numeric keypad toggles WordPerfect between two modes, Typeover and Insert. In Typeover mode, letters typed on the keyboard replace letters at the cursor position. At the bottom left of the screen will be this message

Typeover

In Insert mode, no message is shown. Letters typed on the keyboard are inserted at the cursor position, and all characters to the right of the cursor are pushed to the right to make room.

When you reach the end of a page, WordPerfect inserts a Soft Page Break (displayed as a row of dashes across the screen). If you wish to start a new page before you have reached the bottom of the current one, press the Hard Page Break key (CTRL+ENTER). The Hard Page Break is displayed as a row of equal signs across the screen.

Marking a Block

Various sections in this book discuss the Block command, which designates a section of text for a particular purpose. WordPerfect can perform about 20 different functions on a block of text, including underlining, spell checking, and deleting. To see a complete list of these functions, press the <Help> key (F3) and then the <Block> key (ALT+F4).

To mark a section of text as a block, position the cursor on the first letter you wish to include in the block and press the <Block> key (ALT+F4). The message

Block on

will begin flashing on the screen. Use any of WordPerfect's cursor positioning commands to move to the character *following* the last character you want included in the block. The blocked text will appear highlighted (shown in reverse video).

If you type any single character while defining a block, the cursor will move forward to the next occurrence of that character (within the next 2000 characters). By pressing the ENTER key or a period, you can define a paragraph or sentence as a block. The Search function will move the cursor to the next occurrence of any code or text in the document.

You can also define a block by starting with the cursor positioned *after* the last character to be included in the block and moving it backward in the text *onto* the first character.

While the text you want is highlighted and the "Block on" message is flashing, you can perform any block action.

Deleting Text

There are several methods of deleting text in WordPerfect. The method you choose depends on how much text you want to delete. Some of the major deletion commands will ask for confirmation ("Are you really sure you want to erase all this work?") before actually performing the command. Even after you confirm the deletion of the text, however, you can still bring it back to life with the Undelete function discussed later in this chapter.

Deleting Small Amounts of Text

The two keys used to delete characters one at a time are

DEL   This key is usually located at the bottom of the numeric keypad on the right side of the keyboard. It deletes a single character *at the cursor position* and moves the following text left to close up the space.

BACKSPACE   This key is usually above the ENTER key and is marked with a left arrow. It deletes a single character *to the left of the cursor position* and moves the following text to the left to fill in the space.

Deleting Larger Amounts of Text

There are four key sequences for deleting larger amounts of text:

<**Delete Word**> (CTRL+BACKSPACE)   This key sequence deletes the word at the current cursor location. You can place the cursor anywhere within, or on the space following, the word. After the word is deleted, the cursor is positioned at the first letter of the following word, making it convenient to delete several words *forward*, in succession.

<**Delete Word Left**> (HOME, BACKSPACE)   This key sequence deletes the word that *precedes* the word at the current cursor location. (If the cursor is positioned in the middle of a word when you first press the key sequence, WordPerfect will delete the letters in the word that precede the cursor.) You can use this key sequence to delete several words *backward*, in succession.

<**Delete EOL**> (CTRL+END)   This key sequence deletes all text from

the cursor position to the end of the current line. If the line ends with a Soft Return (a return automatically generated by WordPerfect when the cursor reaches the right margin), text from the following line is brought up to the cursor position. In this way, you can delete several lines of a paragraph in succession.

<Delete EOP> (CTRL+PGDN)   This key sequence deletes all of the text from the cursor position to the end of the current page. The command will ask for confirmation before deleting the text.

Deleting Sentences, Paragraphs, And Pages

You can delete a single sentence, paragraph, or page by using the Move function. To do this, position the cursor anywhere within the sentence, paragraph, or page, and press the <Move> key (CTRL+F4). Type **1** to select a sentence, **2** for a paragraph, or **3** for a page. Then type **3** to delete the selected text.

Using the Block Function To Delete Text

You can also use the Block function to delete text. To do so, use the steps outlined earlier to define the block, and while the "Block on" message is flashing, press the DEL or BACKSPACE key. WordPerfect will ask for confirmation before deleting the text.

Cutting, Copying, and Pasting

To move text from one place in WordPerfect to another, you use the Move function. When you *cut* or *copy* text, it is placed in a buffer (a holding area) until you are ready to *retrieve* (paste) it somewhere else. The text can be retrieved anywhere in the current document, or in another document that you retrieve from disk. There is only one buffer, so each time you execute a Cut or Copy command, the previous buffer contents are automatically cleared. Both Cut and Copy place text *into* the buffer — the only difference between them is that Cut also deletes the text from its original position.

You can use the <Move> key with *block definition off* or with *block definition on*. The menu that appears at the bottom of the screen will differ, depending on which method you are using.

If you press the <Move> key but have not marked a block, you can only cut or copy a single sentence, paragraph, or page. As long as the cursor is positioned anywhere inside any of these units, the Move command will automatically highlight the amount of text you choose to move. You can then choose whether to cut or copy the text, which will be placed in the temporary buffer. (As discussed earlier, you can also choose to delete the selected text.)

By defining a block before pressing the <Move> key, you can move any amount of text, not just one sentence, paragraph, or page. First, mark the block as outlined earlier. Then, while the "Block on" message is flashing, press the <Move> key. A menu will appear at the bottom of the screen, allowing you to either cut or copy the text. After you choose one, the text is placed in the temporary buffer.

After cutting or copying the text, move the cursor to where you want to retrieve it. You can clear the screen and load a new document before retrieving, or use the <Switch> (SHFT+F3) key as described later in this chapter. In fact, you can just go on with your typing and retrieve the text whenever you're ready. The buffer will retain the moved text until you either perform another Move command or exit WordPerfect.

When you are ready to retrieve the text, press the <Move> key and choose **5**, "Retrieve Text." (You can also press the <Retrieve> key (SHFT+F10), and simply press ENTER when prompted for a filename.) The text will be placed at the cursor position.

Undeleting

WordPerfect has a unique, three-level Undelete function that lets you restore text deleted by mistake. Given all of the methods the program has for deleting text, it is inevitable that you will one day accidentally hit the wrong key sequence and delete some portion of text that you want to retain. At this point you will truly appreciate the Undelete feature. It allows you to edit documents quickly, since you don't need to worry about inadvertently deleting text.

No matter how much text you deleted, and no matter which method you used to delete it, you can always bring it back to life with Undelete.

WordPerfect will save up to three levels of deletion in separate buffers. The determining factor in what constitutes a deletion is *cursor movement*. If you delete four words in a row, they would all be considered one deletion. If you were then to move your cursor to the beginning of a line and execute the <Delete EOL> (CTRL+END) key sequence, the entire deleted line would be considered the second deletion. Move your cursor again, delete four characters, and you have the third deletion. If you were to make yet another deletion, the first deletion would be "pushed off the stack" to make room for the latest deletion.

To activate Undelete, press the <Cancel> key (F1) when there is nothing to cancel — in other words, when there are no menus or prompts visible and there is no other function taking place. The first time the key is pressed, the most recent deletion is inserted and highlighted at the cursor position. A menu gives you the choice of either restoring the displayed text or viewing the previous deletion. You can cycle through all three deletions before deciding to undelete one. (The UP ARROW and DOWN ARROW keys can also be used to cycle through the deletions.)

Press **1**, "Restore," to restore the deleted text. You can cancel the Undelete function by pressing <Cancel> a second time.

You can also use the Undelete function as a sort of "quick and dirty" cut and paste function. For example, you can easily delete three words, move the cursor to where you want the words to be pasted, and undelete them. This is frequently faster and more convenient than taking the time to mark a small amount of text as a block.

Text Embellishments

You can add emphasis to your text by adding underlining or boldfacing. There are two ways to do this.

If you have not yet typed the text, press the appropriate function key (F8 for underline or F6 for bold) once, type the text you want emphasized, and press the same key again to turn the emphasis off.

If the text already exists, mark it as a block using the block procedures discussed earlier and, while the "Block on" message is flashing, press the appropriate emphasis key.

WORKING WITH REVEAL CODES

Working with the <Reveal Codes> key (ALT+F3) can be traumatic for first-time users of WordPerfect. Suddenly, the nice "Clean Screen" turns into a mess of seemingly unintelligible abbreviations. Yet the use of the Reveal Codes function is such an important part of working successfully with WordPerfect that you must clear this cloud of confusion.

When you press the <Reveal Codes> key, you see a split screen as in Figure 1-1. The top portion of the screen displays your text as usual, and the bottom portion displays your text with its codes revealed. There are now two cursors on the screen: the normal one in the top portion of the screen, and another thicker one in the Reveal Codes section in the bottom portion of the screen.

You can move the cursors using all of the normal cursor movement commands; both will move simultaneously.

You can easily see where you made formatting changes in your text on the Reveal Codes screen. These changes are represented by bolded codes surrounded by square brackets. As you move your cursor past them, you will see that the cursor jumps from before a code to after it with just one press of an arrow key. This is because the program considers all the letters between each set of brackets to be a single code, although the code may be made up of many characters on the screen.

You cannot insert any text while in Reveal Codes, but you can delete text and codes with both the DEL and BACKSPACE keys. DEL deletes

Doc 1 Pg 1 Ln 1   Pos 10

Figure 1-1.   The Reveal Codes screen

characters and codes that are after the cursor, and BACKSPACE deletes characters and codes that are before the cursor.

While in Reveal Codes, you can see an [HRt] code wherever *you* pressed the ENTER key in your text. [HRt] is an abbreviation for Hard Return. When *WordPerfect* decides where a line should end (when it automatically wraps text to the next line), a Soft Return is inserted, which is indicated by an [SRt] code.

There are basically two types of hidden codes: those that are independent and those that are members of a Matched Pair.

Codes like margin, tab, and spacing changes are independent. They affect all text that follows them until another code of the same type is encountered. Figure 1-2 shows a Reveal Codes screen containing an independent code.

Codes for underlining and boldfacing are examples of Matched Pair codes. These typically use an uppercase letter to designate the beginning of the function and a lowercase letter to designate its end. For example, try pressing the <Underline> key, typing some text, pressing the <Underline> key again, and then pressing the <Reveal Codes> key. At the point in your text where you first pressed the <Underline> key, there appears a [U]; and where you pressed it again, there appears a [u]. Tab Align, Flush Right, Bold, and Center all generate Matched Pair codes.

To remove format choices like these from the text, simply remove the first of the Matched Pair; its match will be automatically deleted. (You

Figure 1-2. An independent hidden code

may need to exit Reveal Codes and press the <Reveal Codes> key again to see that the second matching code has been deleted.) Figure 1-3 shows a Reveal Codes screen containing Matched Pair hidden codes.

With either type of hidden code, it is easy to leave behind a trail of unneeded, potentially troublesome codes. You can see in the following example how this would be a bit of a mess:

`[U][B][u][b][U][B]This is bold and underlined.[b][u][HRt]`

In this case, the user was obviously confused and pressed the bold and underline keys too many times, generating a lot of unnecessary codes. These unnecessary codes should be deleted, even though the text may look fine. In fact, if the user had not pressed the <Reveal Codes> key, the codes might never have been discovered at all. Nevertheless, excess codes should always be found and deleted, since they make the Reveal Codes display much more confusing, and they may cause problems when you print the document.

Here is another example of unwanted codes:

`[Margin Set:10,74][Margin Set:12,56][Margin Set:8,50]Hello`

The user in this case was simply indecisive and tried several different margin settings before finding a satisfactory one. Since the Margin Set

Figure 1-3. Matched Pair hidden codes

code only affects text that follows it *until the next Margin Set code*, the first two settings do not affect any text at all and should be deleted.

Use Reveal Codes to help you position your cursor correctly before you issue a formatting command. For example, let's say you press HOME,HOME,UP to move to the top of your document, enter a Margin Set command, and then scroll down through your text to see how your new margins look. Then, deciding you want to change your margins, you again press HOME,HOME,UP and enter a new Margin Set. When you scroll through your text this time, your new margins are not affecting the text. Why? By using Reveal Codes, you would see that the second time you gave the command to go to the top of the document, you positioned the cursor *just before* the previous Margin Set command, so your new Margin Set command was immediately cancelled by your old one. You should have used Reveal Codes to position the cursor *after* the first Margin Set when you were ready to change the margins the second time. Once the margins were set the way you wanted them, you could go back with Reveal Codes to delete the unwanted Margin Set codes.

You can use the <Search> key (F2) or <Reverse Search> key (SHFT+F2) to find text or codes while in Reveal Codes. (The Search functions are described later in this chapter.) You can also mark a block while in Reveal Codes by pressing the <Block> key (ALT+F4). You will see the [Block] code, which temporarily marks the beginning of a block, appear at the cursor position. You can then position the cursor to the opposite end of the block.

Pressing any key besides the search keys, <Block>, DEL, BACK-SPACE, or the cursor movement controls returns you to the normal editing screen. (Pressing SPACE is a convenient way to exit the Reveal Codes screen.)

LINE FORMATTING

Tabs

When you first use WordPerfect, it uses a default tab setting with a tab stop every five characters. You can change the tab setting at any point in a document by using the Line Format menu. The [Tab Set:] code you generate affects all [TAB] codes that follow it—until the program encounters another [Tab Set:] code. By generating a new [Tab Set:] code before a section of the text that contains [TAB] codes, you can quickly adjust the position of the text.

To insert a new tab setting (define new tab stops), position the cursor at the place in your document where you want the new tabs to take effect. Then, press the <Line Format> key (SHFT+F8), and type **1** for "Tabs." At the bottom of the screen, you will see the Tab Setting area. The row of periods represents the first set of 80 characters across the line. As you move the cursor past the edges of the screen, the setting area will scroll left and right to allow you to set tab stops for wider margins.

Tab Stop Alignment

The four types of tab stops are left-aligned, right-aligned, decimal-aligned, and centered, which are represented in the Tab Setting area by the letters L, R, D, and C, respectively. Decimal-aligned tab stops actually align text to whatever is currently the align character, which normally is a decimal point. (See the "Align Tabs" section later in this chapter for a description of using decimal-aligned tab stops.)

Setting Tab Stops

The three ways to set tab stops are free-form, direct, and incremental.

With the free-form method, move the cursor using the RIGHT ARROW and LEFT ARROW keys to the desired position for the tab stop and type L, R, D, or C (in either lowercase or uppercase).

To enter tab stops with the direct method, type any number and press ENTER. The cursor will move to the specified position and insert a left-aligned tab stop. (If you do not want a left-aligned tab stop, you can press the appropriate letter right after the tab stop has been set to change its type.) You can enter as many tab stops in succession as you like.

Finally, the incremental method allows you to specify a starting tab position and an incremental value. Simply enter the two values separated by a comma. For example, entering **10,8** would place left-aligned tab stops at 10,18,26,34, and so on. To set incremental tab stops of a type other than left-aligned, manually insert a tab stop of the desired type at the starting point of the series and then enter the two values.

Using Tab Stops With Dot Leaders

You can make any of the tab stops (except center tab stops) use a "dot leader" by positioning the cursor onto any L, R, or D tab stop, and typing a period. When a tab stop uses a dot leader, the space before each tabbed item is filled with periods, rather than being left blank.

Deleting Tab Stops

To delete a tab stop in the Tab Setting area, position the cursor on the tab stop you want to delete and press the DEL key. You can also delete many tab stops at once by using the <Delete EOL> command (CTRL+END). This command will delete all of the tab stops to the right of the cursor.

Using Tabs

When you are through changing tab settings, press the <Exit> key (F7) to return to the document editing screen. To move the cursor to a tab stop while you are typing your text, press the TAB key. This key is usually positioned above the CTRL key on the left side of the keyboard and marked with two opposing arrows.

The precise hidden codes that are placed in the document when you press the TAB key depend on the type of the next defined tab stop. If it is a left-aligned tab stop, a [TAB] code is inserted. For right-aligned or decimal-aligned tab stops, a matched pair of [A] and [a] codes is inserted. (In the case of a decimal-aligned tab stop, these are the same codes that are inserted when you press the <Tab Align> key, as discussed in the next section.) For a centered tab stop, a [TAB] code and a matched pair of [C] and [c] codes are inserted.

To display a ruler at the bottom of the screen which displays your current tab settings, see the section titled "Windows" later in this chapter.

ALIGN TABS

Align tabs line up text at the occurrence of a particular character, rather than at the left edge, right edge, or center of the tabbed text. Align tabs are most frequently used to line up a column of numbers properly, but are flexible enough to be used for many different purposes.

You can use Align tabs in two ways. You can define a decimal-aligned tab stop using the steps outlined in the previous section, and then use the TAB key each time you want to use an Align Tab. Or, you can use the <Tab Align> key (CTRL+F6) to use an Align tab with any type of defined tab stop. The first method is better when you know you will be entering a significant amount of data, such as in a table. The second method is helpful when you only occasionally need to use an Align tab, or if you do not want to change your Tab Settings.

Whichever method you use, the program will display

```
Align Char = .
```

Enter the text to be aligned. All the characters you type will move to the *left* of the tab stop until you type a decimal point. Then the characters you type will start appearing to the right of the tab stop. For example, if you enter **1,298.79**, the characters 1,298 would be moved to the left of the tab stop, the decimal point would be lined up right at the tab stop, and the characters 79 would appear after the tab stop. This allows a column of dollar amounts to be lined up correctly on the decimal point. If you want to end the Tab Align function before you have pressed the align character, press TAB, <Tab Align>, or ENTER.

You can change the Tab Align character from a period to any letter, number, or punctuation mark. To change the character, first position the cursor to the place in your document where you want the new align character to take effect. Then, press the <Line Format> key (SHFT+F8), choose "Align Char" from the menu, and enter the character you want to use. From that point on in the document, the Tab Align function (and decimal-aligned tab stops) will respond to the specified character. This versatility allows the Tab Align function to be used for a variety of text applications as well as for lining up numbers. For example, here's a table where the equal sign was used as the align character:

```
      belief = croyance
        boat = bateau
       bulky = volumineux
butterscotch = caramel au beurre
```

Another use for changing the align character would be to have the function use a comma as an align character, since many countries use a comma as a decimal point.

Margins

WordPerfect's margins are set by specifying a number of characters from the left edge of the paper. They are initially set to be 10 from the left for the left margin and 74 from the left for the right margin. The difference between the value for the left margin and the value for the right margin is considered the line length.

To change the margins, position the cursor at the left edge of the first line you want to affect. If you do not position it at the left edge, an [HRt] (Hard Return) will automatically be inserted before the [Margin Set:] code. Press the <Line Format> key (SHFT+F8) and choose "Margins" from the menu. You will see the current margin settings and be prompted for the new value. Enter the value for the left margin and press SPACE or ENTER. Then enter the value for the right margin and again press SPACE or ENTER. A [Margin Set:] code is inserted in the text and all text from that point on, until another [Margin Set:] code is encountered, will be formatted with the margins you entered.

If your margins are wider than the screen, your text will automatically scroll left and right as you type. You can manually scroll the text using the arrow key sequences discussed earlier in "Short Trips."

Spacing

WordPerfect initially produces single-spaced text unless you've modified the program's Initial Settings. To change to another spacing, press the

<Line Format> key (SHFT+F8) and choose **3** for "Spacing," from the menu. The program will then display the current spacing value and prompt you for the new setting. Type the number you want and press ENTER. For example, type **2** for double spacing.

The screen displays, as closely as possible, the spacing as it will appear when your document is printed. There is no way the screen can show half spacing, but the Line Indicator at the bottom of the screen will keep track of half lines. The line spacing shown on the screen will be the next whole number after the value you enter. For example, specifying one-and-a-half line spacing (1.5) produces double spacing on the screen.

Mathematical formulas often contain many superscripted and subscripted characters. You can enter each of these characters with WordPerfect's Superscript or Subscript command, but if you have many superscripts or subscripts, this can be quite tedious. Also, since a character that is superscripted or subscripted does not actually change position on the screen, the resulting formula can be difficult to read.

Changing to half-line spacing can help this process a great deal. To do this, press the <Line Format> key, choose **3** for "Spacing," type **.5**, and press ENTER. The Line Indicator will then reflect only a half-line change between lines on the screen. Use the space bar to position the cursor while typing the formula. In this way, you can see roughly what the text will look like before it is printed, and you can type any number of superscripted and subscripted characters without entering a special code for each one. For example, with half-line spacing you can enter a formula that looks like this:

$$x^2 = y^2 + H\ O_2$$

The printed result will look like this:

$$x^2 = y^2 + H_2O$$

Centering

As with text embellishments, centering may be specified either before or after you have typed the text to be centered.

To center a line before you type it, simply press the <Center> key (SHFT+F6), type the line, and press ENTER. To center a line that has already been typed, position the cursor on the first character of the line and press <Center>. Then, when you move your cursor down, the line will reformat and be properly centered. You can also center many lines at once by marking them as a block and, while the "Block on" message is flashing, pressing the <Center> key. The program will ask you to confirm the centering before it completes the command.

To center text over a column of text or numbers, use a center tab stop (see the earlier section "Tabs").

Indenting Paragraphs

You can use the Indent functions to change the margins for just one paragraph at a time. The Left Indent function brings in the left margin, and the Left/Right Indent function brings in both margins evenly. The Indent functions use tab stops to determine the margin positions of the paragraph. Since tab stops are set at five-space intervals by default, you usually indent a paragraph in increments of five spaces.

Many people think of an indented paragraph as one in which only the first line is indented. To create this type of paragraph, you should use the TAB key as described in the earlier section, "Tabs."

To indent the left margin of a paragraph, simply press the <Left Indent> key (F4) before typing the text of the paragraph, and the cursor will move to the first defined tab stop. You can press the <Left Indent> several times, until your cursor is positioned where you want the left margin of the paragraph to be. At first, it may seem that the Indent function performs the same function as pressing the TAB key. However, when you begin to type the paragraph, you will see that the second and subsequent lines wrap to the same location as the first line.

To indent an existing paragraph, position the cursor on the first character in the paragraph, and press the <Left Indent> key. You may need to press the DOWN ARROW key to make the screen reflect the indentation.

You may wish to type a paragraph number, or some other text, before indenting the paragraph. Then, when you press the <Left Indent> key, the remainder of the paragraph is indented to the next tab stop. You can also press the TAB or <Left Indent> key before entering the paragraph number, useful for numbered sub-paragraphs.

The Left/Right Indent function works exactly the same as the Left Indent, except that the right margin is reduced by the same amount as the left margin. Tab stops are only used to determine the left margin—the right margin is based on the left margin. Therefore, you control the position of both margins only by the location of the tab stop with which the left margin aligns.

For example, to enter a quotation that is evenly indented 10 spaces on both sides—and your tab stops are set at five-space intervals—simply press the <Left/Right Indent> key (SHFT+F4) twice, type the paragraph, and press ENTER.

SEARCHING

WordPerfect has a Search function that looks through your text to find any word, phrase, or other series of letters and codes that you specify. You can have the program search from the cursor position forward (toward the end of the document) or backward (toward the beginning). It is very important to position your cursor appropriately before you issue the Search command.

Using Search

To start the search, press the <Search> key (F2), and enter the *search string* (the text you wish to search for). If you have previously used Search since starting WordPerfect, the program will suggest the previous search string. You can either type a new search string, or you can edit the previous one. When you have entered the desired search string, press <Search> again or ESC. The cursor will then be positioned *after* the next occurrence of the search string. To search for more occurrences of the same text, just press the <Search> key twice. To search backward, follow the same steps as explained, using the <Search Left> key (SHFT+F2) to start the process.

Replacing

Use the Replace function to search for one string of text and replace it with another. This function can be useful if you have consistently misspelled a name or incorrectly typed a phrase. The Replace function works in a similar fashion to the Search function; however, it only works in a forward direction.

To start the Replace procedure, press the <Replace> key (ALT+F2). The program asks whether you want it to stop at each occurrence of the search string and ask for confirmation. If you are sure you want to replace all occurrences, you don't need confirmation, so type **N**. If only some of the occurrences will need to be replaced, type **Y** for confirmation.

You will then be prompted for the search string, which is entered exactly as for the Search command. You can press any of the Search keys or ESC to end the search string. When you do, you will be prompted for a *replacement string*. Enter the text that will replace the search string and press one of the Search keys or ESC again.

If you don't enter anything for the replacement string, all occurrences of the search string will be replaced with nothing—that is, deleted.

To perform the Replace function on a specific amount of text rather than the entire document, simply use the Block function to mark the text before starting the Replace. Only the occurrences of the search string that are found within the blocked text will be replaced.

Searching for Hidden Codes

You can search for codes as well as for text. If you mistakenly try to start a search by pressing the ENTER key, [HRt] appears in the search string. This happens because the [HRt] code is *searchable*—that is, you can use the Search function to find the code in the text. For example, this can be useful if you want to find a phrase that appears on a line of its own (such as a title), if you want to find all paragraphs that begin or end with a certain word, or if you want to find a certain number of blank lines between paragraphs.

To insert other codes into the search string, you can usually press the key sequence that you would normally use to generate them in the text. For example, to search for the next occurrence of a margin change in your document, press the <Search> key (F2), then enter the [Margin Set] code into the search string by pressing the <Line Format> key (SHFT+F8) and choosing **3** for "Margin." Most codes can be entered in this manner, although the menus that appear might look a little different than those that each key would normally produce.

The underline and bold functions each produce a Matched Pair of hidden codes. To enter the code that turns the function on (the [U] or the [B]) into the search string, press the appropriate function key. To enter the code that turns the function off (the [u] or the [b]) into the search string, press the appropriate function key twice, press LEFT ARROW, then BACKSPACE to delete the first code, and then RIGHT ARROW.

Searching for Words

Sometimes a search can turn up unexpected results. For example, if you search for "man," the Search function will not only find all occurrences of the word *man* but also *woman, manager,* and *Comanche.* One way to limit a search to entire words is to put a space before and after the word in the search string. However, this will not always work. Some occurrences of the word might start a new paragraph, in which case they will be preceded by an [HRt] instead of a space. They may end a sentence, which means they would be followed by any of a number of different punctuation marks. Or, they may be enclosed in quotation marks.

Ultimately, there is no good way to limit a search to entire words (as opposed to parts of larger words) without compromising the reliability of the Search. The best bet, then, is to put up with the inaccurate findings, to be sure you are finding all of the occurrences.

Using Wildcards

Another feature of the Search and Replace functions is that the search string can include a *wildcard* character that will match any other character. To insert the wildcard character into the search string, press CTRL+V and then CTRL+X, and you will see ^X appear. For example, **fa^X** will find *far, fat,* and *fad.*

Extended Search

Normally, the Search and Replace functions locate text and codes that appear only in text that is visible on the editing screen. The Extended Search (or Replace) extends the scope to include text in headers, footers, footnotes, and endnotes.

To use the Extended Search, simply press the HOME key before pressing the <Search>, <Search Left>, or <Replace> keys. If an occurrence of the search string is found within a header, footer, footnote, or endnote, the Search will end (or the Replace will pause) within the appropriate screen.

FILE MANAGEMENT

File management consists of the process of saving and retrieving documents to and from disk, as well as deleting, renaming, and copying documents currently on disk. File management functions are simply housekeeping tasks that keep the files on your disks organized.

Saving and Retrieving Documents

All WordPerfect documents are given a file name when they are saved on disk. These file names can be any legal DOS file name; that is, they can consist of a name of from 1 to 8 characters, a period, and an extension of from 1 to 3 characters. The characters can be any letter or number, as well as any of these punctuation marks:

$ ( ) & ' - @ # { } % ~ ! —

You can use the extension to specify a type of document. For example, .LTR might specify a letter, while .AGT might specify an agreement. The <List Files> key, discussed later in this chapter, could then be used to search through all your files to find only your letters or agreements.

Saving

To save the current document on disk, press the <Save> key (F10), type a file name, and press ENTER. If you have previously saved the current document (thereby giving it a name) or you have retrieved the document from disk (instead of creating it from scratch), the Save command will first suggest the known name. If you want to save the document with this name, you can simply press ENTER. Otherwise, you can use the cursor control keys to edit the name, or just type a new name and press ENTER. If a file with the name you specify already exists on disk, the program will ask if you want to replace the file with the current document. Type **Y** to replace the file or type **N** to specify another name.

It is a good idea to save a current version of your document periodically while you work, not just when you are done. This is truly a quick and painless procedure and one every computer veteran does on a frequent basis. The hassle of pressing the <Save> key, ENTER (use the same name), and Y (to confirm the replacement) is trivial compared to the horror of losing a file because it wasn't saved to disk when the lights went out. The saving process can even be reduced to one keystroke with a macro, as discussed in Chapter 10, "Macro Library."

It is also a good idea to use WordPerfect's Timed Backup feature, described in Appendix A, "Installation."

Retrieving

You can retrieve a document into memory (onto the screen) at any time. If the screen is clear when you retrieve, you will only be editing the new document. If the screen already contains a document, you will insert the contents of the retrieved document at the cursor position.

There are two ways to retrieve a document from disk: using the <Retrieve> key (SHFT+F10) and using the <List Files> key (F5).

Using the <Retrieve> key can be quicker, but you must remember the entire file name. To retrieve a document this way, press the <Retrieve> key (SHFT+F10), type the file name, and press ENTER.

The <List Files> key allows you to display a disk's directory and simply point to the file you want to retrieve (see the next section). *Don't forget that unless you want to combine documents, you should clear the screen before retrieving a new document.*

List Files

With the <List Files> key (F5) you can retrieve and print documents as well as perform such DOS-like commands as renaming, deleting, and copying files. A Word Search mode lets you find documents containing specific text, and a Look command lets you take a "quick look" at a document without actually retrieving it.

When you press the <List Files> key (F5), you see a display like this at the bottom of the screen:

```
Dir B:\*.*                    (Use = to change default directory)
```

if you're using a floppy-based computer system, or

```
Dir C:\WP\DATA\*.*            (Use = to change default directory)
```

if you're using a hard disk. At this point WordPerfect is displaying the current *default directory* — that is, the disk or directory that files are retrieved from and stored to, unless you specify otherwise.

There are four actions you can choose from at this point:

- Press ENTER to work with the files on the default directory.

- Edit the directory name, or type a new drive or directory, and press ENTER to work temporarily with the files from that drive or directory.

- Press = (equal sign), and then edit the directory name, or type a new drive or directory, and press ENTER to *change* the default directory. WordPerfect will again display the directory prompt, so you can repeat any of these actions.

- Enter a *filename template,* which is usually a combination of valid DOS file name characters and the two DOS wildcard symbols, ? and *. This template allows you to specify a subset of your current disk or directory files that the List Files function will use. For example, to work with all of your letter files, you could enter *.**LTR** to specify all files with an .LTR extension, or you could enter **GR*.*** to specify all files beginning with GR. (Refer to your DOS manual for a complete description of the wildcard symbols.)

After selecting some combination of these four choices, you will see the List Files display. At the top is some useful information, including the disk or directory, the filename template you specified, the size of your current document, the amount of free space on your current disk, and the current date and time. Below that will appear a list of the files you've specified, in alphabetical order from left to right.

A bar, which you can move with the cursor control keys, is located on an entry labeled ". <CURRENT>" at the top of the column on the left. This bar indicates the file on which you want to perform an action. In addition to using the arrow keys, you can reposition the bar by using <Screen Up>, <Screen Down>, and several of the other cursor positioning controls. Also, if you start typing a file name, the bar will immediately move to the file that most closely matches the letters you type. It will usually find the file after you type the first few letters.

Nine different actions are listed at the bottom of the screen. Pressing a number from 1 to 9 causes the action to be performed, usually on the selected file. You can also perform an action on several files at a time either by marking them individually (positioning the cursor bar and pressing the * key) or by marking all files with the <Mark Text> key (ALT+F5). Once all files have been marked with the <Mark Text> key, you can unmark individual files by positioning the cursor bar and pressing the * key. Marked files can be deleted, copied, printed, and searched.

Let's discuss the nine actions individually:

Retrieve   Retrieves the selected file (like the <Retrieve> key). Remember to clear the screen before retrieving a new document.

Delete   Deletes the file from disk. The program will ask for confirmation before completing the command.

Rename   Prompts you for a new name for the selected file. The name cannot be the same as another file name on the disk or in the current directory.

Print   Prints the selected file. This is one of the three methods of printing documents. Printing is discussed later in this chapter.

Text In   Retrieves the selected file as an ASCII file. This command is discussed in detail in Chapter 8.

Look   Lets you "look" at the selected file or directory. (You can also use the ENTER key to perform this action.) This is a quick way to check the contents of a file without actually retrieving it and disrupting your current editing workspace. It is also much faster than retrieving the file. Once you are looking at a file, you can use the DOWN ARROW key and the <Screen Down> or PGDN key (which in this case perform the same action) to view the file, but you cannot scroll up. When you are finished looking, press any key to return to the List File screen.

If the bar is currently highlighting a directory name instead of a file name when you press ENTER or type **6**, you will first be prompted for a filename template, and then you will "look" at the directory. That is, you will see the contents of the directory in the List Files display, but the directory will not become your default directory.

Change Directory   Allows you to change the default directory and filename template while remaining on the List Files screen.

Copy   Copies the selected file to a specified disk or directory. You can also use Copy to make a duplicate of a file with a different name. This command performs the same action as the DOS COPY command.

Word Search   Prompts you for a text string that WordPerfect will search for in all the files currently listed on the List Files display. A new List Files screen will be displayed showing only the files containing the given text. A complete discussion of how this function is used can be found in Appendix B, "Using Word Search."

Type **0**, or press <Cancel> (F1), <Exit> (F7), or SPACE, to exit the List Files screen and return to your document.

WORKING WITH TWO DOCUMENTS AT A TIME

There are times when you will want to work with two documents simultaneously. Perhaps you're creating a document and need information contained in another WordPerfect document. You may, for example, be writing a letter and need access to a previous letter you have written about the same subject. If you are writing a magazine article, you may want your outline or notes in one file and the article itself in another. Or you may be working on a document and need to write a quick memo or take notes on a phone conversation. WordPerfect makes it easy to edit two documents at once. You can even copy (or cut) and retrieve information between two documents with this feature.

To switch from a document you are working on to a second document, press the <Switch> key (SHFT+F3). The screen will be clear except for the document information in the lower right corner. Instead of "Doc 1," it now says "Doc 2."

At this point you can begin typing a new document or retrieve an existing file. All WordPerfect commands function exactly as they do when you are working with only one file.

What happened to the first file you were working on? Don't worry. It is still there, even if you have not saved it to disk. If you press <Switch> again, you are returned to your first document, exactly where you left off. The <Switch> key acts as a toggle, taking you back and forth between the two documents.

You can work with each document independently, or you can transfer information between them using the Move command. Simply use the <Switch> key after copying or cutting text, but before retrieving it.

Windows

With the Windows function, you can view both Document 1 and Document 2 on the screen at the same time. The separate sections of the screen that show the two documents are called *windows*.

To split the screen into two sections, press the <Screen> key (CTRL+F3) and type **1**, for "Window." You will be prompted for the "# of lines in this window." Type any number from 1 to 24 (a full screen holds 24 lines of text), and press ENTER.

Once you select the window size, you will notice a thick horizontal bar across the screen. This is called the *ruler,* and it shows you the current tab and margin settings according to your cursor position. The little triangles in the middle of the line show the positions of the tab stops. The left and right margin marks are normally displayed as left and right square brackets, but if a margin mark falls at the same place as a tab stop, it is displayed as a curly bracket.

If the tab stop triangles are pointing up, you are working in Document 1, the top window. If they are pointing down, you are working in Document 2, the bottom window. The <Switch> key (SHFT+F3), as always, toggles you between Document 1 and Document 2.

The ruler and the two lines of document information for each window take up a total of three lines. Since there are 25 total lines on the screen, this leaves you with 22 lines of text to be shared by both windows. When you size a window, WordPerfect automatically creates another window that is 22 lines minus the size of the window you created. For instance, if you create a 10-line window, the other window is automatically 12 lines. (Because of this, you can create two equal-sized windows by specifying that either window contains 11 lines.)

To change the size of either window, press the <Screen> key, type **1** for "Window," enter the number of lines that you want the window to be, and press ENTER. Thus, if your current window is 8 lines long and you want it to be 12, you press <Screen>, **1, 12**, and ENTER. The size of the other window is automatically adjusted.

You can eliminate windows altogether by sizing either window to 24 lines. When you do that, the other window (the one that you are not actively working in) disappears from view, but the document is still in the computer's memory. You can switch to that document at any time by pressing the <Switch> key.

To get the ruler without displaying a window, set the size of either window to 23 lines. The ruler will be displayed at the bottom of the screen. Use the <Switch> key to switch between the two documents.

Working with windows can require quite a few keystrokes, but you can automate the steps with macros (see Chapter 10, "Macro Library").

SAVING BLOCKS

You can save a portion of a file by marking it with the <Block> key. There are two ways to save the block: as a file by itself or added to the end of another file.

Saving a Block to a File

To save a block as a separate document, highlight the text with the Block command. While the message "Block on" is flashing, press the <Save> key (F10). WordPerfect will display the "Block name:" prompt. When you enter a file name, the block will be stored on disk as a separate file. Just as with the Save command, if a file with that name already exists, you will be prompted to confirm the file replace. The block will also remain in its original location in the document you are working on.

Appending a Block
To Another File

WordPerfect's Block Append command also lets you add a block of text to the end of another file. This can be useful, for example, for collecting bits and pieces of text into a sort of "scrapbook" file.

To perform the Block Append command, highlight the text with the Block command. While the "Block on" message is flashing, press the <Move> key (CTRL+F4) and choose **3**, "Append." Type the name of the file to which you wish to append the block, and press ENTER. The file must already exist on disk.

CONTROLLING PRINTERS

When you tell WordPerfect to print a document, it generates a *print job*. This print job is placed at the end of the *print queue*, which is simply a list of the documents waiting to be printed.

You manage the print queue from the Printer Control screen, which gives you a complete account of what is going on with your printer: Is it printing? What is it printing? How far along is it? The Printer Control screen provides the answers.

Printing

There are three ways to print a document. All have the same result: they generate a print job, which is added to the print queue.

Printing the Current Document

This method is the easiest because it does not require that the document be saved to disk or that a file name be entered. When you are finished typing the text you want printed, press the <Print> key (SHFT+F7) and type **1** for "Full Text" to print the entire document currently in memory, or type **2** to print just the page the cursor is on.

The other two methods of printing require that the document be stored on disk in the condition in which you want it printed. This means that if you are editing a document on screen and want to print it using one of these methods, you must first save the file on disk. You can be editing any document when either of these print commands is issued.

Printing With List Files

To print with List Files, go to the List Files display by pressing the <List Files> key (F5) and pressing ENTER. Position the bar on the file you want to print and type **4** for "Print," to generate a print job. You can use this method to print one document while you are editing another.

Printing a Document by Name

This method, unlike the other two, allows you to specify a *selection* of pages to print. Press the <Print> key (SHFT+F7), type **4** for "Printer Control," then **P** for "Print." Then enter the name of the file you wish to print. When you enter the file name, you will be prompted for the page(s) to print. You can either press ENTER to use the default of printing the entire document, or you can enter individual page numbers or ranges of pages.

To print individual pages, enter each number separated by a comma. For example, you can type **2,9,15** and press ENTER to print pages 2, 9, and 15 of the specified document. To print a range of pages, enter two page numbers separated by a hyphen. For example, you can type **5-10** and press ENTER to print pages 5 through 10, inclusive. If you omit the first number, printing will start at the beginning of the document. If you omit the second number, printing will continue to the last page of the document.

You can also combine individual page numbers with page ranges. For example, you can type **5,10-15,20** to print page 5, pages 10 through 15, and page 20.

If you have used the New Page Number command to start new sections within a document—for example, to restart numbering for chapters within a book or sections within a manual—you can refer to these sections when printing a range of pages. To do this, simply precede the number of the page within a section with the section number and a colon. For example, to print page 3 of the second section in a document, type **2:3** and press ENTER. To print pages 5 through 9 from the third section, type **3:5-9** and press ENTER.

Managing the Print Queue

Once you generate a print job, it is added to the end of the print queue. After it is printed, the document is removed from the queue. You can inspect and manage the print queue by pressing the <Print> key (SHFT+F7) and choosing **4**, "Printer Control." At the top of the screen is a menu for controlling printers and print jobs, in the middle is a status display that shows what is currently happening, and at the bottom is a list of the three print jobs at the top of the queue. To see a list of all print jobs in the queue, choose **D**, "Display All Print Jobs," from the menu.

If you will normally print only one file at a time, the process of managing the print queue is incidental, unless you encounter problems during printing. However, you can still check the Printer Control screen for information on the status of a print job.

If you generate a print job and the printer doesn't start printing, *don't tell it to print again.* There is probably something wrong that needs correcting before the print job can be restarted. If you generate too many print jobs, you can end up with quite a mess. Instead, check the Printer Control screen to see if you can determine what the problem is, so that you can fix it and restart the print job.

Here is an explanation of the menu choices on the Printer Control screen that affect printing:

C   *Cancel Print Job(s)*
This command cancels a specific print job by number. You can also cancel all the active print jobs either by typing * here and pressing ENTER or by exiting WordPerfect and responding **Y** to the prompt "Cancel all print jobs?"

D   *Display All Print Jobs*
This command clears the screen and displays a list of all print jobs in the print queue.

G   *"Go" (Resume Printing)*
If you need to stop printing (if the printer cover opens or you run out of ribbon, for example), use the Stop Printing command that follows. The

Go command will then start things rolling again, beginning with whatever page you specify. The Go command also starts printing for each page when you are operating in hand-fed mode. This process can be simplified by using a macro, as discussed in Chapter 10, "Macro Library."

R *Rush Print Job*

This command takes the specified print job and puts it at the top of the print queue.

S *Stop Printing*

Typing **S** will stop WordPerfect from trying to print. Since many printers have memory buffers that hold a page or more of text, printing may not stop immediately. It may be necessary to press **S** and then turn off the printer — or reset it, if possible — to actually stop printing immediately. Use Go to start printing again.

Print Options

Print Options allows you to set such options as printing multiple copies of a document, printing to a different printer, or adding a binding width.

With Print Options, you select which Printer Number WordPerfect will use for printing documents. (Where and how the documents will be printed depends on how you have defined the Printer Numbers. See Appendix A, "Installation," for a description of the process.) Initially the selection is Printer Number 1, which is normally the printer/paper feed combination you use most frequently.

You can also specify how many copies of a document will be made and whether a *binding width* will be included. A binding width is a page offset that alternates sides between pages so the document can be bound in book format.

There are two ways to set the Print Options: temporarily (for one print job) or for the rest of the WordPerfect session. To set them temporarily, press the <Print> key (SHFT+F7) and enter **3** for "Change Options." When you have changed the desired options, you will be returned to the <Print> menu. The options you changed will only be in effect if you generate a print job immediately, from this menu. Once you exit the menu and return to your document, the options will be reset to what they were before you changed them.

To set the Print Options for the rest of the session, press the <Print> key, type **4** for "Printer Control," and **1** for "Select Print Options." The menu is identical to the Change Print Options menu.

The Print Options menus do not generate codes in the text as formatting commands do. Instead, they will affect any document that is printed, whether it is printed from disk or from the screen in either Document 1 or Document 2.

Previewing a Document

WordPerfect does not display on the editing screen such document elements and formatting features as headers, footers, footnotes, endnotes, page numbering, line numbering, and right justification. Instead, these are normally visible only when you print a document. However, the Print Preview function allows you to see these things on the screen, without the need to print.

To preview a document on the screen, press the <Print> key (SHFT+F7), and type 6 for "Preview." Type 1 to preview the entire document, or type 2 to preview the page on which your cursor is currently positioned. WordPerfect actually formats your document just as it will when it is printed, saving the resulting text to disk rather then sending it directly to the printer. Then, it displays the previewed text.

At the lower left corner of the screen, you will see the word "PREVIEW." This reminds you that you are currently in a special Preview Mode. You cannot make any additions or changes to the previewed text — however, you can use the <Switch> key (SHFT+F3) to return to the document itself, and the <Switch> key again to return to the Preview. In this way, you can easily switch back to the document to inspect the Reveal Codes screen and compare it to the previewed text.

You can use all of the normal WordPerfect cursor control keys to scroll through the previewed text, and you can use the <Search> functions to locate text.

When you are finished looking at the previewed text, press the <Exit> key (F7) to return to the document. The <Switch> key will then return to its normal function of switching between Document 1 and Document 2.

SPELL CHECKING

WordPerfect's built-in spell checker has a 120,000-word dictionary that allows you to check the spelling for an entire document, a page, a single word, or a marked block of text. Before initiating the spell-check procedure, floppy disk users may have to insert the Speller Disk in one of the disk drives. (See Appendix A, "Installation.")

Checking Text

To begin the spell-checking procedure for the entire document, press the <Spell> key (CTRL+F1) and type **3**, "Document." The cursor may be positioned anywhere when you issue this command. To check the current word or page, position the cursor accordingly, press <Spell>, and choose "Word" or "Page." To check a block of text, mark the text first with the <Block> key (ALT+F4) and then press <Spell>.

WordPerfect will begin to read through the selected text, checking each word against its own dictionary and your personal dictionary. If it finds a word that isn't in one of the dictionaries, it tells you that the word was "Not found" and presents you with a list of alternative spellings. You must first determine if the word is indeed misspelled or if it is a proper name or other correctly spelled word that is not in WordPerfect's dictionary. If the word is correct, press **2** to "Skip" over that word or press **3** to add the word to your personal dictionary. Once a word is added to your personal dictionary, WordPerfect no longer considers it a misspelling.

You will be presented with a list of possible spellings. If you see the correct spelling, simply select the letter adjacent to the word; WordPerfect will make the correction for you and continue checking the document. (If the same misspelling is found again in the document, it will automatically be replaced with the correction you selected for the first occurrence.)

If you do not see the correct spelling in the list, you can select **4**, "Edit," and make the correction yourself. (You can also simply begin to move the cursor using one of the arrow keys, and you will enter Edit mode automatically.) In the Edit mode, you can move the cursor to the left and right and delete and insert characters. Press ENTER to return to the spell check.

If the spell checker highlights a word that contains numbers, you have the option of editing the word, skipping it, or ignoring words that contain numbers for the rest of the search.

WordPerfect also notifies you if it finds two identical words in succession, which is a common typing error. If it does, you will have the option of skipping the double words, deleting the second word, or disabling double word checking. You can also edit the text in the same manner as with a misspelling.

When the spell checker is finished it tells you the total number of words in the document. This feature is handy for writers whose work must be within a certain word length. Pressing any key will return to the

Spell menu. To generate a word count without checking the spelling of a document, choose "Count" from the Spell menu.

If you need additional help to correct misspellings, you can use WordPerfect's Look Up or Phonetic spelling aids. They can both be used in two ways. If the Spell function is displaying the message "Not found," you can choose either "Look Up" or "Phonetic" from the menu. Choosing "Look Up" will prompt you for a *word pattern,* while choosing "Phonetic" will begin a phonetic search of the highlighted word. (See the sections that follow for a description of each of these functions.)

Alternatively, you can press the <Spell> key (CTRL+F2) and choose "Look Up" from the menu. In this case, the program will prompt you for a "Word or Word Pattern:". If you enter a word, the phonetic search will begin. If you enter a word pattern, the program will perform the Look Up procedure.

The Phonetic Search

The Phonetic Search function allows you to search for the correct spelling of a word based on how it sounds. For example, if you don't know the correct spelling of "straight," you can press the <Spell> key, choose **5**, "Look Up," and enter **strate**. WordPerfect will present you with a list of words that are phonetically similar, including "straight." When WordPerfect is highlighting a misspelled word, choosing "Phonetic" will start a search based on the word.

The Look Up Function

The Look Up function allows you to type in part of a word so that WordPerfect can provide you with a list of correct words that contain those letters. You do this by using the question mark (?) and the asterisk (*) as wildcards. The question mark is used to represent any single character and the asterisk is used to represent any number of characters.

For example, say you don't know how to spell "necessary" but you know that it begins with "nec." Choose "Look Up" from the Spell menu and enter **nec***; you will see a list of about 80 words that begin with "nec." Once you find the correct spelling, simply type the letter adjacent to the word; WordPerfect automatically makes the correction.

If you know the end of a word, you can precede that string with an *. For example, if you don't know how to spell "alkaloid" you can enter ***oid** and get a rather long list of words ending in "oid."

You can even use this feature for letters that appear in the middle of a word. Specifying ***and*** will find all words with "and" in the middle, including "archimandrite." Entering **pres**ed** will present a list of all words that begin with "pres" and end with "ed."

You can limit the words that will be displayed even more by using the question mark. Entering **??ed** would produce a list only of four-letter words that end in "ed." Entering **lik??** would produce a list of words that start with "lik" and have no more than five letters.

FILE ENCRYPTION

WordPerfect can help you keep your secrets. By using the program's file encryption feature, you can "lock" your files so that no one can retrieve or print them without entering the correct password.

To lock a document with File Encryption, save it by pressing the <Text In/Out> key (CTRL+F5) and choosing **4**, "Save a Locked Document." The program than asks you to enter a password. Select any word or phrase of up to 75 characters and press ENTER. You are then prompted to reenter the password. You need to type the password exactly as it was first entered and then press ENTER. This is WordPerfect's way of verifying that you have entered the password correctly. At this point you are prompted to enter a file name. If the document has been previously named, you can simply press ENTER. Otherwise, type a new name for the document and then press ENTER.

You retrieve locked files as you do all WordPerfect files, except that WordPerfect will ask you to "Enter Password:". If you fail to enter the password correctly, the program will say "ERROR: File is locked," and you will be prevented from accessing the file. Without the password, you cannot use WordPerfect to print the file, nor can you read it from within DOS. If there is a way to access a locked file without knowing the password, we haven't figured it out. Therefore, if you are going to lock your files, make sure you remember your password. Even WordPerfect Corporation cannot help you access a locked file without it.

Another way to retrieve a locked file is to press the <Text In/Out> key (CTRL+F5) and choose **5**, "Retrieve a Locked Document."

You save a locked file exactly as you save any other file. When WordPerfect prompts for a password, enter the password you wish to use and press ENTER. Reenter the password for confirmation, then press ENTER again. To unlock a file — that is, save it without a password — use the <Save> key and press ENTER when prompted for a password.

2 MACROS

Imagine driving your car and seeing a sign that says: "Remove foot from the accelerator, depress brake pedal, look for oncoming traffic, wait for the traffic to clear, remove your foot from the brake, depress accelerator, proceed." Fortunately, you have been programmed to perform all those tasks when you see a sign that simply says "STOP."

A macro is like that Stop sign—simply a shortcut. It is either a typed word or a keystroke or two that can substitute for any longer sequence of keystrokes.

Built into WordPerfect is a macro facility that lets you store keystrokes—whether for commands or text—and play the keystrokes back at any time, for any number of times. You can think of a macro as a "typing robot": if you teach it to perform a task once, it will remember the steps and automatically repeat them for you.

When you create a macro to perform a task, all the keys you press are stored on disk in a file with the name of your choice. You can specify whether the macro will be started with a single keystroke or with a name. The keystroke method is faster, but the more descriptive name method helps you remember what the macro does.

You can use macros either to type commonly used phrases like long company names or to execute a sequence of formatting commands, such as margin and tab changes. You can also use macros to perform procedures that would be too tedious to perform by hand. For example, newspaper articles often need special typesetting codes inserted in the text before they are submitted. You could create a macro to go through each finished article and add all the appropriate codes.

Macros are one of WordPerfect's most powerful features. The more you learn about the program, the more you will discover uses for them. They can help with day-to-day tasks as well as with infrequently performed, complex procedures. Once you are familiar with the basics of macro naming, definition, and invocation, you will find macros an invaluable tool in the writing process.

MACRO NAMES

WordPerfect allows you to assign a name to each macro. Once that name has been assigned, the macro is stored as a file on disk with .MAC added as a file extension. You can execute the macro at any time, regardless of which document you are currently editing. This allows you to use the same macro with many different documents.

Macros are normally stored on the default disk or directory. Thus, if you subsequently change the default disk or directory, WordPerfect will no longer be able to find your macros. There is a solution to this problem, however.

If you store your macros on the *system disk* or *directory* (where the WordPerfect program files are stored), the macros will be accessible no matter what your default directory. To store your macros this way, change the default directory to the system disk or directory before starting the macro definition.

On a floppy disk system, the system disk is usually the one that is kept in the A drive. You don't normally want to store files on the system disk, but macros are typically small enough not to cause a problem. On a hard disk, the program files are normally stored in a directory called C: \WP or C: \WORD.

There are three different ways to name a macro: the ALT Key method, the Longer Name method, and the Temporary Name method.

ALT Key Macros

Use the ALT Key method to name macros that will be invoked frequently, since it requires the fewest keystrokes. To name a macro with this method, hold down the ALT key and type any letter while the program is displaying the "Define Macro:" prompt. (You do not need to then press ENTER.)

When you use the ALT Key method, you must keep track of which functions each macro performs, as its single-letter name will not help to remind you. Since macros cannot be retrieved or edited like normal WordPerfect documents, it is a good idea to keep a written list of macros that you have created with the ALT Key method.

You can specify up to 26 ALT key macro names for each hard disk directory or floppy disk — one for each letter of the alphabet. Use a letter that indicates the macro's purpose. A macro to control the printer, for example, might be named with ALT+P while a macro to save a file might be named with ALT+S.

ALT Key macros are saved on the disk as ALT plus the single letter plus the .MAC extension. A macro named with the ALT key and P, then, would be stored as ALTP.MAC.

Longer Name Macros

Use the Longer Name method for more complex macros that will not be invoked frequently. To name a macro in this way, type the name and press ENTER while the program is displaying the "Define Macro:" prompt.

The name can be two to eight characters long and can consist of any characters that are legal for DOS file names (letters, numbers, and some punctuation marks).

The disadvantage of the Longer Name method is that it requires a minimum of four keystrokes to invoke the macro; the ALT Key method takes only two. The advantage of the Longer Name method is that you can pick a name that describes the macro's purpose. The Longer Name macro is saved on disk with the selected name and the .MAC extension.

Temporary Macros

You will usually need to save your macros for future use, but you may occasionally want to create a macro for use during a single session only. To create a temporary macro, type a single letter (without the use of the ALT key) followed by ENTER, or simply press ENTER, while the program is displaying the "Define Macro:" prompt.

There are 27 possible temporary macro names—26 for the letters of

You type		*Result*	*Method*
ALT+S	→	ALTS.MAC	ALT Key method
find	→	FIND.MAC	Longer Name method
A	→	*Not Saved*	Temporary Macro, Named
ENTER	→	*Not Saved*	Temporary Macro, Unnamed

Table 2-1.   Examples of Macro Names

the alphabet, plus the one that is used when ENTER is pressed by itself. Temporary macros are not saved on disk and will be lost when you next exit WordPerfect. This avoids unnecessary disk clutter.

See Table 2-1 for examples of macro naming methods.

DEFINING MACROS

To define a macro, first press the <Macro Def> key (CTRL+F10). You will see this prompt at the bottom of the screen:

```
Define Macro:
```

The program is asking you to provide a name for the macro. You can use any one of the three methods described earlier:

- *ALT Key Macros*   To create a macro with an ALT key name, hold down the ALT key and type any single letter. You do not need to press ENTER.

- *Longer Name Macros*   To create a macro with a longer name, type any name two to eight characters long and press ENTER.

- *Temporary Macros*   To create a temporary macro, you can either type any single letter (without the ALT key) and press ENTER, or you can press ENTER by itself.

If the macro name you specify already exists on the disk and you are using the ALT Key or Longer Name method, you will be asked whether you want to replace the existing macro with the one you are about to define. Be careful—it is easy to forget which function a macro performs, so you might accidentally delete a lot of work with just one keystroke. When a temporary macro is being replaced, the program will not ask for confirmation.

After you have named the macro, this message will begin to flash at the bottom of the screen:

`Macro Def`

It will continue to flash for as long as you are defining your macro. (It may disappear if you enter one of WordPerfect's menus, but it will always reappear when you return to the document.) While the message is flashing, everything you type, including both text and WordPerfect commands, will be stored in the macro.

When you are through entering the keystrokes you want contained in the macro, press the <Macro Def> key again to stop the macro definition. If you used the ALT Key or Longer Name method, the macro will be stored on disk. If you defined a temporary macro, it will be stored in memory.

Clear the screen (by pressing the <Exit> key (F7) and typing **N** and **N**). Then try the following exercise using the Longer Name method to identify the macro:

1. Press the <Macro Def> key (CTRL+F10).

2. Type **respond** and press ENTER.

   You will see the flashing "Macro Def" on the screen.

3. Type **Please respond to our request**

   Include a space after the word "request".

4. Press the <Underline> key (F8).

5. Type **as soon as possible**

6. Press the <Underline> key again.

7. Type **.** and press ENTER.

8. Press the <Macro Def> key again.

   The flashing "Macro Def" will disappear.

Your screen will look like Figure 2-1.

Please respond to our request <u>as soon as possible</u>.

Doc 1 Pg 1 Ln 2   Pos 10

Figure 2-1.   Creating a macro

Here you have combined a frequently used phrase with the WordPerfect underlining function. When you pressed the <Macro Def> key the second time, the macro was saved on disk as RESPOND.MAC. You can use the <List Files> key (F5) to verify this if you are distrustful. In the next section, you will use the macro you just defined.

INVOKING MACROS

The procedure you use to invoke a macro (that is, to play back your keystrokes) varies, depending on the method you chose in naming it.

ALT Key Macros

When you want to invoke an ALT Key macro, simply hold down the ALT key and type whatever letter you used to name the macro. All your keystrokes will be played back. As mentioned earlier, this is the quickest and easiest way to invoke a macro.

Longer Name Macros

If you use the Longer Name method to create a macro, you can invoke it by following these three steps:

1. Press the <Macro> key.

2. Type the macro name.

3. Press ENTER.

As you can see, this method requires more keystrokes than the ALT Key method, but it makes it much easier to keep track of your macros.

To use the Longer Name macro you have just defined, follow these steps: Press the <Macro> key (ALT+F10), type **respond**, and press ENTER. The sentence you typed earlier, underline and all, will appear on the screen.

The macro is now on disk and is accessible from any document. If you wish, you can use the <List Files> function to delete the macro, as you would any other file.

Temporary Macros

To invoke a temporary macro,

1. Press the <Macro> key.

2. Either type the single letter and press ENTER or simply press ENTER.

MACRO PRACTICE—MASS UNDERLINING

Let's create a more complex macro. Suppose you have a document in which you've used the word "palazzo" (Italian for "palace") hundreds of times, and you are told one day that it must be underlined, since it is a foreign word. What should you do? Spend hours going through your document to correct the errors? You can use the Search function, but you would still have to underline each occurrence individually. Instead, you can use a macro to handle this situation.

The first step is to decide on the steps *you* would follow to perform the same procedure that the macro will perform. The best way, after moving the cursor to the top of the document, is to

1. Use the Search function to find "palazzo".

2. Mark "palazzo" as a block.

3. Use the <Underline> key to underline the word.

A macro will follow the same steps. It can also repeat the steps as you would until it can find no more occurrences of the given text. (This type of macro, called a looping macro, is discussed in the next section.) First, you will create a macro that underlines one occurrence at a time, using the simple steps just listed.

To start, you should place some text on the screen to work with. Clear the screen and type the following:

Inside the palazzo, the well-equipped royal guard anxiously watched the court-yard. A ring of horses slowly surrounded the palazzo. Beyond the duck pond, the palazzo gates were giving way to the thrusts of the angry mob. Soon, the palazzo would be overrun by screaming activists.

For the purposes of this exercise, imagine that this short paragraph is in fact a novel spanning over 350 pages in which you have used the word "palazzo" liberally. Save the paragraph on disk with the name of your choice for later use in this chapter. Then position the cursor at the top of the document by pressing HOME, HOME, UP ARROW.

Now you should decide on an appropriate name for the macro you will create. You probably won't use it again since you are not likely to repeat the same mistake, so give the macro a temporary name following these steps.

Note: If you make a mistake while entering the steps of the macro, press the <Macro Def> key to stop the "Macro Def" message from flashing at the bottom of the screen. Then reposition your cursor at the top of the document and start again from step 1. You may also need to clear the screen and reload the paragraph from disk.

1. Press the <Macro Def> (CTRL+F10) key.

2. Type **p** and press ENTER.

Now you will search for the word "palazzo" in your paragraph.

3. Press the <Forward Search> key (F2).

4. Type **palazzo** and press ESC.

   The cursor will now be positioned after the last letter of the first occurrence of the word "palazzo".

5. Press the <Block> key (ALT+F4).

   Flashing wildly at the bottom of the screen will be this message:

   ```
   Block on  Macro Def
   ```

   To mark the word as a block so that it can be underlined, use the <Word Left> key.

6. Press the <Word Left> key (CTRL+LEFT).

   The word "palazzo" will now be highlighted.

7. Press the <Underline> key (F8).

   The word "palazzo" will now be underlined.

8. Press the <Word Right> key (CTRL+RIGHT).

   This positions the cursor after the occurrence of "palazzo" that was just underlined. If you were to omit this step, the first occurrence of "palazzo" would be found and underlined each time you executed the macro.

9. Press the <Macro Def> key to end the macro definition.

   And that's it! While defining the macro, you underlined the first "palazzo" in the text. Now let's use the macro to underline the next one.

1. Press the <Macro> key (ALT+F10).

2. Type **p** and press ENTER.

If everything goes as planned, the next "palazzo" will be underlined as

```
Inside the palazzo, the well-equipped royal guard anxiously
watched the courtyard.  A ring of horses slowly surrounded the
palazzo.  Beyond the duck pond, the palazzo gates were giving way
to the thrusts of the angry mob.  Soon, the palazzo would be
overrun by screaming activists.
```

                                            Doc 1 Pg 1 Ln 3   Pos 20

Figure 2-2.   Underlined sample text

shown in Figure 2-2. Try the macro a few more times to underline the remaining occurrences.

    In the preceding example, you located the text, marked it as a block, and underlined it. More precisely, you taught WordPerfect how to perform for you what would otherwise have been a laborious task. Are your fingers still tired from pressing the <Macro> key, though? In the next section, you will see how a macro can perform even more work.

LOOPING/BRANCHING MACROS

You can instruct a macro to perform its task once and then either repeat itself or invoke another macro. If it repeats itself, it is called a *looping macro,* and if it invokes another macro, it is called a *branching macro.* The instruction that tells a macro to repeat itself or to begin another macro is usually the last instruction in the macro. (You will learn about the exception to this rule, the conditional branching macro, later in this chapter.) In other words, one macro cannot invoke another and then continue with more steps once the second macro has finished. After the second macro has been invoked, the first one relinquishes control.

The Search function prevents a macro from falling into an *endless loop*. This undesirable situation occurs when the macro is performed over and over, endlessly. When a search included as a macro step is no longer able to find the specified text, either the macro is terminated (as in a looping macro) or another macro is invoked (as in a conditional branching macro). Thus, whenever the purpose of a macro is to find some text repeated throughout a document and manipulate it in some way, this termination/branching feature will allow the macro to execute until all occurrences have been processed and then stop searching for that text.

Note: This rule does not apply to the Replace command, which can be used several times within a macro without causing it to terminate.

The Looping Macro

The looping macro repeats a procedure as many times as necessary to complete a given task. For example, in the "palazzo" exercise, you need a way for the macro to underline *each* occurrence of the word "palazzo" until the Search function cannot find another occurrence. This would allow you to start the macro and then sit back while it churns away.

Let's create a temporary looping macro to do this job. First, clear the screen and retrieve the "palazzo" document. (You saved it, didn't you? If not, retype the text.) Position the cursor at the top of the document and follow these steps to redefine the macro:

1. Press the <Macro Def> key (CTRL+F10), type **p**, and press ENTER.
   Remember that when a temporary macro name is reused, the program does not confirm its replacement.

2. Press the <Forward Search> key.

3. Type **palazzo** and press ESC.

4. Press the <Block> key.

5. Press the <Word Left> key.

6. Press the <Underline> key.

7. Press the <Word Right> key.

8. Press the <Macro> key, type **p**, and press ENTER.

   This additional step causes the macro to loop.

9. Press the <Macro Def> key to end the macro definition.

Now let's try out the macro. Clear the screen and retrieve the document. Then press the <Macro> key, type **p**, and press ENTER. All occurrences of the word "palazzo" will now be underlined. Let's see how it happened.

First, the macro searched for "palazzo". It found the first occurrence and positioned the cursor at the end of the word. The macro then defined "palazzo" as a block and underlined it. Next, the cursor was positioned after the word again in preparation for the next execution. Finally, the macro invoked a macro—itself—and the steps were repeated until no more occurrences of "palazzo" could be found. Then the macro gracefully came to a halt.

The Branching Macro

A branching macro transfers control to *another* macro, rather than beginning again. There are two types of branching macros: unconditional and conditional.

The Unconditional Branching Macro

The last step of an *unconditional branching macro* invokes a second macro. You can use this type of macro to piece together several macros into one *routine*. For example, you may need a macro to perform some preliminary formatting steps on a document before transferring control to a looping macro for a repetitive task. Or you might want a macro to return to a "main" macro that handles a macro menu for a specific application. (See Chapter 3, "Merge," for an example of a macro menu system.)

The Conditional Branching Macro

The *conditional branching macro* provides a *conditional loop* for the macro programmer. (Are you surprised to be called a programmer? The steps contained in this type of macro are quite similar to functions found in many popular programming languages.) One step of this macro is to search for some text. If the text is found, the macro will follow one course of action. If the text is not found, the macro takes another course.

You specify a *fail macro* name at the beginning of a conditional branching macro. This must be the *first step* after providing a macro name. In this *one instance,* invoking another macro is not the macro's last step. Instead, the program merely keeps the name of the second macro "in mind" until it is needed. When the search fails (when the text can no longer be located), the fail macro is invoked (see Figure 2-3).

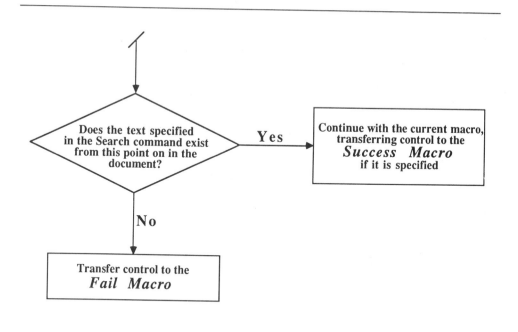

Figure 2-3.   The conditional branching macro—the conditional statement

The *success macro* (see Figure 2-3) is simply the macro that is invoked as the last step in the conditional branching macro. If the search is successful (the text is located), the macro continues to perform its next steps. Any new macro invoked as one of these steps is only performed if the search is successful. That macro is called the *success macro*. Figure 2-4 shows the sequence of macro steps.

In its simplest form, the conditional branching macro contains only the fail macro, the Search command, and either additional steps or the success macro. Usually, however, you will specify both the steps to be performed if the search is successful and a success macro, since typical applications involve processing the found text in some way and then repeating the macro using the success macro.

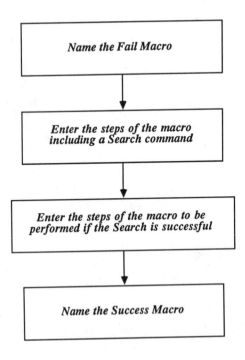

Figure 2-4.   Elements of the conditional branching macro

If you have some previous programming experience, you will notice similarities between the conditional branching macro and conditional loops, common in most programming languages. The difference is mainly in the format (the way the loop is set up) and the type of condition that can be tested (text found or not found as opposed to a numeric or alphabetic equation or comparison).

Let's create a conditional branching macro with the "palazzo" exercise. The macro will first perform the same function as the macro in the previous section: It will underline all occurrences of the word "palazzo" in the sample paragraph. When the search for "palazzo" fails, a second macro will be invoked to divide the four sentences into separate paragraphs.

Start by clearing the screen and retrieving the paragraph. Make sure the cursor is located at the top of the document. First, redefine the macro that underlines "palazzo" to include the branching step.

1. Press the <Macro Def> key (CTRL+F10), type **p**, and press ENTER.

2. Press the <Macro> key, type **r**, and press ENTER.

    This step names "R" as the fail macro, which does not exist at this time, but will be defined later.

3. Press the <Forward Search> key.

4. Type **palazzo** and press ESC.

5. Press the <Block> key.

6. Press the <Word Left> key.

7. Press the <Underline> key.

8. Press the <Word Right> key.

9. Press the <Macro> key, type **p**, and press ENTER.

    This step invokes the success macro, which will only be performed if the search in step 3 is successful. Since the macro invokes itself, the whole process will repeat until the search fails. When it does, the "R" fail macro specified in step 2 is invoked.

10. Press the <Macro Def> key to end definition of the "P" macro.

Now define the fail macro, "R," to perform the next step.

1. Press the <Macro Def> key, type **r**, and press ENTER.

2. Press HOME, HOME, UP ARROW.

This step positions the cursor at the top of the document in preparation for the Replace command in the next step, which always searches forward.

3. Press the <Replace> key (ALT+F2).

4. Type **N** (for No confirmation).

5. Type **.** and press SPACE, SPACE, ESC.

This step locates the end of each sentence.

6. Type **.** and press ENTER, ENTER, ESC.

This step breaks the sentences into paragraphs, with a blank line separating them.

7. Press the <Macro Def> key to end definition of macro "R".

When the "P" macro is invoked now, it will underline all occurrences of "palazzo" and then invoke the "R" macro, which will break the sentences into separate paragraphs.

Now clear the screen and retrieve the document once again. Go ahead and try the macro.

AVOIDING MACRO PITFALLS

Before you begin creating your own macros, you should learn how to avoid some common pitfalls.

Assumptions

A macro may *assume* certain conditions when it is invoked. These can include the position of the cursor, whether the printer is ready, and even whether there is a document on the screen.

It is important to consider the conditions under which a macro is created. Will it rely on these conditions to work properly when it is executed? For example, will the macro assume that the cursor is at the top of the document, or will it move the cursor to the top as its first step?

As you know, a looping macro will repeat itself over and over as it goes through your text. If you include a HOME, HOME, UP sequence as the first step of such a macro, the cursor will move to the top of the document each time a loop executes. This will probably disable whichever function the macro is trying to perform. In this case, then, you must *not* include HOME, HOME, UP. Instead, you must make the *assumption* that the macro will be started with the cursor already at the top of the document.

Cursor Navigation

When you use the cursor control keys during normal editing, you can see where the cursor goes at all times. For example, you can tell which characters are being included in a block definition by noting the on-screen highlighting. If something unexpected happens because of your document layout, you can easily correct the situation. However, a macro cannot make corrections for you during execution. You will have to write macros that move the cursor appropriately in all text situations.

For example, say you need to write a macro that searches for a particular phrase, marks it as a block, and then makes it bold. However, one word in the phrase is underlined in some of the occurrences. As you know from the discussion on Reveal Codes in Chapter 1, the cursor moves past a hidden code (like the Underline Begin and Underline End codes) as it would a letter. When marking the phrase as a block, then, you would have to use an arrow key two more times for an occurrence including an underlined word than you would for one that did not. The only reliable way to mark the phrase as a block would be to use the <Word Left> key in your macro instead of the arrow keys, since the cursor would then jump by entire words, avoiding the problem of hidden codes in the text.

There are many other situations where it helps to use cursor positioning controls that do not depend on your own decision making. Whenever possible, then, use the END, HOME, <Word Left>, and <Word Right> keys in macros to "feel" your way around the text.

THE PAUSE THAT REFRESHES

WordPerfect's macros gain tremendous flexibility with the combined Delay/Pause command, which provides four important features:

Pause for Input   You can insert a pause in a macro that allows it to stop temporarily; it will wait for you to enter information from the keyboard before continuing. You can therefore write a macro in a general format and customize it each time it is invoked. For example, you can create a macro that issues the keystrokes necessary to go to a menu and then pauses to let you make your choice from that menu.

Keystroke Delay   You can slow down a macro so that actions (including typed text) are executed at a speed slow enough for you to read the screen. The *delay factor*—the length of time between each keystroke of the macro—can be from 0.1 to 25.4 seconds.

Macro Visibility   You can make a macro either "visible"—that is, text, menus, and prompts will be shown on the screen while the macro is executing—or "invisible"—which means the screen will clear and "∗ Please Wait ∗" will appear at the bottom of the screen. Unless you specify otherwise, macros are normally invisible.

Timed Pause   You can insert a pause in a macro for a period of from 0.1 to 25.4 seconds. You can use this pause to view a particular screen or menu before the macro moves on.

The <Pause> key sequence (CTRL+PGUP) initiates all of these functions. The one performed depends on the keystrokes that follow the <Pause>.

Pause for Input

The Pause for Input function stops the macro during execution and waits for user input. You can pause the macro at any point—for example, when WordPerfect needs a response to a menu choice or prompt. When you execute the macro, it stops at the pause, beeps, and waits for you to enter something and press ENTER before it continues.

To insert a pause for input into a macro, create the macro in the usual way until you get to the place where you want the macro to pause for user input. Then press the <Pause> key (CTRL+PGUP) and then ENTER. This begins the pause. (Pressing ENTER instead of entering a number—as you will for the other three functions performed by the <Pause> key—indicates that this is an instruction to pause for input.)

WordPerfect will now wait for you to enter an *example* of the text that will be entered. Then press ENTER again to end the pause. This example will not be stored with the macro. It is necessary to enter an example only if your macro needs *something* entered here to work properly during macro definition. If you do not need or want to enter an example, simply press CTRL+PGUP and ENTER twice to insert the pause for input. In either case, you can now define the rest of your macro.

For practice, now create a macro to automate the steps for changing the number of copies of a document to be printed. (A discussion of this and other Print Options can be found in Chapter 1, "Basics Refresher.") With the cursor anywhere in your document:

1. Press the <Macro Def> key (CTRL+F10).

2. Press ALT+C (hold down the ALT key and type **C**).

   This will create a macro called ALTC.MAC. If you previously defined a macro with this name, the program will ask for confirmation to overwrite it.

3. Press the <Print> key (SHFT+F7).

4. Type **4** for "Printer Control."

5. Type **1** for "Select Print Options."

6. Type **2** for "Number of Copies."

7. Press the <Pause> key (CTRL+PGUP) and press ENTER twice.

   This step inserts the pause for input.

8. Press ENTER.

   This ENTER is the one that you would normally press after entering the number of copies you want.

9. Press ENTER.

   This exits from the Select Print Options menu to the Printer Control screen.

10. Press ENTER.

    This exits from the Printer Control screen to the document.

11. Press <Macro Def> to end the macro definition.

Now let's invoke the macro.

1. Press ALT+C.

   The macro will beep and pause at the Select Print Options menu, waiting for you to type the number of printed copies you want.

2.   Type **2** and press ENTER.

This specifies that you want two printed copies. The macro will continue running until it has completed the remaining keystrokes.

You can see how much easier this is than entering all of the steps manually each time. From now on, anytime you want to print several copies of a document, you are only a few keystrokes away.

Keystroke Delay and Macro Visibility

The *Keystroke Delay* and *Macro Visibility* functions are both specified with the same procedure. To enter either function into a macro, press the <Pause> key sequence. WordPerfect will beep, indicating that the program is waiting for you to type a number and then press ENTER.

The number must be from 1 to 254. The selected number creates a delay between keystrokes measured in tenths of a second. For example, enter 10 to indicate a one-second delay between keystrokes and 15 to indicate 1.5 seconds. Specifying a delay anywhere in a macro causes the entire macro to become visible. A delay of two-tenths of a second makes typed text just about readable. This delay is especially useful for preparing demos and tutorials.

Enter a 0 (for a zero-second delay) to indicate a *visible* macro that is executed at top speed. To make the macro *invisible* at any point (for the rest of the macro or until another Keystroke Delay command), enter 255.

While you type the number and press ENTER, no keystrokes are recorded on the screen. In fact, there is no way to verify that you are pressing the right keys, so remember what you are typing.

Now try an exercise that uses the Keystroke Delay function to type text at a readable speed. Make sure the screen is clear.

1.   Press the <Macro Def> key (CTRL+F10).

2.   Type **t** and press ENTER.

3.   Press the <Pause> key (CTRL+PGUP).

4.   Type **2** and press ENTER.

5.   Press ENTER five times; then press the <Center> key (SHFT+F6).

6.   Type **Thank you for joining our tutorial.**

7.   Press ENTER three times; then press the <Center> key.

8. Type **It's been a**

9. Press SPACE and then the <Bold> key (F6).

10. Type **pleasure**

11. Press the <Bold> key.

12. Press SPACE and type **to have you with us.** Press ENTER.

13. Press the <Macro Def> key to end macro definition.

Clear the screen and then execute the macro. The macro will be visible, and the text will be typed at a readable speed.

Timed Pause

You enter a *Timed Pause* function by inserting a long keystroke delay and then a short one, which slows the macro down for one step (the pause) and then speeds it up again. Here is an exercise that creates a five-second delay:

1. Press the <Macro Def> key (CTRL+F10).

2. Type **p** and press ENTER.

3. Press the <Help> key (F3).

4. Press the <Cancel> key (F1).
   You see the Help screen for the Cancel function.

5. Press the <Pause> key (CTRL+PGUP).
   The system beeps and waits for input.

6. Type **50** and press ENTER.
   This step will cause the macro to pause for five seconds.

7. Press the <Pause> key.

8. Type **255** and press ENTER.
   This returns the macro to top speed and invisibility.

9. Press ENTER.
   This will exit the Help screen.

10. Press the <Macro Def> key to end macro definition.

Now invoke the "P" macro. It will display the Help screen for the Cancel function for five seconds and then return to the document.

USING DOCUMENT 2

WordPerfect can work with two separate documents at once, as discussed in Chapter 1. This dual-document editing capability can be quite handy when used in conjunction with macros.

If you make an assumption that Document 2 will be available when a macro is invoked, then the macro can use it as a temporary editing work space. This work space provides a perfect area either for storing gathered bits of text or for performing any other action that requires the use of an editing environment but would disrupt the flow of text in Document 1.

You can, for instance, write a simple macro that will copy whatever line of text the cursor is on (or copy a sentence, paragraph, or other block of text), retrieve (paste) it into Document 2, and return to Document 1. If you try this, you will see that when the macro is executed, the cursor disappears for less than a second while it copies the text. It then becomes a simple matter to browse through your document, find the lines you want to collect, and execute the macro once for each line. When you are done, all of the lines you selected will be gathered in one place— Document 2.

You can also use Document 2 as a temporary holding place for a mass search operation—if, for example, you want to write a macro that searches a document, finds all of the footnote references, and combines them into a single separate document.

There are several ways to perform this task. One good method is to create a macro that uses the Edit Footnote function for the first footnote, marks its text as a block, copies the block, exits Edit Footnote, and retrieves (pastes) it into Document 2. Then the macro returns to Document 1 to repeat the procedure with the next footnote. Switching back and forth between the two documents is instantaneous, and block copying requires a minimum of disk access, so this is a fairly fast process.

USING OTHER MACRO PROGRAMS

There are several general-purpose, *memory-resident* utilities available, such as Prokey and Superkey, that function much as WordPerfect's macros do.

Most of these programs can be used with WordPerfect. They provide a lot more flexibility in *redefining* the keyboard (making one key act like another) than do WordPerfect's macros. However, WordPerfect's macros provide such features as conditional looping and pausing for input, which are sometimes impossible or difficult to implement with the general-purpose programs.

For a more complete discussion on the use of these programs with WordPerfect, see Chapter 10, "Macro Library."

EDITING MACROS WITH M-EDIT

The WordPerfect Library includes a macro editing program called M-Edit, which provides a powerful macro editing environment that displays keystrokes in the macro with full word descriptions. This display makes it possible to change the steps of a macro—an operation that cannot be performed from within WordPerfect. You can also add comments to the macro steps.

For a discussion of M-Edit, as well as other programs included in the WordPerfect Library package, see Appendix D, "WordPerfect Library."

3 MERGE

WordPerfect's Merge function allows you to create one "form" document (called a *primary document*) and use it repeatedly with information that is filled in either automatically (from a list of items stored in a *secondary document*) or manually (from the keyboard).

The most common application of the Merge function is a *mailmerge* operation. In this case the primary document is a form letter, and the secondary document contains a mailing list. The Merge function will combine the two documents, generating a new letter for each person on the list. Each personalized letter can be printed as it is generated, or the merge can save the letters to be printed later, in one batch.

The Merge function can also be used for a variety of other tasks. You may, for example, want to have information about a book collection printed both as a series of index cards in a specific format and as a columnar report of the book titles. Using WordPerfect's Merge function, you could maintain the actual data for all your books in a secondary file and then create several primary files that would format the data in different ways.

Most database programs design reports in a similar fashion. In fact, the Merge function is similar to a database program in many ways. You may find, after reading this chapter, that the Merge function is flexible enough to make unnecessary the purchase of an additional program for database work.

Although in its simplest form the Merge function is easy to use, it is also, in its more advanced forms, one of the most complex of WordPerfect's functions. In Chapter 1 you saw the benefits of WordPerfect's *clean screen* (that is, with no control codes shown). With the Merge function, you will notice an exception to the rule. After all, you are ready to learn the Merge function, one of the program's most advanced features; you should also be ready to bend a little in your expectation of the way WordPerfect appears on the screen.

BASIC MERGE COMPONENTS

The most basic form of the merge operation combines a single document with a list of information. To perform this task, you must create two files on disk: the primary document and the secondary document. Each of these documents has its own set of rules about the placement of text and about special *Merge codes* that will direct the merge operation.

Although it may not seem logical, it will be easier for you to understand the different layouts of the primary and secondary documents if the secondary document is discussed first.

The Secondary Document

The secondary document contains the information to be inserted into the primary document when you execute the Merge. For example, the secondary document might contain a list of names and addresses for use in a form letter merge operation. The secondary document is divided into *fields* and *records*. A field contains a single piece of information, like a name. A record contains a set of fields, like a person's name, address, phone number, date of birth, and salary. Special Merge codes separate the fields and records from one another.

You mark the end of a field by pressing the <Merge Return> key (F9), which inserts ^R and a Hard Return into the text at the cursor position. This key is identified as <Merge R> on the keyboard template.

Fields are, for most purposes, unlimited in length. They can consist of many lines, since the field ends only when the program encounters the

Note: Letters preceded by a caret (^) are usually referred to as if they had been entered using the CONTROL key. Thus, ^R is referred to as CONTROL R, even though in this particular case you have not pressed the CONTROL key. Do *not* enter this or any other Merge code by typing a caret followed by the single letter, since it would not be recognized by the Merge function. When marking the end of a field, you must always use the <Merge Return> key (F9).

^R [HRt] combination. For most applications, however, fields are only one or two lines long.

Mark the end of a record by pressing the <Merge End-of-Record> key (SHFT+F9), which inserts ^E and a Hard Return into the text at the cursor position. (This key is identified as <Merge E> on the keyboard template.) Records are also unlimited in length. They can contain as many fields as you want, but the number of fields in each record of a secondary document should always be the same.

The secondary document, like the primary document, is simply a standard WordPerfect file with some special codes inserted. Its potential size, then, like that of any other WordPerfect document, is determined by a combination of available disk space and cache memory (RAM). The number of records that can be stored in a secondary document is limited only by the total document size.

WordPerfect will internally number the fields sequentially, starting with 1 for the first field in each record. When the merge is actually executed, these numbers are used to pull information from the secondary document and place it into the primary document. Since WordPerfect will extract the information by counting the fields in each record, it is important that you keep the number of fields the same for each record. Therefore, if a field will be blank in one of the records, you still need to press the <Merge Return> key to insert a Merge Return code into that field. The field will not contain any text, but inserting the Merge Return code will keep the field numbering accurate.

Merge Practice — Creating A Secondary Document

As a simple example of a secondary document, let's create a file that contains a mailing list of only two people. Be sure the screen is clear before beginning the lesson.

1. Type **John** and press <Merge Return> (F9).

2. Type **Kent** and press <Merge Return>.

3. Type **Amalgamated Steel** and press <Merge Return>.

4. Type **334 Main St.** and press <Merge Return>.

5. Type **Toledo, OH 09332** and press <Merge Return>.

6. Press the <Merge End-of-Record> key (SHIFT+F9).

7. Type **Jan** and press <Merge Return>.

8. Type **Frankenbaumer** and press <Merge Return>.

9. Press <Merge Return>.

Notice that in this record, you simply press <Merge Return> for the second field, since there is no company name.

10. Type **554 Pine Ave.** and press <Merge Return>.

11. Type **Eureka, CA 94543** and press <Merge Return>.

12. Press the <Merge End-of-Record> key.

13. Press the <Save> key (F10).

14. Type **list** and press ENTER.

Your screen should like the one in Figure 3-1. (Note that the ^R and ^E codes are usually the only two Merge codes that are inserted into a secondary file.)

In this secondary document, field 1 is the first name, field 2 is the last name, field 3 is the company name, field 4 is the street address, and field 5 is the city, state, and ZIP code. (You should keep a written list of the fields and their corresponding field numbers whenever you create a secondary document. See the section entitled "Using Field Names" later in this chapter for an alternative to using field numbers.) You can see that if you want to specify a full name in the primary document, you will need to use both field 1 and field 2. Note that in the first record, field 3 contains a company name, while in the second record, field 3 is empty.

Now let's see how this data is used in the primary document.

The Primary Document

There are two ways of using WordPerfect's Merge function: the *simple method* and the *flexible method.* In this section, you will learn how to create a primary document for a simple merge. The flexible method, discussed later in the chapter, can perform some interesting tricks. However, it requires more effort and patience to implement.

```
John^R
Kent^R
Amalgamated Steel^R
334 Main St.^R
Toledo, OH 09332^R
^E
Jan^R
Frankenbaumer^R
^R
554 Pine Ave.^R
Eureka, CA 94543^R
^E

-
```

Doc 1 Pg 1 Ln 13   Pos 10

Figure 3-1.   A sample secondary document

Create the primary document exactly as you want the final printed document to appear. That is, type the document using WordPerfect's formatting commands (like Bold, Tab, and Center). The only difference is that you will insert one of the Merge codes into the text at each point where you want variable information to be entered. The variable information will come from either a secondary file or the keyboard. (Entering information from the keyboard during a merge operation is discussed later in this chapter, in the section "Give and Take — The Keyboard Merge.")

To insert any Merge code into the text of the primary document, press the <Merge Codes> key (ALT+F9). At the bottom of the screen a menu will appear that looks like this:

```
^C; ^D; ^F; ^G; ^N; ^O; ^P; ^Q; ^S; ^T; ^U; ^V:
```

This is probably the most cryptic of WordPerfect's menus. Each of the letters indicates a specific Merge function. To implement a simple merge, you need only the ^F Merge code.

^**F**   *Insert Field*

This code extracts a specific numbered field from the secondary document and inserts it into the primary document at the place where the code was inserted.

Here are three things to remember about inserting the ^F Merge code into a primary document:

- You do not need to insert every field in your secondary document into your primary document.

- You do not need to insert fields in numerical order.

- You can include any field as many times as you want.

To enter the ^F Merge code, type **F**. WordPerfect will respond by requesting a field number. Type the number of the field you want to include and press ENTER. The ^F code, followed by the field number you specified and a final ^, will be inserted into the text at the cursor position. For example, to insert field 1 of the secondary document into the primary document at the cursor position, press the <Merge Codes> key (ALT+F9), **F** for Field Number, **1** for field 1, and ENTER. The code ^F1^ will be inserted in the text.

When the merge is actually executed, it deletes the entire ^F code sequence and inserts the text from the specified field exactly where the sequence was located. You can place formatting commands (like Center, Underline, Flush Right, Align Tab, and so on) into the primary document before and after the ^F code sequence. The inserted text will be affected by these commands.

If, for example, you want the text from a specific field underlined in the final document, press the <Underline> key in the primary document before pressing the <Merge Codes> key. After entering the ^F code, press the <Underline> key again. The ^F code sequence will appear underlined (or marked for underlining depending on your monitor). When the primary document is merged with a secondary document, the text from that field will be underlined.

Suppressing Blank Lines

Sometimes, you need to insert a field in a primary document which may or may not contain information, depending on the record that is being merged. For example, you may have a field for company name, but not all of the people on your list are associated with a company. To avoid having a blank line in your merged document when a field is empty, simply include a question mark after the field number. For each record, merge will look to see whether or not the field is empty. If it is, the entire line on which the field appears will be deleted, suppressing the blank line. (Because of this, you should be careful about using the question mark for a field that appears on the same line with text or other ^F merge codes.)

For example, if the field that may or may not contain information is field 2, insert the ^F merge code by pressing the <Merge Codes> key (ALT+F9), typing **F** for Field, typing **2?**, and pressing ENTER. The merge code sequence ^F2?^ will appear at the cursor location. The merge codes for the entire address, then, would look similar to this:

```
^F1^
^F2?^
^F3^
^F4^  ^F5^
```

When the merge is executed, only those records with information in field 2 will have a line for the field. For records which do not have information in field 2, merge will skip right from field 1 to field 3.

Merge Practice—Creating A Primary Document

To create a primary document that will generate form letters for the list you made earlier, clear the screen and enter the text as shown in Figure 3-2. To insert the ^F merge codes into the letter, press the <Merge Codes> key (ALT+F9), type **F**, type the appropriate field number, and press ENTER.

December 23, 1986

^F1^ ^F2^
^F3?^
^F4^
^F5^

Dear ^F1^:

We are very sorry to inform you that all of the tickets for the
All-Star Spectacular at the Grenoble Theater this Friday, October
14, have been sold out. Enclosed, please find a refund for the
deposit you left with us last July.

We regret that you will be unable to attend, as we have always
appreciated the patronage of the ^F2^ family. Thank you for your
patience and your consideration.

Sincerely,

The Management of the Grenoble Theater
-
                                        Doc 1 Pg 1 Ln 24   Pos 10

Figure 3-2.   The primary document with merge codes

Performing the Simple Merge

The process of executing the simple merge procedure is what its name
indicates — simple. After following the steps just described, you press the
<Merge/Sort> key (CTRL+F9), choose "Merge," and enter the names
of the primary and secondary documents. Then the merge begins. To
stop a merge before it is complete, press the <Cancel> key (F1).

In a simple merge like this, WordPerfect combines the primary file
and the secondary file to make *one big merged document*. This file will
contain one copy of the primary document for each record that is found

December 23, 1986

John Kent
Amalgamated Steel
334 Main St.
Toledo, OH 09332

Dear John:

We are very sorry to inform you that all of the tickets for the
All-Star Spectacular at the Grenoble Theater this Friday, October
14, have been sold out. Enclosed, please find a refund for the
deposit you left with us last July.

We regret that you will be unable to attend, as we have always
appreciated the patronage of the Kent family. Thank you for your
patience and your consideration.

Sincerely,

The Management of the Grenoble Theater

                                    Doc 1   Pg 1   Ln 1   Pos 10

Figure 3-3.   Merged document

on a new page.

Make sure the screen is clear before you begin performing the merge.
It is very important to do this since the on-screen document is used to
generate the merged document. (Any text that is on the screen when a
merge is executed will be included in the final merged document.) Follow
these steps:

1. Press the <Merge/Sort> key (CTRL+F9).

2. Type **1** for "Merge."

3. At the "Primary file:" prompt, type **letter** and press ENTER.

4. At the "Secondary file:" prompt, type **list** and press ENTER.

The screen will clear, and this message will be displayed briefly at the bottom of the screen:

```
* Merging *
```

5. Press HOME,HOME,UP ARROW to move to the top of the merged document. Your screen should look like the one in Figure 3-3.

The Merge function has now created a two-page document containing two versions of the primary file. Scroll through the document to see how the data from the two records in the secondary file has been incorporated into the text. Notice that the address is four lines long in the first letter but three lines long in the second letter. Also notice that the longer last name in the second record caused the last paragraph of the letter to be formatted differently from the first record. WordPerfect automatically reformats paragraphs while performing the merge operation. If you printed the document now, you would have two personalized letters.

THE FLEXIBLE MERGE

With the simple merge procedure, WordPerfect performs many functions automatically. For instance, it generates a Hard Page Break between copies of the primary document, and it moves successively to each record in the secondary document. With the flexible merge, these operations are not performed automatically. If you want a Hard Page Break inserted, you have to put it in yourself. You also need to specify when the merge should move to the next record in the secondary file.

The procedure for using WordPerfect's flexible merge is similar to that for computer programming. When you create a primary document, you are essentially writing a "program" that will lead WordPerfect through a series of instructions when the merge procedure is initiated. When you execute a merge and specify a primary document, you are "running" the program. The program places output into the merged document as it executes. This output consists of text that is entered in the primary file, fields that are requested from a secondary file, and keyboard input.

As the merge executes, it examines each character in the primary document. Text (like the body of a form letter) is passed directly into the merged document. The Merge function processes field codes (like $^\wedge$F1$^\wedge$) by deleting the code, extracting the specified field number, and placing it in the merged document.

Beyond this, there are several Merge codes that control the merge operation, telling it when to move to the next record in the secondary file and whether it should switch to a new primary or secondary document.

Flexible Merge Codes

The flexible merge is implicitly selected when you use any one of three Merge codes in the primary document: $^\wedge$N, $^\wedge$P, or $^\wedge$S. As soon as the merge operation encounters one of them, the simple merge cycle is cancelled. Thereafter, you must use the Flexible Merge codes to manually perform many of the functions that are performed automatically by the simple merge.

The $^\wedge$N code performs a step that is normally handled by the simple merge:

^N *Next Record*
This code tells the Merge function to start using the next record in the current secondary document. All subsequent $^\wedge$F codes will retrieve information from this next record. When there are no more records, the merge operation ends.

The $^\wedge$P code instructs the system to continue the merge operation using a new primary file. This primary file can be the same one that you specified when the merge was originally executed (which means the merge would be repeating the same steps, as with the simple merge). The new primary file can also be different from the one originally specified. In this case, the control of the merge operation is transferred to the new document. This document is then processed like the first one.

^P *Primary Document*
This code specifies a new primary document for the merge to use. It is entered in Matched Pair form. The name of the primary document is entered between two $^\wedge$P codes, without any spaces. For example, $^\wedge$Pform.ltr$^\wedge$P instructs the merge to begin using the "form.ltr" primary

file. If no file name is entered between the codes (that is, ^P^P), the merge will reuse the primary file currently being used.

If you can use the ^N and ^P codes to perform the same functions as the simple merge, you may wonder why you can't *always* use the simple merge. In fact, you can completely simulate the simple merge cycle using Flexible Merge codes. However, the flexible merge performs many functions that could not be performed by the simple merge.

For example, the flexible merge can suppress the Hard Page Break that the simple merge automatically inserts between copies of the primary document. With the Hard Page Break suppressed, the copies will not appear on separate pages in the final merged document. To perform this function, add these codes to the end of a primary document:

```
^N^P^P
```

These codes tell the merge to use the next record in the secondary document and then to continue the merge reusing the current primary document. When the merge encounters this string of codes at the end of a primary document, the simple merge cycle is cancelled, and no Hard Page Break is inserted. This might be useful in a number of situations.

Instead of writing form letters, you may want to see a report showing only the names of everyone on your mailing list. You want the names to appear one after the other, not on separate pages.

Clear the screen and create a short primary document consisting only of these Merge codes:

```
^F1^ ^F2^
^N^P^P
```

Save the file with the name "report", clear the screen, and execute the merge. Use "report" as the primary file name and "list" (the file from your previous exercise) as the secondary file name. After the merge is complete, you will see the names of the two people on your list. (Naturally, with a larger mailing list you would see more names.) After a report like this is generated, you could move the cursor to the top of the document and retrieve a "report header" document that consists of a title and field names for the report.

You can make a report like this more elaborate by adding more fields separated by Tab or Tab Align codes or by adding print enhancements like Bold and Underline. (Pressing <Tab Align> and then entering the ^F Merge code for a field that contains numbers causes the numbers to line up properly in the final merged document.) You can generate some fancy columnar reports using this technique.

Suppression of the Hard Page Break code, however, is only one of many abilities the flexible merge affords you. You can also use the ^P codes to combine many smaller documents into a final document. This is possible because control returns to the original primary document when the merge has completely processed a new primary document specified with the ^P codes. (This will not occur if control is transferred again or if the merge stops while processing the new primary document.)

Remember that when a primary document is "processed," any text the document contains will be passed into the final merged document. Therefore, if the new primary document that you specify contains only text, the file is simply "retrieved" and added to the merged document; processing continues with the original primary document. In this way, you can combine several documents into one final document.

For example, you could write several standard paragraphs, saving them as separate files on disk with names like "salut" for salutation and "body.4" as one of four possible paragraphs for the body of a letter. Then you could combine the paragraphs into a custom form letter by building a primary document like this one:

```
^Pheader^P
^Psalut^P
^Pbody.4^P
^Pbody.1^P
^Pconclude.2^P
^Psignoff^P
```

After saving this document and specifying it as a primary file in a merge, you would have a letter that included all of the paragraphs you specified.

The ^S code is similar to the ^P code, except that it specifies a new secondary document for the merge to start using, instead of a new primary document. You might want to use the ^S code to maintain two separate secondary documents that you often use together.

^S *Secondary Document*
This command specifies a new secondary document for the merge to use. The file name is specified exactly as with the ^P code. You must always specify a name.

Perhaps you have one secondary document that contains a list of people with IBM computers and another of people with Compaq computers. You frequently use the lists separately but occasionally need to perform a mailmerge using both lists at once. By inserting a set of ^S codes that specify the name of the second list at the end of the first list, you can perform the mailmerge on both lists with the same merge instruction.

Merging to the Printer

The simple merge creates one large document that can then be saved, printed, or otherwise processed. However, if you are using a secondary file that contains a large number of records, the resulting merged document can often become too big to handle. In fact, you may simply be unable to create a document as large as the one that would be produced by the simple merge.

The solution to this problem is the flexible merge. With it, the Merge function can automatically print each copy of the primary document after it has been merged with a record from the secondary document.

To merge to the printer, use the ^T Merge code:

^T   *Type (Print) Merged Document*
This command will generate a Full Text Print of the merged document, and then it will clear it from memory.

This code generates a print job, exactly as if you had pressed the <Print> key and selected "Full Text." This means that, as with all documents, the printer will automatically advance to the next sheet of paper (if you are using continuous paper) after the document has been printed. You do not want to use the simple merge, which would force an extra Hard Page Break between records, causing a blank piece of paper to be ejected between pages.

The ^T Merge code, then, does not invoke the flexible merge itself, but its use requires other codes that do. To avoid the extra Hard Page Break, use the ^N and ^P^P sequences to perform the actual merge loop. Use the <Merge Codes> key to place this sequence at the end of a primary document for executing a merge to the printer, as shown here:

```
^T^N^P^P
```

This code sequence prints the merged document and clears it from memory (^T), advances to the next record in the secondary file (^N), and cycles back to the beginning of the same primary file (^P^P).

Give and Take — The Keyboard Merge

There are two Merge codes that provide interaction between you and WordPerfect during the merge process. They are ^C, for "input from the Console," and ^O, for "Output to the screen."

^C *Input from the Console/Keyboard*

When the system encounters this code during the actual merge operation, the merge will pause and wait for you to enter data. After entering the data, press the <Merge Return> key (F9). (Think of pressing the <Merge Return> key here as ending a field, in the same way that you would end a field in the secondary document.)

^O *Output to the Screen*

The text that appears between two ^O codes will be placed at the bottom of the screen when the merge encounters the sequence. This is a Matched Pair Merge code.

Note that you can place both these codes in either the primary or secondary document. If you want the Merge function to pause for input once for every record in the secondary file (or if there will be no secondary file), insert the code into the primary file at the appropriate location. To have it pause for only selected records, insert the code into the secondary file within the appropriate records.

The ^O and ^C codes are commonly used together. For example, you can remind yourself of the type of information to be entered from the keyboard before stopping the merge for input. To do this, use the ^O code to output a message to the screen. The ^C code requests the input:

```
^OEnter client's 1985 donation^O^C
```

When the merge encounters this sequence, it will delete the ^O codes and all text between them, display the text at the bottom of the screen, and wait for input. The input will actually be placed in the document at the location of the first ^O, since everything else will be deleted during the merge.

These codes can be used to execute a fill-in-the-blanks type of operation. Perhaps you have a standard document that you use frequently. Only key information, like the client's name and dollar amounts, will change each time. You can use the keyboard merge to prompt you for these variable pieces of text. Simply enter a code sequence like the one just shown anywhere in the document that text should be entered manually during the merge.

If a ^C code appears between a set of ^G, ^P, or ^S Matched Pair codes, the text that you enter when the merge pauses will specify the macro or the primary or secondary file name, depending on which Matched Pair codes you used. (The ^G code, used to execute a macro, is described later in this chapter.)

You may choose to enter part of the file name after the ^C code — for example, the file extension — and then enter the first part of the file name (which might vary each time) when the merge pauses for input. This is useful if there are several related files from which you need to choose. For instance, to have the merge stop and prompt for one of a set of related primary files, enter a sequence like this:

```
^P^C.rld^P
```

This tells the merge that a new primary file will be specified, that it should prompt for a text string, and that it should combine that text string with ".rld" to produce the complete file name.

If you enclose a series like this with a set of ^O codes (with a text prompt), then the prompt will appear at the bottom of the screen (instead of "Primary name:" or "Secondary name:" or "Macro:"). You will also enter the inputted text at the bottom of the screen (instead of wherever the ^C code happens to be placed in the primary document). This is the most elegant way to enter a file name during a merge.

To have the merge prompt for a new primary document at the bottom of the screen, enter this into a primary document:

```
^OWhich letter would you like to use? ^P^C^P^O
```

Providing this type of "custom prompt" makes the procedure easy to understand, which is especially helpful when it will be executed by another person.

When you use the ^C code in this way, you need to press only the ENTER key to continue with the merge operation. Pressing the <Merge Return> key is not required.

Other Merge Codes

Here are several other Merge codes that can be useful in the merge process:

^D *Insert Date*
This code inserts the current date, as set by the computer's system clock, into the merged document. This code produces a result similar to pressing the <Date> key (SHFT+F5) and choosing "Insert Function."

^Q *Quit Merge*
When the system encounters this code, the Merge function stops executing. If you place it just before the ^E code in the last record you want to process in a secondary file, it will halt the Merge function after processing the record.

^U *Update Screen*
This code "rewrites" the screen, performing the same function as pressing the <Screen> key (CTRL+F3) and choosing "Rewrite." Usually, the Merge function will not display an accurate screen while the merge is being performed. The ^U code allows you to see the state of the document at a certain point in the merge.

USING THE MERGE FUNCTION WITH MACROS

Merges and macros can work together to form a powerful alliance. Each has the ability to invoke the other. However, a macro ends when a merge is started, and a merge ends before a macro is started. Therefore, only one is functioning at a time, which means that you cannot execute several merge procedures with a given macro, nor can you execute several macros from within a single merge. You can, however, "chain" several macros and merge procedures together.

Macros and merge procedures can both be considered languages of control. They operate in very different ways, with different strengths and weaknesses. For most purposes, macros are the best device for automating a procedure, but the Merge function does have some abilities that macros do not. Together, they can do just about anything.

To execute a macro from within a merge, insert the ^G Merge code into a primary document:

^G *Goto (Execute) a Macro*

This command specifies a macro that will be executed when the merge is complete, even if the primary document is changed during the merge with a ^P code. The macro will not execute until the merge has been completed, regardless of whether it is a simple or flexible merge or where the code is inserted in the primary document. It is a Matched Pair code.

Here is a sequence of codes that will execute a macro when a merge is complete:

```
^GALTM^G^T^N^P^P
```

Here, the string "^GALTM^G" specifies that the ALTM.MAC macro will execute when the merge is complete. The "^T^N^P^P" performs the normal flexible merge control, printing the documents one at a time. It is important to put the set of ^G codes specifying the macro name before the set of ^P codes.Otherwise, the ^G codes will never be processed—control will have passed to another primary document before the merge encounters the codes. However, once the merge has encountered a set of ^G codes with a macro name, it will remember which macro to execute after the merge, no matter which primary document is being processed. When the merge is complete, the macro will be executed (unless another set of ^G codes is encountered).

To execute a merge from within a macro, simply enter the normal steps to execute the merge while you are defining the macro. When the merge procedure begins, macro definition automatically ends. Because of this, executing a merge is always the last step of a macro. You may wish to include a Pause for Input command at either the "Primary file:" or "Secondary file:" prompt (see Chapter 2, "Macros").

The macro menu that is discussed in the next section, "Menu Magic," shows you how you can use macros and the Merge function together to perform some interesting and complex tasks.

MENU MAGIC

You have already seen how to use the Merge function in many ways besides the traditional combining of a single document with a list of information. Another way in which you can use the Merge function to make your life easier is to create a menu system.

You can use the menu to select from several macros that execute frequently performed word processing tasks. You can also use the menu in the middle of a mailmerge operation to prompt you for a new primary or secondary file name.

You create a menu with the technique described in the "Give and Take" section of this chapter. That is, you place a prompt string, as well as a Matched Pair code like ^P, ^S, or ^G, and finally a ^C code, between two ^O codes. The ^C code is used to prompt for the file or macro name.

The only difference between a normal keyboard merge and creating a menu is that for the menu, the prompt string is several lines long. When the merge encounters a multi-line prompt string, it scrolls each line up from the bottom of the screen until it comes to the line containing the ^C code, where it stops. It is this last line that is actually used for the prompt string at the bottom of the screen. In this way, the menu choices constitute the first part of this string, and a prompt like "Enter your choice:" constitutes the final part.

Let's create a macro menu that lets you choose from several commonly performed tasks. (Use only spaces to format the menu, not the TAB key.) Clear the screen and follow these steps:

1. Press the <Merge Codes> key (ALT+F9) and type **O**

2. Press ENTER six times.

3. Press ESC, type **34**, and press SPACE.

4. Type **Main Menu** and press ENTER.

5. Press ESC, type **34**, and press SPACE.

6. Type --------- and press ENTER twice.

7. Press ESC, type **28**, and press SPACE.

8. Type **1. Start mailmerge** and press ENTER twice.

9. Press ESC, type **28**, and press SPACE.

10. Type **2. Document Assembly** and press ENTER twice.

11. Press ESC, type **28**, and press SPACE.

12. Type **3. Print mailing labels** and press ENTER.

13. Press ESC, type **28**, and press SPACE.

14. Type **4. Backup files** and press ENTER twice.

15. Press ESC, type **28**, and press SPACE.

16. Type **5. Quit WordPerfect** and press ENTER seven times.

17. Press ESC, type **28**, and press SPACE.

18. Type **Enter your choice:** and press SPACE.

19. Press the <Merge Codes> key and type **G**

20. Press the <Merge Codes> key and type **C**

21. Type **menu**

22. Press the <Merge Codes> key and type **G**

23. Press the <Merge Codes> key and type **O**

Notice that "menu" appears after the ^C code but within the ^G codes. When the merge encounters this, it will execute a macro whose name starts with the number chosen from the menu and ends with "menu".

Save this primary file as "menu" and then clear the screen. To complete this menu system, define macros that perform the various functions listed on the menu, and give them names like "1menu," "2menu," and so on. You can call the menu to the screen (whether or not the macros have been defined) by following these steps:

1. Press the <Merge/Sort> key (CTRL+F9).

2. Type **1** for "Merge."

3. Type **menu** and press ENTER twice.

Your screen will look like the one in Figure 3-4. To execute a macro from the menu, you would simply type the corresponding number and press ENTER. If the macro you request has not been defined, the message "ERROR: File not found" will be displayed.

```
                            Main Menu
                            ---------

                    1.  Start mailmerge

                    2.  Document Assembly

                    3.  Print mailing labels

                    4.  Backup files

                    5.  Quit WordPerfect




                    Enter your choice: _
```

Figure 3-4.   Macro menu example

As an example, "Start mailmerge" is the first choice in the menu shown above. You would want this choice to enter all the keystrokes necessary to initiate a commonly performed merge procedure (like a form letter and customer list). The macro, named "1menu," would start the merge and enter the primary and secondary file names for you. When you choose "1" from the menu, the macro "1menu" is executed, starting the merge procedure.

You might also define an ALT key macro (like ALT+M for "Menu") to call up the menu by executing the merge. The first steps of the macro should be to insert the merge code ^Q into the current document, and then to press the LEFT ARROW key once. After you enter a menu choice, the ^Q code will halt the merge, leaving the cursor in its same position in the document. And, since there is no text in the primary menu file outside of the ^O codes (and all text within ^O codes is automatically deleted during a merge), the menu text will not disturb the text in the current document.

With a menu like this one, you can use a macro (ALT+M) to execute a merge (the menu) that executes a macro (1menu.mac), which in turn executes a merge (the mailmerge operation), which might then execute a macro (ALTM) to return to the menu. (You executed the menu macro manually by holding down the ALT key and typing **M**, but to specify the same macro in a primary document you would enter "^Galtm^G".)

You can also use a menu like this to select from several primary or secondary files during a merge procedure. Simply create a menu like the preceding one for macros but containing ^P or ^S codes and names of primary or secondary documents instead. Then include the entire sequence of text between the ^O codes in a primary document; when it is encountered, the menu will appear. When you choose from the menu, the merge will continue with the new primary or secondary document.

THE DUAL MERGE

With the Dual Merge, the primary file is combined with the secondary file to create another primary or secondary file. This feature, although somewhat complicated, provides abilities that would not otherwise be possible.

Suppose you have a standard contract with four pieces of information that will change each time they are used: name, contract date, dollar amount, and location. You would use the Merge With Keyboard function discussed earlier, right? Yes, but what if the name appears 24 times in the document, the dollar amount 5 times, and the location twice. You would have to repeatedly enter the same information throughout the document. To avoid this, use the dual merge.

What you want is a merge that will prompt you for the correct entries, *creating* a secondary file that will then be merged with the contract.

The key to the dual merge is the ^V Merge code:

^V *Insert Merge Code*
^V is a Matched Pair Merge code. A set of ^V codes acts as a "shield" for Merge codes that appear between them. When you execute the merge, the ^V codes are deleted, but any Merge codes that appear between them will be transferred, unprocessed, into the merged document.

Note: Most of WordPerfect's Merge codes have some logic behind their single-letter nomenclature. ^V is so named because "CTRL+V" has traditionally meant "insert control codes" in the microcomputer industry.

Now create a primary file that, like the preceding example, will generate a secondary file. (When typing the ^R and ^E codes in this lesson, press <Merge Codes> and then type **R** or **E**, rather than pressing

<Merge Return> and <Merge End-of-Record>; this avoids insertion of an [HRt].) Enter this sequence of text and codes:

```
^OEnter client's name^O^C^V^R^V
^OEnter the date of the contract^O^C^V^R^V
^OEnter the dollar amount^O^C^V^R^V
^OEnter the location of the property^O^C^V^R^V
^V^E^V
```

Save this file as "contract.inp" and then clear the screen. Execute the merge by pressing <Merge/Sort>, typing **1** for "Merge," entering **contract.inp** for the primary file, and just pressing ENTER for the secondary file. You will be prompted for each of these items. Press the <Merge Return> key to move to each new field. After you have entered all of the information, what you see will look just like a single record in a secondary file, with the ^R code at the end of every field and the ^E code at the end of the record.

Here is what happened: The Merge function first processed each set of ^O codes by displaying the text at the bottom of the screen and then deleting the text and the codes. Next it paused for you to enter the field contents. When you pressed the <Merge Return> key, the system went on to process the string "^V^R^V". The ^V codes were deleted, and the ^R code was left intact. The ^E code was also left intact when the merge encountered it at the end of the file.

You end up with a formatted record that can be saved and used as a secondary file for a merge with the contract as the primary file. In this way, the information that you entered once can be spread through the contract as many times as necessary. Simply create the contract as a primary file that has ^F codes at appropriate places to retrieve one of the four items in the file you just created, and then execute the merge. You might want to create one macro to start the first merge, and another to save the created secondary file, clear the screen, and start the second merge. In this case, you would include a set of ^G codes, with the name of the secondary macro, in the primary file listed above.

The functions of the Merge codes are summarized in Table 3-1.

SORTING AND SELECTING DATA

You can sort records stored in secondary documents with WordPerfect's Sort function—for example, to print a set of mailing labels in ZIP code order. You can also select specific records from the secondary document

^F   *Insert Field*
Inserts a specific numbered field from the secondary
document into the primary document.

^N   *Next Record*
Tells the Merge function to start using the next record in the current
secondary document. When there are no more records, the merge operation ends.

^P   *Primary Document*
Specifies a new primary document for the Merge function to use.

^S   *Secondary Document*
Specifies a new secondary document for the Merge function to use.

^T   *Type (Print) Merged Document*
Generates a Full Text Print of the merged document and then clears it from
memory.

^C   *Input From the Console/Keyboard*
Pauses and waits for you to enter data. Continue with <Merge Return>.

^O   *Output to the Screen*
Places text at the bottom of the screen.

^G   *Goto (Execute) a Macro*
Specifies a macro that will be executed when the merge operation is
complete.

^D   *Insert Date*
Inserts the current date, as set by the computer's system clock.

^Q   *Quit Merge*
Causes the Merge function to stop executing.

^U   *Update Screen*
Rewrites the screen.

^V   *Insert Merge Codes*
Allows merge codes to be ignored during a merge for a dual merge.

Table 3-1.   Summary of Merge Codes

for use in a merge operation, such as printing labels for a specific ZIP
code range.

The sort/select operation also works with individual lines (like a
profit and loss statement) or paragraph text (like bibliographic entries).
You can sort the data based on a specific column or word in the text.

Starting the Sort/Select Operation

Unlike the merge operation, you can sort and select information that is either in memory or stored on disk. To start the procedure, clear the screen and follow these steps:

1. Press the <Retrieve> key (SHFT+F10).

2. Type **list** and press ENTER.

   This is the secondary document that you created earlier in the chapter.

3. Press the <Merge/Sort> key (CTRL+F9).

4. Type **2** for "Sort."

   Here the program prompts you to enter the name of the file containing the information you want to sort. Note that the default response is (Screen). If you press ENTER to use the default, the document currently on screen will be used as the source for the sorting and selection process.

5. Press ENTER.

   Here the program prompts you to enter the name of a file to contain the result of the sorting and selecting process. Note that the default for this prompt is (Screen) as well. If you press ENTER to use the default, the result will be placed in the current document after the original text has been deleted. If the name of the file you specify already exists on disk, the program will ask for confirmation before continuing.

6. Press ENTER.

You will see the sort/select display on the screen, as in Figure 3-5.

In addition to sorting a file on disk or a document in memory, you can sort a block of text. To do this, mark the text with the <Block> key and then press the <Merge/Sort> key. The program immediately shows the sort/select display. The result of the sort/select process will replace the marked text.

The screen is divided into two parts. At the top, you can see ten lines of the current document. At the bottom is the sort/select display. At the top of this display you can see the type of sort that is currently active:

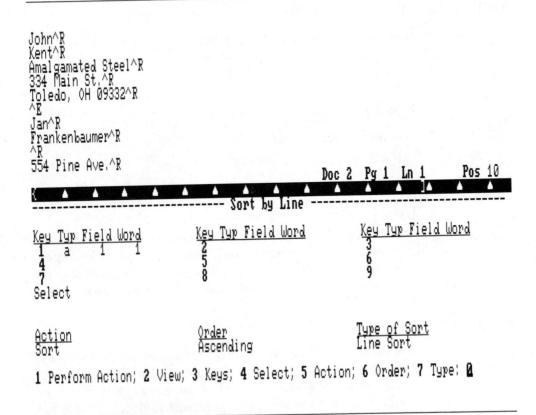

Figure 3-5.   The sort/select display

Line, Paragraph, or Secondary Merge. Some parts of the display will change depending on which type of sort you select. Initially, the function will be set to "Sort by Line." Along the bottom of the screen is a menu.

If at any time during the sort/select process you need to see more of the document than the ten lines shown, type **2** for "View." The cursor will move into the document area, and you can scroll the document using any of WordPerfect's cursor positioning commands. (You cannot enter or edit the text of the document in this mode.) To return to the sort/select screen, press the <Exit> key (F7).

Now specify the type of sort/select you will need to work with the "list" file.

7. Type **7** for "Type."

This allows you to specify the type of sort/select you want.

8. Type **1** for "Merge."

The title of the sort/select display becomes "Sort Secondary Merge File."

You are now ready to begin the sort/select process.

Specifying Keys

Before WordPerfect can rearrange or select records from your data, you need to tell it exactly which part of the data will be used for performing the sort or selection. You do this by specifying *keys*. A key is simply a word that has been isolated within your data. The program will first sort using the word specified with key 1; then the records that have identical words in key 1 will be sorted with key 2, and so on. You can define up to nine keys.

To specify a key, type **3** to select "Keys" from the sort/select display. The cursor will move to the middle of the display, where the key definitions are shown. You specify keys by entering four pieces of information about the data. The first is type, which is either alphanumeric (text) or numeric. Second is the field number that the word appears in. Third is the line of the field number that the word appears in (for example, the second line of a two-line address). Fourth is the position of the word within the line of the field number specified. If the number is positive, the words are counted from the left. If it is negative, the words are counted from the right. Similarly, if the line number is positive, the lines are counted from the top. If it is negative, they are counted from the bottom.

To insert a key, position the cursor with the arrow keys and press INS. To delete a key, press DEL.

For example, to specify the first key as the second field in your document, last name, follow these steps:

1. Type **3** to select "Keys" from the sort/select display.

This moves the cursor to the definition for key 1.

2. Press ENTER to use "a" for alphanumeric type.

3. Type **2** and press ENTER.

This specifies field 2.

4. Press ENTER to use 1 for the line number.

5. Press ENTER to use 1 for the word number.

The cursor moves to the definition for key 2.

6. Press the <Exit> key (F7) to stop specifying keys.

Performing the Sort

To perform the sort, type **1** for "Perform Action." To sort the records in descending order instead of ascending order, you could type **6** for "Order" and select "Descending" before selecting "Perform Action." A message will appear briefly at the bottom of the screen to show the number of records that have been examined. When the sort is done, you are returned to the document screen. Notice that the two records have reversed positions.

Specifying Selection Criteria

To perform a selection on a list of data, you use the same keys that are specified for sorting. Once you have defined these keys, you use them in a comparative statement that WordPerfect can use to determine which records will be included in the output.

When entering the selection criteria, you specify which key you are comparing by typing "key" followed immediately by the key number. For example, if you have key 1 defined as the last name (as you have done for the exercise), then you use "key1" in the selection criteria. When you choose **4** for "Select," a message at the bottom of the screen shows the allowable operators that you can use for comparative purposes in the selection criteria.

The selection criteria is entered as a logical statement. You need to first think about how you would state a request to yourself and then translate that request into a statement that WordPerfect can understand.

Perhaps you want to perform a merge using only those people whose ZIP codes are higher than 80896. First, you need to define the ZIP code as key 1. Then the statement would be translated to "key1 > 80896" or "all those records where key 1 is greater than 80896." Let's perform the steps to change key 1's definition and enter the selection criteria.

1. Press the <Merge/Sort> key (CTRL+F9).

2. Type **2** for "Sort" and press ENTER twice.

3. Type **3** for "Keys."

4. Press ENTER to use "a" for alphanumeric type.

   Even though a ZIP code consists of numeric digits, it is usually considered alphanumeric. The numeric type should only be used with numbers that you might use to perform some mathematical function.

5. Type **4** to specify Field Number 4.

6. Press ENTER to use 1 for line number 1.

7. Type **−1** to specify the last word of the line.

   The sort/select function will look backward from the end of the line to locate a space when you use a negative number as the word number. The word that follows the first space it finds is used for the key.

8. Press ENTER and then <Exit>.

   Now you are ready to enter the selection criteria.

9. Type **4** for "Select."

   The cursor moves below the "Select" prompt in the middle of the sort/select display.

10. Type **key1 > 80896** and press ENTER.

When you enter selection criteria, the Action indicator changes from "Sort" to "Select and Sort." If you prefer to use the selection criteria without also sorting the data, you can press **5** for "Action" and choose "Select Only."

Performing the Selection

Be very careful when performing the selection. If you are replacing a file on disk or are working with a document on screen, you might lose some of your data by entering an incorrect selection criteria since the old text will be *replaced* by the selected text. (For example, if you had entered **key1 > 99654** as the selection criteria for this document, you would be presented with a blank screen when the selection was complete — none of the records would have matched the criteria.)

Make sure that you are not replacing the only copy of a secondary document. Also be sure that you have saved the document, if you are working with one in memory, before executing the selection.

To extract from your file all of the records whose ZIP codes are higher than 80896, simply type **1** for "Perform Action." The sort/select screen will disappear, and you will be returned to the document. Only Jan Frankenbaumer's record remains on the screen, since John does not live in the targeted area.

Advanced Selection Criteria

The selection criteria can actually be much more complex than the example just shown. There, you used only one comparative statement. However, you can join several comparative statements using special symbols in the selection criteria.

If you wanted to produce a list of clients whose ZIP codes were within the range of 46553 and 74554, for instance, you would need to combine two statements with an "and" operator. In other words, you want "all those records where key 1 is greater than 46553 *and* key 1 is less than 74554." To specify this, use the * (asterisk) for the "and" character. Parentheses are also used to make the statement more understandable. Thus, the selection criteria would be as follows: "(key1 > 46553) * (key1 < 74554)".

Another logical operator is "or." To specify "or" in the selection criteria, use the + (plus) character. If you wanted a list of people with ZIP codes of either 95446 or 94704, then the selection criteria would be "(key1 = 95446) + (key1 = 94704)".

You can use any combination of the nine keys in the selection criteria. If, for example, you have defined key 1 as the salary and key 2 as the city, you could enter the following criteria to produce a list of people who earn between $20,000 and $30,000 and live in Dayton: "((key1 >= 20000) * (key1 <= 30000)) * (key2 = Dayton)".

There is one special key that is used in selecting records. The *global key* is used to specify text that might appear anywhere within a record. This key is identified as "keyg" in the selection criteria.

The operators that can be used in the selection criteria are summarized in Table 3-2.

+ (OR)	Separates two key statements when only one or the other must be true to match
* (AND)	Separates two key statements when both must be true to match
=	equal to
<>	not equal to
>	greater than
<	less than
>=	greater than or equal to
<=	less than or equal to

Table 3-2.   Summary of Selection Criteria Operators

Sorting/Selecting Lines and Paragraphs

The only difference between using the sort/select feature with secondary merge files and with lines and paragraphs is in defining the keys.

When using the feature with lines, you specify keys with just a field number and a word number. You separate fields in a line with either a Tab code or an Align Tab code. The first field (column) in a line is field 1. Specify the word number in the same way as with merge files. Records are separated by a Hard or Soft Return.

With paragraphs, you specify keys with line, field, and word numbers. Specify line numbers as with merge files. Field and word numbers are specified as with lines. Records are separated by two or more Hard Returns. Use the paragraph sort to sort and select bibliographic references.

EDITING SECONDARY MERGE FILES WITH NOTEBOOK

WordPerfect Library, which is sold separately from WordPerfect, includes a program called Notebook that allows you to manipulate secondary merge files more easily. With Notebook, you can view records in the merge file either in a custom-designed screen form or in a row-and-column format. Files saved from Notebook can be used in a WordPerfect merge operation without prior translation.

For a discussion of Notebook, as well as of other programs included in WordPerfect Library, see Appendix D, "WordPerfect Library."

USING FIELD NAMES

Normally, you indicate which fields to include in a primary file by using field numbers. Unfortunately, it can be difficult to remember which field numbers correspond to which fields. If you use the Notebook program from WordPerfect Corporation (see Appendix D, "WordPerfect Library") to manage your secondary documents, you can refer to the fields using the names you specified there. However, even if you don't use Notebook, you can still use field names if you prepare the secondary document properly. (Early versions of WordPerfect 4.2 had a problem with this function—be sure you are working with the latest release.)

To name your fields manually, you create a *header record* in the secondary document—that is, the first record will be a special one containing the names of the fields. This record will not be included as normal data when you perform a merge operation.

To insert a header record, first retrieve the secondary document you wish to use. Then, with the cursor at the top of the document, press the <Merge Codes> key (ALT+ F9), type **N**, and press ENTER. This inserts the ^N merge code, which tells WordPerfect during a merge that it should go to the next record.

Then, for each field in your secondary document, press the <Bold> key (F6), type the field name, press the <Bold> key again, and press ENTER. Each field name must be bolded separately, and followed by a Hard Return. After you've entered all of the field names, and pressed ENTER for the last one, press the <Merge Return> key (F9).

Now, you must create empty fields to complete the header record. There must be as many fields in this header record as there are in each normal record in the secondary document. (You've already entered one field—the list of field names ending with ^R.) To create each additional empty field, press the <Merge Codes> key, type **N**, and press the <Merge Return> key.

Once you've entered all of the empty fields, press the<Merge End-of-Record> key (SHIFT+ F9). The line after the the one with ^E should be the first line of your actual data. Save the document.

To use the field names in a primary file, simply enter a name at the "Field?" prompt, instead of a number. WordPerfect will insert the ^F merge code, the field name you entered, and a caret (^). For example, to enter the Name field into a primary file, you would press the <Merge Codes> key, type **F** and then **Name,** and then press ENTER. The program will insert ^FName^ at the cursor location.

4 OUTLINE AND PARAGRAPH NUMBERING

WordPerfect's Outline and Paragraph Numbering functions allow you to assign a number automatically to outline entries or individual paragraphs and larger blocks of text. These functions provide two important advantages over entering numbers manually:

• If outline entries or numbered paragraphs are moved from one location in the document to another, all of the affected numbers will be recalculated instantly.

• Specific formatting required for the various *levels* of the outline or paragraphs is performed automatically. Legal documents, for example, often contain numbered parts. A section may be level 1, a paragraph level 1.1, and a subparagraph level 1.1.1. Outlines typically use a combination of Roman numerals, uppercase letters, numbers, and lowercase letters to distinguish the levels of the headings.

Figure 4-1 is an example of a three-level outline. Figure 4-2 shows a typical application of the Paragraph Numbering function in a legal document that uses three levels.

Although the Outline and Paragraph Numbering functions can use letters as well as numbers, the code that is inserted into the text when you use these functions is called a *number code,* and the number or letter generated by the code is called a *number.*

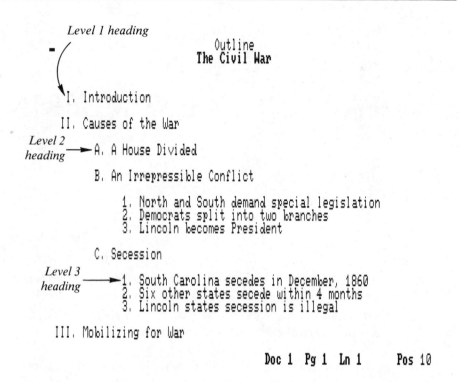

```
                              Outline
                          The Civil War


             I. Introduction

             II. Causes of the War
                A. A House Divided

                B. An Irrepressible Conflict

                    1. North and South demand special legislation
                    2. Democrats split into two branches
                    3. Lincoln becomes President

                C. Secession

                    1. South Carolina secedes in December, 1860
                    2. Six other states secede within 4 months
                    3. Lincoln states secession is illegal

             III. Mobilizing for War

                                    Doc 1  Pg 1  Ln 1      Pos 10
```

Level 1 heading

Level 2 heading

Level 3 heading

Figure 4-1.   A three-level outline

You can specify how the number or letter will be punctuated. For instance, a level 1 paragraph number can appear as a number followed by a period, and a level 2 paragraph number can appear as a lowercase letter followed by a parenthesis.

You can also use the Paragraph Numbering function to number a list of items automatically. You could assign a paragraph number to each step of a tutorial (like the ones in this book) so that if they were rearranged, the program would recalculate the numbers. A simple macro can be created to insert a number code quickly.

In an outline, you indicate the levels by preceding each number code with [TAB] codes. A code number entered at the left margin produces a

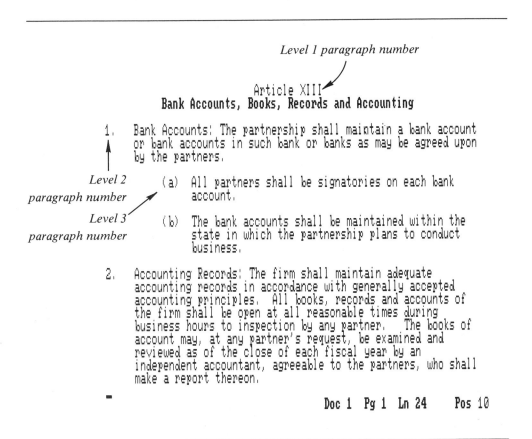

Level 1 paragraph number

Article XIII
Bank Accounts, Books, Records and Accounting

1. Bank Accounts: The partnership shall maintain a bank account
    or bank accounts in such bank or banks as may be agreed upon
    by the partners.

Level 2
paragraph number

(a) All partners shall be signatories on each bank
     account.

Level 3
paragraph number

(b) The bank accounts shall be maintained within the
     state in which the partnership plans to conduct
     business.

2. Accounting Records: The firm shall maintain adequate
    accounting records in accordance with generally accepted
    accounting principles. All books, records and accounts of
    the firm shall be open at all reasonable times during
    business hours to inspection by any partner. The books of
    account may, at any partner's request, be examined and
    reviewed as of the close of each fiscal year by an
    independent accountant, agreeable to the partners, who shall
    make a report thereon.

Doc 1　Pg 1　Ln 24　　Pos 10

Figure 4-2.　A three-level numbered legal document

level 1 entry, a code entered after one [TAB] produces a level 2 entry, and so on. With the Paragraph Numbering function, you can indicate the level of a number code either by inserting [TAB] codes before the number code or by specifying the level directly.

DEFINING A FORMAT

Before using either the Outline or Paragraph Numbering function, you must specify the format that you desire for the different levels. First position the cursor anywhere in the text *preceding* the place where you

```
Paragraph Numbering Definition

    1 - Paragraph Numbering, e.g. 1. a. i. (1) (a) (i) 1)
    2 - Outline Numbering, e.g. I. A. 1. a. (1) (a) i)
    3 - Legal Numbering, e.g. 1. 1.1. 2.2.1 etc.
    4 - Other

Selection: 0

Levels:                1  2  3  4  5  6  7
    Number Style:      4  3  1  4  3  1  4
    Punctuation:       1  1  1  3  3  3  2

Number Style                            Punctuation
0 - Upper Case Roman                    0 - #
1 - Lower Case Roman                    1 - #.
2 - Upper Case Letters                  2 - #)
3 - Lower Case Letters                  3 - (#)
4 - Numbers
5 - Numbers with previous levels separated by a period

Starting Paragraph Number (in Legal Style): 1
```

Figure 4-3.   The Paragraph Numbering Definition screen

want to use paragraph numbering or begin your outline. Then press the
<Mark Text> key (ALT+F5), type **6** for "Other Options," and type **1** for
"Define Paragraph/Outline Numbering." The Paragraph Numbering
Definition screen is displayed. This screen is shown in Figure 4-3.

You will use this screen to specify the format for both outline and
paragraph numbers. The menu at the top of the screen shows three
common settings for the numbering formats, plus a fourth choice that lets
you specify the format for each level manually. For example, if you select
choice **1**, your first level will be identified by a number followed by a
period (1.), your second level by a lowercase letter followed by a period
(a.), your third level by a lowercase Roman numeral followed by a period
(i.), and so on.

If one of the three preset formats meets your needs, type the number of that choice.

If not, type **4**, for "Other." The cursor will move to the Level Format Specification area in the middle of the screen. You can specify the format for up to seven levels. For each level, you define two attributes: "Number Style" and "Punctuation."

The choices for "Number Style" are listed in the lower-left corner of the screen. You can select from Roman numerals (uppercase and lowercase), letters (uppercase and lowercase), and Arabic numbers.

Punctuation choices are also listed at the bottom of the screen.

Enter your choices of number style and punctuation for the levels you want to use. You can simply press ENTER for levels that contain a default setting with which you are satisfied. You must go though all the levels to get out of the menu, even if you won't be using all seven levels in your document.

When you are finished defining the formats for numbering, you will be prompted for a "Starting Number." Besides allowing you to provide a starting number, this function will also allow you to specify the level at which numbering will begin. This is helpful for continuing numbering in another document, or for restarting numbering within a document.

If you want numbering to start at 1 (or I for Roman numerals, A for letters), simply press ENTER. Otherwise, you can type another starting number and press ENTER. Use the Legal format (numbers with previous levels separated by periods) to specify the number, as well as the desired level. For example, to start with paragraph "3.", section "b." (Paragraph Numbering style), type **3.2** and press ENTER.

After you have entered the starting number, you are returned to the document. A [Par#Def] code is inserted in the text at the cursor position. You can restart numbering at any point in the document by positioning the cursor, and repeating the definition process.

USING THE OUTLINE AND PARAGRAPH NUMBERING FUNCTIONS

Although number codes for the Outline and Paragraph Number functions are the same, they are implemented differently.

Outline Mode

To use the Outline function, you must put WordPerfect into a special *Outline mode*. Move your cursor to the point where you want to begin typing your outline. Then press the <Mark Text> key (ALT+F5) and type **1** for "Outline." At the bottom of the screen, you will see

`Outline`

The menu choice acts as a toggle. When you are finished creating your outline, press <Mark Text> and type **1** again to turn off Outline mode.

In Outline mode, an Outline Number code is automatically inserted into your text every time you press the ENTER key (or generate a Hard Page Break). After you press ENTER (or CTRL+ENTER), your cursor will be at the left margin. The Outline function generates a level 1 code at the left margin. To increase the code's level, press the TAB key. (Even though the cursor will appear after the number code, the [TAB] codes are inserted before the number code.) With each press of the TAB key, the level increases by one, and the number format changes to reflect the new level. When the number is at the desired level, you can continue with your typing. (Normally, you will precede text with an indent or a space or two.)

After typing the outline entry, press ENTER to return the cursor to the left margin for the next entry. A new outline number appears before the cursor. If you want to insert a blank line before the next outline entry, press ENTER again. You can insert as many blank lines as you want.

Clear the screen and try this exercise to create a simple two-level outline:

1. Press the <Mark Text> key (ALT+F5).

2. Type **6** for "Other Options."

3. Type **1** for "Define Paragraph/Outline Numbering."

   You will see the Paragraph Numbering Definition screen.

4. Type **2** for "Outline Numbering," then press ENTER.

   You will return to the document.

5. Press the <Reveal Codes> key (ALT+F3).

   You will see the [Par#Def] code.

6. Press ENTER to clear the Reveal Codes screen.

7. Press the <Mark Text> key and type **1** for "Outline."

"Outline" will appear at the bottom of the screen.

8. Press ENTER.

The Roman numeral I will appear before the cursor.

9. Press SPACE and type **Introduction**

10. Press ENTER and then TAB.

A level 2 number code, A, will appear before the cursor.

11. Press SPACE and type **How are you?**

12. Press ENTER and then TAB.

13. Press SPACE and type **Nice to see you again.**

14. Press ENTER and then SPACE and type **Conclusion**

15. Press ENTER and then TAB.

16. Press SPACE and type **See you later.**

17. Press ENTER and then TAB.

18. Press SPACE and type **Goodbye.**

19. Press the <Mark Text> key and type **1** for "Outline."

"Outline" will disappear from the bottom of the screen.

20. Press ENTER.

Your screen should look like the one in Figure 4-4.

To reduce the level of an outline entry (to change a level 4 heading to a level 3 heading, for instance), press the Margin Release key (SHIFT+TAB) when the cursor is to the right of an entry's number code. You can also delete one or more of the [TAB] codes which precede the number code. Start by moving the cursor to just before the number code. Use the Reveal Codes screen to help position the cursor. There should be at least one [TAB] code to the left of the flashing cursor. Press BACK-SPACE as many times as needed to reduce the entry's level. Each time you press BACKSPACE to delete a [TAB] code, the entry is reduced one level.

When the entry is at the level you desire, press the RIGHT ARROW key to position the cursor after the number code. You will see the changed level on the screen. You can then continue with the text for the entry, if you have not already typed it.

```
I. Introduction
    A. How are you?
    B. Nice to see you again.
II. Conclusion
    A. See you later.
    B. Goodbye.

-
```

                                              Doc 1 Pg 1 Ln 8   Pos 10

Figure 4-4.   Example of a simple outline

To increase the level of an outline entry, simply insert a [TAB] code before the entry's number code. Position the cursor to just before the code and press TAB. Press RIGHT ARROW to see the changed level.

Try deleting some lines from the outline you created to see how the other entries are affected. You can insert [TAB] codes before some of the entries to see how that affects the rest of the codes.

Paragraph Numbering

Paragraph numbers, like outline entries, are each assigned a specific level. This level can be specified manually or assigned automatically.

Designating Levels Manually

If your paragraph numbers will appear in irregular locations (as in the middle of a heading) or if you will not be indenting to differentiate among the levels, you will need to specify the number's level manually. Position the cursor where you want the number to appear and press the <Mark Text> key. Type **2**, for "Para#." You will be prompted for a paragraph level number. Type the desired level and press ENTER. The number will be inserted in the text at the cursor position. This process is an excellent application for a macro.

Designating Levels Automatically

If your paragraph numbers will be more structured (for example, if all level 1 paragraphs will start at the left margin and all level 2 paragraphs will be indented), you can let WordPerfect assign the paragraph number level for you. First insert the correct number of [TAB] codes for the desired level. (You indicate levels with automatic paragraph numbering just as you do in an outline: with [TAB] codes.) Then press the <Mark Text> key and type **2**, for "Para#." When you press ENTER, an automatic paragraph number will be inserted at the cursor position.

ALIGNING OUTLINE OR PARAGRAPH NUMBERS

You can use the Tab Align function (or a right-aligned tab stop) to line up outline or paragraph numbers as shown in Figure 4-5. The [A] code inserted by these functions does not increase the level of the number code as the [TAB] code does. However, it does position the number at the next tab stop; you may need to adjust your paragraph number definition so that the format of the number codes is what you intended.

The align functions do not recognize a period in the outline or paragraph number format as an Align Character. Because of this, you must end the alignment so that you can continue with the text for the line. You press the <Indent> key (F4) to end the function, and then you use the BACKSPACE key to delete the Indent code. Since you need to generate the code, even though it will be deleted, you must have a tab stop defined following the one you plan to use for alignment.

```
                              Outline
                          The Civil War


   I.  Introduction

  II.  Causes of the War

 III.  Mobilizing for War

  IV.  The Home Fronts

   V.  Results of the War
```
— Outline numbers are aligned at the period

```
                        Doc 1  Pg 1  Ln 15    Pos 10
```

Figure 4-5.   Aligning outline entries

To align paragraph numbers using a right-aligned tab stop, follow these steps:

1. Set a right-aligned tab stop at the column you wish to use for alignment. Be sure to include another tab stop after this one.

2. Press the TAB key.

3. Press the <Mark Text> key (ALT+F5).

4. Type **2** for "Paragraph Number," and either press ENTER for automatic level or type a level number and press ENTER.

5. Press the <Indent> key (F4) to end the alignment.

6. Press BACKSPACE to delete the extraneous Indent code.

7. Press SPACE twice or the <Indent> key (F4), and enter the text.

8. Press ENTER to end the line or paragraph.

You may want to create a macro that will perform steps 2 through 7. To align outline numbers, follow these steps:

1. Set a right-aligned tab stop at the column you wish to use for alignment. Be sure to include another tab stop after this one.

2. Press the <Mark Text> key (ALT+F5) and type **1** for "Outline" to turn on Outline mode.

3. Press ENTER to generate an outline number.

4. Press TAB (if necessary) until the number is one tab stop before the desired position (although its format should reflect the correct *level*).

5. Press LEFT ARROW to position the cursor before the number code.

6. Press the <Tab Align> key (CTRL+F6).

7. Press RIGHT ARROW to position the cursor after the number code.

8. Press the <Indent> key (F4) to end the Tab Align function.

9. Press BACKSPACE to delete the extraneous Indent code.

10. Press SPACE twice or the <Indent> key (F4), and enter the text.

11. Press ENTER to end the line and insert a new outline number, or press <Mark Text> and type **1** to turn off Outline mode.

5 DOCUMENT ACCESSORIES

WordPerfect can help you to create a variety of *document accessories*—sections of your document that are ancillary to the main body of text. These consist of the following:

- An *index*

- A *table of contents*

- A *table of authorities*

- Up to five separate *lists* (of illustrations, figures, etc.)

- *Footnotes* and *endnotes*.

These accessories are commonly used in academic and legal documents as well as in book manuscripts and publications. For each of them, the program allows you to design the format so you can create a "look" similar to what you would see in a final published document. (The Table of Authorities function is discussed in Appendix E, "Legal Features.")

The Index, Table of Contents, and List functions work in basically the same manner. For all of them, you

1. *Mark* as a block the text that you want to include in the index, table, or list.

2. Place your cursor at the location where you want the index, table, or list to appear and *define* the style you want to use.

3. *Generate* the index, table, or list.

CREATING AN INDEX

WordPerfect can compile an index for you from text in a document. This index can include subtopics as well as main topics. WordPerfect lets you create the index either with or without page numbers.

You can decide which words to include in the index either after the document has been written or while you are writing it. If you determine that a word or phrase should be included, you need to mark it as an index entry. You can also specify the words and phrases you wish to index in a separate *concordance file*.

Marking the Text

You can use text from your document as an index entry, or you can manually enter the text. In either case, WordPerfect will insert a hidden code in your document when you create the entry. The page that the hidden code falls on determines the page number for this entry in the completed index.

Using Text From Your Document

To use text from your document, move the cursor so that it is anywhere on the word you wish included in the index. If your entry contains two or more words, mark the entry as a block using the <Block> key.

Then press the <Mark Text> key (ALT+F5) and type **5** for "Index." (Notice that the Mark Text menu varies slightly, depending on whether you have marked the text as a block.) WordPerfect will then ask for the index *heading* and *subheading*. Before you can go on, it is necessary to understand the meaning of these two terms.

An index heading is the main reference to an index item. Each entry must have an index heading. A subheading is any one of many items included under a heading. (You do not need to specify a subheading for each entry.) For example, imagine you are creating an index for a cookbook. You might specify one heading to be *Chicken,* with subheadings for *baked, broiled,* and *fried.* When readers look up *Chicken* in the index, they are directed to the type of chicken that interests them. In this example, *Chicken* would be an index heading and *baked, broiled*, and *fried* would be subheadings. WordPerfect automatically capitalizes the index headings.

WordPerfect first suggests the text that you marked as a block (or the word that the cursor was on) as the index heading. If this is correct, press ENTER. Otherwise, edit the text or type the correct heading, and press ENTER.

If you typed your own text for the Heading, the text you marked on the screen will be suggested for the subheading. Press ENTER to use the suggested text.

If you pressed ENTER to accept the suggestion for the heading, then the subheading prompt will be blank. You can press ENTER if you do not need a subheading, or you can type a subheading and press ENTER.

Thus, to mark a single word as a heading for an index (without a subheading), simply position the cursor anywhere within the word, press the <Mark Text> key, type **5** for "Index," and press ENTER twice. To mark several words as a heading for an index (without a subheading), mark them as a block, press the <Mark Text> key, type **5** for "Index," and press ENTER twice.

Manually Creating Index Entries

To manually create an index entry, move the cursor to the place in your document to which you want the entry to refer. Then, press the <Mark Text> key (ALT+F5), and type **5** for "Index." Enter the heading and subheading for the entry. If the program suggests the word at the cursor location for the heading, simply type over the suggestion. Then, when it suggests the same word as a subheading, you can edit the text, type over the subheading, or press BACKSPACE and then ENTER to create an index entry without a subheading.

That's all there is to marking the text. WordPerfect inserts an [Index:] hidden code immediately before the word or phrase you specified. You can view this code by pressing the <Reveal Codes> key (ALT+F3).

Notice that this method of marking text is unlike many of the other ways in which WordPerfect marks text. Instead of placing a matched pair of hidden codes around the text (as with such functions as Bold, Underline, and Center), WordPerfect duplicates the marked text and inserts it into a hidden code. Within the code, the heading text and subheading text are separated by a semicolon.

Using a Concordance File

WordPerfect gives you the option of maintaining a concordance file, a document which contains a list of words and phrases that the program will include in a compiled index. This is especially useful for entries which appear frequently throughout the document. If you wish, you can use the concordance file in addition to marking specific entries in the text of a document.

Creating Entries

To create entries for a concordance file, start with a blank screen. Type each entry on its own line, and press ENTER. When the index is generated, WordPerfect will build an index entry for each occurrence in the document of an entry in the concordance file. Continue typing entries in this manner until you have entered all of the words and phrases you wish to include. Since the file will be saved as a normal WordPerfect document, you'll be able to retrieve and modify it at any time.

Modifying the Generated Entry

Normally, WordPerfect will use the text from the entry in the concordance file to build the entry for the index. However, you can choose to have the program use a different word or phrase for the actual entry than the one it used to match occurrences in the text. For example, you may want the words *moose, deer,* and *antelope* to all generate the index entry *Animals, four-legged.*

To do this, insert an Index code (as described in the previous section "Manually Creating Index Entries") on the same line as the entry in the concordance file, after the entry but before the Hard Return. For the example above, you would position the cursor on the line that contained *moose*, press the END key to be sure that you are at the end of the line, press the <Mark Text> key, type **5** for "Index," type **Animals** for the heading and press ENTER, and type **four-legged** for the subheading and press ENTER.

Creating Multiple Entries

If you wish, you can have one match of a word or phrase in the concordance with an occurrence in the document generate a series of index entries, instead of just one. For example, you may want occurrences of *moose* to be indexed not only on *Animals, four-legged,* but also on *Animals, hooved* and *Canada, animals.*

```
Index Definition

    1 - No Page Numbers
    2 - Page Numbers Follow Entries
    3 - (Page Numbers) Follow Entries
    4 - Flush Right Page Numbers
    5 - Flush Right Page Numbers with Leaders
```

Figure 5-1.   The Index Definition screen

To do this, simply enter as many index entries as you wish at the end of the line which contains the entry in the concordance file. When the entry matches an occurrence in the document, an index entry will be generated for each index code that exists at the end of the entry's line in the concordance file.

Saving the File

When you have entered all of the entries and associated index codes you wish to include in the concordance file, save it using the <Save> key (F10). You might want to give the concordance file a name that will remind you for which document it was created. For example, you may want to adopt ".con" as a standard file extension for a concordance file, so that it can share the same filename as the document you are indexing.

Positioning the Index
And Defining Its Format

Once you have specified all the words and phrases to be indexed, the next step is to indicate where you want the index to appear and how you want it to look.

Move your cursor to the position in your document where you want the index to appear. When WordPerfect generates the index, it will only process marked entries that appear before the definition code that this command produces. Therefore, you would normally position the cursor at the end of the document. When you have properly positioned the cursor, press the <Mark Text> key (ALT+F5), type **6** for "Other Options," and type **5** for "Define Index." Type the name of the concordance file you wish to use, and press ENTER. If you will not be using a concordance file, simply press ENTER. The Index Definition screen appears, as shown in Figure 5-1.

Now you have to decide how you want the index to look. Press the number corresponding to the format you desire.

With options 4 and 5, the page number appears flush right (at the right margin). If you change the margin settings, the page numbers move accordingly. This allows you to reformat the index easily.

After you type a number to specify the index format, you are returned to the document. A [DefMark:Index] hidden code is placed into the text at the cursor position.

Generating the Index

After defining a format, you generate the index by pressing the <Mark Text> key (ALT+F5), typing **6** for "Other Options," and **8** for "Generate Tables and Index." The cursor can be anywhere in the document.

Before the program begins the generation process, it will ask for confirmation that you wish to replace any previously generated tables and index with the new ones. If you wish to save one of the tables or the index, type **N** at the prompt and the generation process will abort. Copy the desired tables of index to another document and restart the generation. If you wish to replace the old ones with new versions, type **Y**.

It can take some time for the program to find all of your marked references and arrange them appropriately, especially if you are using a concordance file. As WordPerfect reads through your document, it keeps you posted on its progress by means of a counter. (This counter has no known relevance to anything within the document.) When the program is finished, the index appears in the document where you placed the

Index definition code.

Reformatting the Index

WordPerfect formats the index using a combination of Left Indent, Left/Right Indent, and Margin Release hidden codes, all of which depend on tab settings to position the text. Thus, it is important to set tab stops appropriately.

There are three important tab positions in an index:

- The first tab stop should always be at the left margin. This is where the heading is positioned.

- The second tab stop is where the subheading is positioned. Typically, this is set two to five characters from the left margin.

- The third tab stop is where the second and subsequent lines of both the heading and the subheading will wrap around if the entry is too long for one line. Typically, the third tab stop is set the same distance away from the second tab stop as the second tab stop is from the left margin (and the first tab stop).

Formatting an Index With Columns

Here is an example of how to format an index within two even columns.

Let's assume that you are indexing a document with the default margins of 10 left and 74 right. First, mark all of the index entries in your document. Then position the index and define its format by using the Define Index command. Then generate the index.

Using the Reveal Codes screen, position the cursor just before the [Defmark:Index] hidden code that appears in your document where you defined the index format. Exit the Reveal Codes screen. Then define two evenly spaced newspaper-style columns that are five spaces apart, and turn on Column mode (see Chapter 6, "Columns," for a description of this process).

For columns of the size you have defined, you need a tab stop at the left margin, another tab stop two spaces to the right, and another two more spaces to the right. You also need tabs stops at the same intervals for the second column. Therefore, you should now set tab stops at the following positions: 10, 12, 14, 45, 47, and 49. Delete all other tab stops. When you exit the Tab Setting area, the index should be properly formatted.

CREATING A TABLE OF CONTENTS

A table of contents is handled in a similar fashion to an index. You begin by marking the text that you want included in the table. Then you define a format and generate the table.

Marking the Text

Unlike the Index function, the Table of Contents function requires that you use the <Block> key to mark an entry. After the text has been marked as a block, press the <Mark Text> key (ALT+F5). Type **1** for "To C" to mark the entry. WordPerfect then asks you to indicate the "To C Level:."

There are up to five *levels* for the table of contents. A level indicates the position on the page (relative to the left margin) where the item will appear. Use level 1 for major headings and higher levels for lesser divisions within the document.

For example, level 1 might be used for chapter headings, level 2 for major divisions within chapters, and level 3 for minor divisions within the major divisions. You do not have to use all the levels.

Type a level number from 1 to 5 and press ENTER. [Mark] and [EndMark] codes are placed around the blocked text. These codes also contain the level that you specified for the entry.

Positioning the Table of Contents
And Defining Its Format

When you have finished marking all of the entries for the table of contents, move your cursor to the location where you want the table to appear and press the <Mark Text> key (ALT+F5). (This location should

```
Table of Contents Definition

Number of levels in table of contents (1-5): █


                              Page Number Position
        Level 1
        Level 2
        Level 3
        Level 4
        Level 5


Page Number Position
1 - No Page Numbers
2 - Page Number Follow Entries
3 - (Page Numbers) follow Entries
4 - Flush Right Page Numbers
5 - Flush Right Page Numbers with Leaders
```

Figure 5-2.   The Table of Contents Definition screen

be near the top of the document, *before* all entries marked for inclusion in the table of contents.) Type **6** for "Other Options," and then **2** for "Define Table of Contents." The Table of Contents Definition screen is displayed, as shown in Figure 5-2.

Enter the number of levels you want in your table of contents. This number should be the same as the highest level number you used when marking text in your document for the table of contents. Make sure that you specify enough levels; if you don't, you will have to go through the definition step again. You can always define more levels than you have used (or plan to use) in your document.

The program will then ask if you want to display the last level in wrapped format. The Wrapped Level option combines entries at the last level into paragraph form, with the entries separated by semicolons. Figure 5-4 shows an example on the screen of a table of contents with the last level in wrapped format. This format can save space in the table of contents and may be appropriate when the last level contains minor

```
                    Table of Contents
                     The Civil War

Introduction . . . . . . . . . . . . . . . . . . . .        1
Causes of the War . . . . . . . . . . . . . . . . .        5
    A House Divided . . . . . . . . . . . . . . . .        6
An Irrepressible Conflict . . . . . . . . . . . .         10
        North and South demand special legislation;
        Democrats split into two branches; Lincoln becomes
        President
    Secession . . . . . . . . . . . . . . . . . .         19
        South Carolina secedes in December, 1860; Six
        other states secede within 4 months; Lincoln
        states secession is illegal
    Mobilizing for War . . . . . . . . . . . . . .        32



    -




                        Doc 1  Pg 1  Ln 16     Pos 10
```

Figure 5-3.   A table of contents with the last level wrapped

topics. Type **Y** if you want to use wrapped format for the last level, or type **N** if you do not.

The cursor will then move to the middle of the screen, where you indicate the format you want for each level in the table of contents. Simply press ENTER if you are satisfied with the default. The default setting is 5, for "Flush Right Page Numbers with Leaders." The options are the same as for the Index function described earlier in this chapter.

If you indicate that you want the last level of the table of contents in wrapped format, the default setting for the last level will be 3, "(Page Numbers) follow Entries." Also, when you choose a format for your last level, the option menu will display only the first three format choices. This is because the flush right format of the last two choices is inappropriate for the paragraph format of the wrapped level.

When you have selected a format for each level, you are returned to your document.

Generating the Table
Of Contents

When you are ready to generate the table of contents, press the <Mark Text> key, type **6** for "Other Options," and then **8** for "Generate Tables and Index." The cursor can be anywhere in the document.

As when you create an index, WordPerfect will confirm the replacement of any old tables, lists, or indexes. Type **Y** to proceed with the generation, or type **N** to abort. A counter shows the program's progress.

CREATING LISTS

WordPerfect's List function allows you to maintain up to five separate lists of items in a document. For example, you may want to have a list of illustrations and a list of tables that appear after the table of contents.

The List function works in almost exactly the same fashion as the Index function. The major difference is that with the List function, you *must* mark the entries with the <Block> key.

Marking the Text

To mark an entry for a list, mark the text as a block, press the <Mark Text> key (ALT+F5), and type **2** for "List." You can have up to five numbered lists per document. Instead of prompting you for a heading and subheading (as with the Index function), the List function simply asks for the number of the list to use for the selected entry. Type a number from 1 to 5.

Positioning the List and Defining Its Format

The processes of positioning a list and of defining its format are identical to the same processes for an index. To position the list, move the cursor to the place in your document, *before* all marked entries, where you want

```
List 1 Definition

     1 - No Page Numbers
     2 - Page Numbers Follow Entries
     3 - (Page Numbers) Follow Entries
     4 - Flush Right Page Numbers
     5 - Flush Right Page Numbers with Leaders




     Selection: ▮
```

Figure 5-4.   The List Definition screen

the list to appear. Press the <Mark Text> key, type **6** for "Other Options," **3** for "Define List," and then a number from 1 to 5 to designate the list number you wish to define. The List Definition screen will appear, as shown in Figure 5-4.

Type the number that corresponds to the format option you desire for the list. These options are explained in the "Creating an Index" section earlier in this chapter. After you enter the number of a format, you are returned to the document.

Generating the List

After you have marked all of the entries for your lists and have located and defined a format for them, you are ready to generate the lists. The cursor can be anywhere in the document. Press the <Mark Text> key (ALT+F5), type **6** for "Other Options," and then **8** for "Generate Tables and Index." WordPerfect will confirm the replacement of any old tables, lists, or indexes. Type **Y** to proceed with the generation or type **N** to abort. A counter shows WordPerfect's progress as it creates your lists.

FOOTNOTES AND ENDNOTES

WordPerfect's Note function will automatically number footnotes and endnotes for you. When the document is printed, the program will place footnotes at the bottom of the page and endnotes at the end of the file. If you add or delete notes, all subsequent notes will be instantly renumbered. The Note function is flexible in that it lets you select from a variety of note options to customize the note format to your satisfaction.

Although you can customize the note format if you want, you can also create notes without doing so. All the options have default values, which can be changed from the "Set Initial Settings" choice on WordPerfect's Setup menu. (See Appendix A, "Installation.")

Creating Notes

Each note is automatically assigned a number that will appear in the text as a *note* reference, as well as with the note text at the bottom of the screen or end of the document. To create a note, move the cursor to the place in your document where you want the note reference to appear. Then press the <Footnote> key (CTRL+F7). Type **1** for "Create" to create a footnote or type **5** for "Create Endnote" to create an endnote. The Note Text screen will appear, as shown in Figure 5-6.

You will see the note number appearing just before the cursor. If this is the first note in the document, the number will be 1. Otherwise, it will be the next sequential number after the number of the previous note. You can now enter the text for the note. (You may want to separate the note number from the text with a few spaces.)

The note number is actually a hidden code, [Note #], that you can see by pressing <Reveal Codes>. Although the Reveal Codes function shows nothing more than the [Note #] code, the screen shows an indent of five spaces and the number. In the printed document, the number is also

1_

Press **EXIT** when done   Ln 1   Pos 16

Figure 5-5.   The Note Text screen

superscripted. You can change the note number format with the Note Options screen discussed later in this chapter—for example, to start every note with the note number, a period, and two spaces.

The text of the note can be virtually any length—up to 16,000 lines. With footnotes, WordPerfect puts as much of the text as possible onto the same page as the footnote reference. If it needs to break the note onto two pages, WordPerfect will keep at least three lines of the note on the first page. (The number of lines to keep together can also be changed with the Note Options screen.)

While entering the text, you can use most of WordPerfect's editing and cursor-control commands. However, some commands perform differently in the Note Text screen from the way they ordinarily do. For example, pressing the TAB key simply inserts five spaces instead of a

[TAB] code. If you accidentally delete the note number, you can make a new one simply by pressing the <Footnote> key (CTRL+F7).

When you have finished entering the text of the note, press the <Exit> key (F7) to return to the document. The note reference appears in the text just before the cursor. When the document is printed, the number will be superscripted. Press the <Reveal Codes> key to see the [Note:Foot] or [Note:End] code that the Note function generated. The hidden code will display the first 50 characters of the note. To see more of it, use the Edit function described in the next section. You can delete a note by deleting its hidden code.

As you create more notes, they are automatically numbered in sequence. (Footnotes and endnotes are numbered independently of each other.) If you add or delete a note, all subsequent notes will be renumbered.

Editing Notes

Since notes are created on the special Note Text screen, you must also edit them there by using the Edit Note command. Your cursor can be anywhere in the document.

To edit a note, first press the <Footnote> key (CTRL+F7). If you want to edit a footnote, type **2**. If you want to edit an endnote, type **6**. In either case, the program then asks you for a note number. (The default note number will be the number of the note following the cursor position. For example, if the cursor is located between notes 8 and 9, then the default note number will be 9.) Type the number of the note you wish to edit and press ENTER. The desired note appears on the Note Text screen. (If WordPerfect cannot find the note you requested, it will display the "* Not Found *" message.) Make any changes to the note that you need to, and then press the <Exit> key.

When you return to your document, the cursor will be placed immediately after the note's hidden code in the document. If you were to press the <Footnote> key and choose "Edit" or "Edit Endnote" again, the default note to edit would be the next one in the document. This makes it easy to edit many notes in succession or to write a macro that manipulates all the notes in a document.

Specifying a New Starting Number

At any point in a document, you can specify a new starting number for footnotes. This can be useful if you want to reset numbering at the beginning of each chapter or if you want one document to pick up numbering where another left off. The next footnote the system encounters will be given the number you specify, and subsequent footnotes will then be numbered sequentially.

To specify a new starting number, first position the cursor before the footnote you want to renumber. Then press the <Footnote> key (CTRL+F7) and type **3** for "New #." Type the new note number and press ENTER. All subsequent notes will be renumbered.

Setting Note Options

To customize the format of your footnotes and endnotes, first position the cursor before the notes that you want to change. When you are finished changing the format, WordPerfect will generate a code that will control the format of all subsequent notes. Press the <Footnote> key and type **4** for "Options." The Footnote Options screen will appear, as shown in Figure 5-7.

As you can see, each of the options is assigned a default value. To change an option's value, type its number or letter, enter the new value, and press ENTER.

Here is an explanation of each of the note options:

1. Spacing within notes

Enter a number for the line spacing of each note. This number is entered in the same way as with the Line Spacing function.

Default: 1 (Single-line spacing)

2. Spacing between notes

Enter a number to indicate how many lines there should be between each note.

Default: 1

3. Lines to keep together

Enter the number of lines that should be kept together if a note needs to be split across a page break. (This works exactly like the Condi-

Footnote Options

```
1 - Spacing within notes                      1
2 - Spacing between notes                      1
3 - Lines to keep together                     3
4 - Start footnote numbers each page           N
5 - Footnote numbering mode                    0
6 - Endnote numbering mode                     0
7 - Line separating text and footnotes         1
8 - Footnotes at bottom of page                Y
9 - Characters for notes                       *
A - String for footnotes in text        [SuprScrpt][Note]
B - String for endnotes in text         [SuprScrpt][Note]
C - String for footnotes in note              [SuprScrpt][Note]
D - String for endnotes in note         [Note],
```

```
For options 5 & 6:              For option 7:
    0 - Numbers                     0 - No line
    1 - Characters                  1 - 2 inch line
    2 - Letters                     2 - Line across entire page
                                    3 - 2 in. line w/continued strings
```

Selection: **0**

Figure 5-6.   The Footnote Options screen

tional End-of-Page command.) Specifying "3" for this option causes three lines of each footnote to be kept on the first page.

Default: 3

4. Start footnote numbers each page

Type **Y** for "Yes" or **N** for "No" to specify whether footnote numbering should be reset for each page. If you specify "Y," the first footnote number on each page will be "1" (if your footnotes use numbers), "a" (if your footnotes use letters), or a single character (if your footnotes use characters). The descriptions of options 5, 6, and 9 show you how to change the note numbering mode.

Default: No

5. Footnote numbering mode

Select a mode from the menu at the lower left of the screen to specify whether you will use numbers, letters, or other characters.

Default: 0 (numbers)

6. Endnote numbering mode

Select a numbering mode for endnotes as with option 5.

Default: 0 (Numbers)

7. Line separating text and footnotes

Select a format from the menu at the lower right of the screen for the line that appears above the footnote text.

Note: You can further customize the two-inch line and the line across the entire page using the Printer program. See Chapter 9, "Using Printers," for a description of this program.

Default: 1 (Two-inch line)

8. Footnotes at bottom of page

Type **Y** for "Yes" or **N** for "No" to specify whether blank lines should be inserted automatically to place the footnote text at the bottom of the page when the page isn't full. If you type **N**, the footnote text will immediately follow the last line of text on the page.

Default: Yes

9. Characters for notes

If you select "1" for option 5 (Character mode), enter the character that you want the function to use. For the first note, one of the characters is used; for the second, two of them are used; for the third, three are used, and so on. You can also enter up to five different characters (e.g., "*#+"). If you do, the function will use one of each character first (*, #, +), then two of each (**, ##, ++), then three (***, ###, +++), and so on.

Default: *

A. String for footnotes in text

When you create any note entry, two strings are generated based on the settings for options A and C (for footnotes) or options B and D (for endnotes). The first string (A or B) is what will appear in the text where the note reference is made, and the other (C or D) is what will appear in the note text area.

When you want to change one of the strings, type the corresponding letter. The prompt "Replace with:" appears at the bottom of the screen. Type the string and press ENTER.

The strings can consist of the following:

- Spaces or characters
- A [Note] code which represents the note number
- Superscript and Underline commands.

You insert codes into the string in the same way that you insert codes into a Search string for the Search function. To insert the [Note] code, press the <Footnote> key (CTRL+F7) and type **1** for "Footnote/Endnote." To insert a Superscript command (which prints the next character one half line higher than the rest of the line), press the <Super/Subscript> key (SHFT+F1) and type **1** for "Superscript." A [SuprScrpt] code appears in the string.

To underline part of the string, press the <Underline> key where you want underlining to start. An [Undrline] code appears in the string. Enter the text (or [Note] code) to be underlined; then press <Underline> again to end underlining. When you press ENTER to end input of the string, a [u] code (which ends underline) is placed in the string where you pressed the <Underline> key a second time. If you did not press the <Underline> key a second time, the program will insert the [u] at the end of the string.

You cannot use any codes other than [Note], [Undrline], and [SuprScrpt] in the string. If you insert any other codes, WordPerfect will ignore them.

Default: "[SuprScrpt][Note]"   (superscripted numbers)

B. String for endnotes in text

Enter a string that will appear in the text where an endnote reference is made. See option A for a description of the string.

Default: "[SuprScrpt][Note]"   (superscripted numbers)

C. String for footnotes in note

Enter a string that will precede the footnote entry at the bottom of the page. See option A for a description of the string.

Default: "   [SuprScrpt][Note]"   (superscripted numbers with a five-space indent)

D. String for endnotes in note

Enter a string that will precede the endnote entry at the end of the document. See option A for a description of the string.

Default: "[Note]." (numbers followed by a period)

Here is an example of setting note options with strings. If you want the note numbers not to be superscripted in the note text area at the bottom of the page, you type **C** for "String for footnotes in note," type five spaces (if you want a five-space indent), press the <Footnote> key (CTRL+F7), type **1** for "Footnote/Endnote," and press ENTER. You could also type a period and one or two spaces after the [Note] code.

Here are some examples of note format strings and the note formats they generate:

String	*Example*
"[Note]. "	"1. "
" [Note]:"	" 1:"
"Note #[Note]: "	"Note #1: "

Reformatting Notes

Note text uses the margin settings that are in effect when you create the note. If you go back and change the margin settings after you have created the note (that is, you generate a [Margin Set:] code before a note), you must reformat all of the subsequent notes if you want the notes to use the new margin settings. (Tab settings do not affect notes, since pressing the TAB key while entering a note simply inserts five spaces.)

Strangely enough, you can reformat notes with the Word Count function of the Speller. (You may need to switch disks first—see Appendix A, "Installation.") Simply press the <Spell> key (CTRL+F2) and type **6** for "Count." All of the notes in the document will be reformatted with the appropriate margins.

Chapter

6 MULTIPLE COLUMNS

WordPerfect can arrange your text into columns, up to 24 across a page. There are two types of columns you can produce:

- Parallel columns, which allow you to have separate pieces of text next to each other on a page.

- Newspaper-style columns, which allow you to have text that continues from the bottom of one column to the top of the next.

PARALLEL COLUMNS

With parallel columns, separate pieces of text are placed side by side on a page, like this:

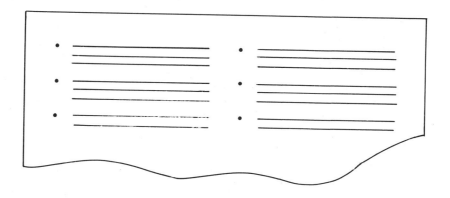

Each of these pieces of text is called a parallel column *entry*. A series of these across a page (one per column) is called a *group* of entries. Parallel columns are useful when you want to compare bulleted lists of features or important points, such as the highlights of two different pieces of property in a real estate transaction. Parallel columns are also useful when you are typing tabular information that consists of many lines—for example, a list of personal information on clients in which one of the entries consists of a four-line address but each other entry is only one line long. Parallel columns can also help with script writing by allowing editor's notes to be placed next to dialogue.

Without the Parallel Columns function, you would have to create these documents by using the TAB key to separate the columns, like this:

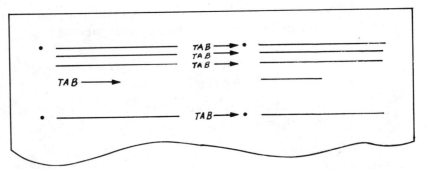

This method makes it nearly impossible to reformat the text, since the column entries are not treated as separate and distinct sections of text.

With the Parallel Columns function, however, each entry is an independent section of text and will be formatted separately from the other entries on the page.

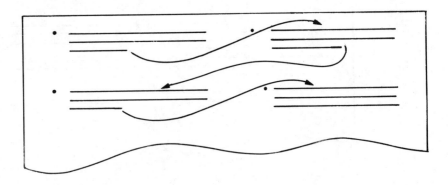

```
Columns:  The Column function        Thesaurus:  With the Thesaurus
allows you to format text into       function you can ask
columns that will be displayed       WordPerfect to look up
on screen as well as on the          synonyms for any word,
printed output,

Indexing:  You can mark              Shell:  You can temporarily
individual words or phrases to       exit WordPerfect and perform
be included in an index,             any DOS command without having
                                     to save and re-load your
                                     document,

Undelete:  Three levels of           Word Search:  You can use the
deleted text are stored in           Word Search function to search
memory and can be "recovered",       through the files on your disk
                                     to find a particular word or
                                     phrase,

■


                 Col 1  Doc 1  Pg 1  Ln 19     Pos 10
```

Figure 6-1.   Parallel columns

When text is edited, deleted, or inserted, it reformats only within its entry. Parallel column entries are never broken over page boundaries. They are held together by [BlockPro:On] and [BlockPro:Off] codes, which are inserted automatically around each group and keep the group on a single page. If any one entry in a group extends past the end of a page, the entire group will be moved to the next page. Figure 6-1 shows an example of a document on the screen with parallel columns.

NEWSPAPER-STYLE COLUMNS

Use newspaper-style columns when you want to have continuous columns with text that "snakes" from one to the other. That is, text will flow from the top of the first column to the bottom of the page, then to

```
There is a distribution for a          The number of shares
mutual fund.                           reinvested is added to the
                                       reinvested shares-to-date
The records of all those               amount.
transactions where the client
has purchased shares in the            A client purchases shares in a
fund must be updated as to the         mutual fund.
current distribution amounts.
                                       Operator is prompted for
The current distribution               client name, mutual fund name,
amount is added to the                 date and amount of investment,
distributions-to-date amount           the original share price, and
for each transaction.                  whether the client has
                                       requested reinvestment of
Also, all those mutual fund            distributions for this
transactions that specifiy a           transaction.
client request for
reinvestment of shares                 The Client DBMS will then
distributed must maintain the          calculate the number of shares
amount of the current                  purchased based on the
reinvestment as well as the            investment amount and the
share price and number of              original price per share.
shares involved as of the
transaction date.
```

Col 2 Doc 1 Pg 1 Ln 23   Pos 45

Figure 6-2.   Newspaper-style columns

---

the top of the next column, then to the bottom of the page, and so on. When you have filled the last column on the page, text will continue on the first column of the following page. (You can also end a column at any point with the <Hard Column> key, as you will see later in this chapter.) You can right justify each of the columns independently, giving the final document a professional appearance. Figure 6-2 shows an example of a document on the screen formatted with newspaper-style columns.

USING COLUMNS

To use either type of column, you must follow these steps:

1. Set your margins to leave enough room for all the columns.

2. Define the column layout, including the number of columns to be used.

3. Turn on Column mode.

4. Enter the text.

5. Turn off Column mode.

DEFINING THE FORMAT

Before you can use columns in your document, you need to define the column layout. This step tells WordPerfect how many columns you will use, which type they are, and where they will be placed on the page.

To define column formats, position the cursor at the place in your document where you want columns to begin. If you want WordPerfect to calculate the column margin settings for you, set the margins first. The left margin setting will control the position of the left edge of the far-left column, and the right margin setting will control the position of the right edge of the far-right column. Make sure your margins are far enough apart to accommodate all your columns. During the column definition in the next step, margin settings for the individual columns will be determined.

Press the <Math/Columns> key (ALT+F7) and type **4** for "Column Def." The Text Column Definition screen is displayed, as shown in Figure 6-3. You need to answer the questions shown (as well as specify the column margin settings) for WordPerfect to set up your columns properly.

The first question asks whether you want evenly spaced columns. If you do (and you probably will), type **Y**. The function will then prompt you for the number of spaces to be placed between the columns. Enter the

Text Column Definition

```
Do you wish to have evenly spaced columns? (Y/N) N
If yes, number of spaces between columns:
Type of columns: 1
        1 - Newspaper
        2 - Parallel with Block Protect

Number of text columns (2-24): 0

Column   Left     Right    Column   Left     Right
   1:                        13:
   2:                        14:
   3:                        15:
   4:                        16:
   5:                        17:
   6:                        18:
   7:                        19:
   8:                        20:
   9:                        21:
  10:                        22:
  11:                        23:
  12:                        24:
```

Figure 6-3.   The Text Column Definition screen

number of spaces and press ENTER. If, instead, you type **N** in answer to the first question, the second will be skipped.

Next, you are asked whether you want newspaper-style or parallel columns. Type **1** if you want newspaper-style columns, or type **2** if you want parallel columns.

Finally, you are asked for the number of columns you want across the page. Enter a number from 2 to 24 and press ENTER. The cursor will then move to the first setting in the column margin settings area of the screen.

Notice that if you specified evenly spaced columns, WordPerfect has calculated the column margins for you. To do this, it first figured the total line length, using the margins that were current when you entered the Text Column Definition screen. Then, taking into account the number of columns specified, it subtracted the number of spaces to be between columns. It divided the remaining number by the total number of columns to determine each column's width and, finally, it calculated the margin settings for each column.

Press ENTER when the cursor is at any margin setting that you are satisfied with, or type a new value and then press ENTER. If you are satisfied with all of the suggested margin settings, simply press the <Exit> key (F7).

If you did not choose evenly spaced columns, you need to enter a margin setting for each of the columns you requested and then press ENTER.

When you are through entering margin settings for the columns, you are returned to your document. A [Col Def:] code will have been inserted into the text at the cursor position. Any columns of text that follow the code will use the format you entered, until the program encounters another such code.

CREATING COLUMNS

After defining the column format, you create the columns by entering WordPerfect's Column mode.

Entering Column Mode

To enter Column mode, press the <Math/Columns> key (ALT+F7), and type 3. Unlike other WordPerfect modes (such as the Insert or Overwrite mode), entering Column mode places a hidden code [Col on] into the text at the cursor position. To stop using columns, press <Math/Columns> and type 3 again. A hidden code [Col off] is placed in the text. When the cursor is located anywhere between a [Col on] code and a [Col off] code, WordPerfect will be in Column mode. When you move the cursor out of this area, WordPerfect will not be in Column mode.

When WordPerfect is in Column mode, the indicator line at the bottom of the screen includes a "Col" reference, like this:

```
Col 1   Doc 1   Pg 4   Ln 31        Pos 10
```

This indicates that the program is ready to use columns.

Once you have defined the column format, you can go in and out of Column mode as often as you like without having to redefine the format each time. For example, you can create a headline that stretches across several columns. You can use any combination of column text and normal text within a single document or page.

Continuing Into the Next Column

When you are in Column mode, the <Hard Page> key (CTRL+ENTER) becomes the <Hard Column> key and is used to force the beginning of a new column. The key sequence produces slightly different results depending on which type of column you are using.

Parallel Columns

If you are using parallel columns, press the <Hard Column> key to create a new entry normally in the next column. When you have entered text in the last column, the new entry starts a new group of entries at the left margin. In this situation, Column mode is temporarily turned off, returning the cursor to the beginning of the next line; a Hard Return is inserted, separating your entries with a blank line; and Column mode is turned back on. The system also inserts Block Protection codes at this point. You can then type the next group of entries.

When Column mode is turned off (either manually or automatically during the Hard Column sequence), the cursor is placed one blank line below the bottom line of the longest entry in the current group. For example, say you are working with three columns. Your first entry is 6 lines long, your second entry is 12 lines long, and your third entry is 4 lines long. If you press the Hard Column key, the cursor will appear two lines below the second entry, which is 12 lines long.

Newspaper-style Columns

With newspaper-style columns, text continues in the next column when it reaches the bottom of the page. Pressing the <Hard Column> key, however, forces the column to end before it normally would, just as pressing the <Hard Page> key (when not in Column mode) forces the *page* to end before it normally would. Text then continues in the next defined column to the right. If you are in the last column when you press the <Hard Column> key, the function generates a Hard Page Break, and the text continues with the first column of the next page.

When you turn off Column mode, the cursor is placed below the bottom line of the columns, at the left margin. (No extra blank line is inserted, unlike the procedure with parallel columns.) You can then type text without columns within the current margin settings. When you want to begin typing text in columns again, turn Column mode back on.

Cursor Control in Column Mode

Most of WordPerfect's cursor-control functions work in the usual way when in Column mode. However, some will be confined to the current column. For example, pressing the END key will move the cursor to the end of the line *within the current column.*

To move the cursor to the next column, press the <Goto> key (CTRL+HOME), and then press RIGHT ARROW. To move the cursor to the last column, press the <Goto> key, press the HOME key, and then press the RIGHT ARROW key.

To move the cursor to the previous column, press the <Goto> key, and then press LEFT ARROW. To move the cursor to the first column, press the <Goto> key, press the HOME key, and then press the LEFT ARROW key.

SOME PRACTICE EXAMPLES

Here are some examples to give you practice using parallel and newspaper-style columns.

Parallel Columns

Make sure the screen is clear. Then follow this exercise first to define the column format for two columns with five spaces between them and then to produce a document with parallel columns in the format you have defined.

1. Make sure your margins are set for 10,74.

2. Press the <Math/Columns> key (ALT+F7).

3. Type **4** for "Column Def."
   You will see the Text Column Definition screen.

4. Type **Y** to request evenly spaced columns.

5. Type **5** and press ENTER to specify the spacing between columns.

6. Type **2** to choose parallel columns.

7. Type **2** to specify two columns across the page and press ENTER.

8. Press the <Exit> key (F7) to use the suggested margin settings.

9. Type **3** to turn on Column mode.

   You will see the "Col 1" indicator at the bottom of the screen.

10. Type ***** and press the <Indent> key (F4).

11. Type the following text:

    All of the text that follows will, in fact, be completely contained within the first column.

12. Press the <Hard Column> key (CTRL+ENTER).

    The cursor moves to the top of the next column (which starts at position 45), creating a new entry.

13. Type ***** and press the <Indent> key.

14. Type the following text:

    This text will appear in the second column, right next to the text we typed for the first column.

The screen will look like the one in Figure 6-4.

```
    *    All of the text that          *    This text will appear in
         follows will, in fact, be          the second column, right
         completely contained              next to the text we typed
         within the first column.          for the first column._
```

                              Col 2 Doc 1 Pg 1 Ln 4   Pos 71

Figure 6-4.   Creating parallel columns

15. Press the <Hard Column> key and press ENTER.

16. Type * and press the <Indent> key.

17. Type the following text:

    This is the first entry of the second group of entries on this page.

18. Press ENTER twice and then press the <Indent> key.

19. Type the following text:

    This is a second paragraph that is also a part of the first entry of the second group of entries.

20. Press the <Hard Column> key.

21. Type * and press the <Indent> key.

```
*   All of the text that         *   This text will appear in
    follows will, in fact, be         the second column, right
    completely contained              next to the text we typed
    within the first column.          for the first column.

*   This is the first entry      *   This is the second entry
    of the second group of            in the second group.
    entries on this page.

    This is a second
    paragraph that is also a
    part of the first entry
    of the second group of
    entries.


-
```

                         Col 1 Doc 1 Pg 1 Ln 17   Pos 10

Figure 6-5. Creating parallel columns with several groups of entries

22. Type the following text:

   This is the second entry in the second group.

23. Press the <Hard Column> key.

The screen will look like the one in Figure 6-5.

Newspaper-style Columns

Clear the screen, and then follow these steps to produce a document using newspaper-style columns:

1. Press the <Math/Columns> key (ALT+ F7) and type **4** for "Column Def."

2. Type **Y** for evenly spaced columns.

3. Type **5** and press ENTER.

4. Type **1** for newspaper-style columns.

5. Type **2** and press ENTER to select two columns, then press the <Exit> key (F7).

6. Type **3** to turn on Column mode.

   Now that you have defined the column format and turned on Column mode, you are ready to enter the column text. To reduce the amount of text you will need to type, first reduce the page length to five lines.

7. Press the <Page Format> key (ALT+F8).

8. Type **4** for "Page Length," and **3** for "Other."

9. Type **5**, press ENTER, type **5**, and press ENTER.

10. Press ENTER to clear the menu.

11. Type the following text:

   Also, all those mutual fund transactions that specify a client request for reinvestment of shares distributed must maintain the amount of the current reinvestment as well as the share price and number of shares involved as of the transaction date.

Notice that when you reach the end of a page (which is only five lines long in this case), the text automatically continues at the top of the second column.

12. Press ENTER.

Since the text above ended on the last line of the second column, pressing ENTER generates a Hard Page Break. Text continues at the top of the first column on the second page.

13. Position the cursor on the first letter in the word "Also" at the top of the first column on the first page. (Use Reveal Codes to ensure that the cursor is positioned after the hidden codes.)

14. Type the following text:

The number of shares reinvested is added to the reinvested shares-to-date amount.

15. Press SPACE twice to separate the sentences, and press DOWN ARROW once to reformat the text.

The screen will look like the one in Figure 6-6.

Notice how the text from the second column "snaked" to the first column of the second page.

LIMITATIONS OF THE COLUMN FUNCTION

Many of WordPerfect's functions can be used when you work in Column mode. For example, the Tabs, Align Tabs, Flush Right, and Center functions all work normally, within the confines of the current column.

However, there are some functions that cannot be used when you are in Column mode. These include the following:

- Footnotes (Endnotes work fine, however).

- Margin Changes.

- New column format definitions (turn Column mode off before defining a new column format).

- Advance Up, Advance Down, and Advance Line (super- and subscripts work, though).

```
The number of shares          specify a client request for
reinvested is added to the    reinvestment of shares
reinvested shares-to-date     distributed must maintain the
amount.  Also, all those      amount of the current
mutual fund transactions that reinvestment as well as the
-----------------------------------------------------------------
share price and number of
shares involved as of the
transaction date.
```

```
                              Col 1  Doc 1  Pg 1  Ln 5      Pos 19
```

Figure 6-6.   Creating newspaper-style columns

When you press the <Move> key (CTRL+F4), choice 4 is "Retrieve Column." On this menu, "Column" *does not* refer to the multiple columns discussed in this chapter. Rather, it refers to columns that are separated with [TAB] codes. You should *not* use this command with parallel or newspaper-style columns. You can, however, use the normal commands (Move Sentence, Move Paragraph, Move Page, or Block Move) to move text within, between, into, and out of columns.

You can speed up scrolling and rewriting text in columns by pressing the <Math/Columns> key (ALT+F7), typing **5** for "Column Display," and typing **N** at the prompt "Display columns side by side?"

Chapter

7 MATH

Although WordPerfect's Math function lacks the sophistication of a spreadsheet program, it can nonetheless perform many types of calculation on numbers within a document. With this function, you can total and subtotal columns; you can even create simple mathematic formulas that add, subtract, multiply, and divide the numbers in the columns.

For example, WordPerfect can calculate a billing statement for you. The program could total current and past services, subtract payments received, and present a grand total for the payment due. An example of a statement of this type is shown on the screen in Figure 7-1. The Math function can also be used to calculate totals of sales figures that you have arranged in columns.

THE MATH PROCESS

To use the Math function, you follow these basic steps:

1. Set tab stops for the columns you plan to use.

2. Define your *math columns.*

3. Turn on Math mode.

4. Enter text and numbers into the *math area.*

5. Calculate the *math area.*

6. Turn off Math mode.

```
                          Law Offices of
                     Jablonski and Kurtweiler

          CURRENT SERVICES

          Client meeting, Jones - 6/2/84              65.00
          Telephone - 3/4/84                          34.00
          Telephone - 5/2/84                          23.00

          Total Current Services                     122.00+

          PAST SERVICES

          Court Appearance - 1/4/84                   87.00
          Telephone - 2/12/84                         23.00

          Total Past Services                        110.00+


          TOTAL SERVICES RENDERED                     232.00=
          PAYMENTS RECEIVED                         T-110.00

          TOTAL AMOUNT DUE                           122.00*
          -
                                    Doc 1  Pg 1  Ln 24      Pos 10
```

Figure 7-1.   Example of a math document

You can have as many math areas as you want in your document. Simply repeat the steps listed above for each math area that you want to define. If the tab settings and math columns have been previously established in your document, you can skip the first two steps.

There are two ways the Math function can calculate numbers for you: down columns and across lines. You enter special *math operators* to calculate different types of totals down individual columns, and you enter *formulas* to compute totals and to perform other calculations across individual lines.

PREPARING TO USE THE MATH FUNCTION

Before you can actually start using the Math function, you must set tab stops to position the math columns, create and define the columns in the column definition process, and then turn on Math mode.

Setting Tabs

The tab stops you set determine the position and width of your math columns. If you later want to reposition the math columns, you can change the tab stops by inserting a new [Tab Set:] code after the old one.

Set your tab stops where you want the decimal points in each column to be aligned. If you will not be using decimal points in your numbers, set the tab stops where you want to right align the numbers. You need to make sure that the tab stops you set leave enough room for the numbers that the Math function will calculate. If you do not, the results of the calculations will not be accurate, since the numbers will overlap.

The first math column (column A) will have its numbers aligned at the first tab stop you define. You cannot use numbers entered at the left margin (before pressing TAB) in your calculations. However, you can enter *labels* at the left margin for lines that contain numbers in math columns to the right.

Note: To keep track of the column positions when you use the Math function, use the Window function to show a ruler at the bottom of the screen. The ruler will always display the current tab settings. To use a ruler, press the <Screen> key (CTRL+F3), type **1** for "Window," type **23**, and press ENTER.

After you have positioned your columns, you may want to type text at the top of each one to label it. For example, you may want to type "Sales" at the top of a column containing sales figures or "Price" at the top of a column containing prices. You should type in these labels after setting tabs but *before* turning on Math mode because some keys work differently when you are in Math mode.

Defining Math Columns

After you have set the tab stops you plan to use (and entered any necessary column labels), you need to define the Math columns. The Math column definition process allows you to specify whether each column will contain numbers or text. You also specify how many digits you want to the right of the decimal point in numbers calculated by the Math function, as well as whether negative numbers should be preceded by a minus sign or enclosed in parentheses. If you will be calculating across lines, as described later in the chapter, you also enter the formulas you plan to use.

The default settings for the Math column definition are for all columns to contain numbers, for calculated numbers to contain two digits to the right of the decimal point, and for negative numbers to be enclosed in parentheses. If these defaults are satisfactory and you do not plan to calculate across lines, you can skip the entire definition process and proceed with turning on Math mode as described in the next section.

To define the Math columns, move the cursor to where you want the math area to begin (making sure it is after any column labels), press the

```
Math Definition            Use arrow keys to position cursor

Columns                    A B C D E F G H I J K L M N O P Q R S T U V W X

Type                       2 2 2 2 2 2 2 2 2 2 2 2 2 2 2 2 2 2 2 2 2 2 2 2

Negative Numbers           ( ( ( ( ( ( ( ( ( ( ( ( ( ( ( ( ( ( ( ( ( ( ( (

# of digits to             2 2 2 2 2 2 2 2 2 2 2 2 2 2 2 2 2 2 2 2 2 2 2 2
the right (0-4)

Calculation   1
Formulas      2
              3
              4

Type of Column:
      0 = Calculation    1 = Text     2 = Numeric    3 = Total

Negative Numbers
      ( = Parenthesis (50.00)          - = Minus Sign  -50.00

Press EXIT when done
```

Figure 7-2.   Math Definition screen

<Math/Columns> key (ALT+F7), and type **2** for "Math Def." The Math Definition screen appears, as shown in Figure 7-2.

You can have up to 24 math columns, each identified with a single letter from A to X. Across the top of the screen are the letters that indicate the individual columns. Below each letter are settings for that particular column. You need to change the settings only for those columns you intend to use, and only for those that differ from the default settings. While the Math Definition screen is displayed, you can freely move the cursor to any setting using the arrow keys.

Note: While working with the Math function, you may find it difficult to keep track of how you have defined each column. To help you with this, keep a written copy of the column definitions handy.

When you are finished entering your math column definition, press the <Exit> key (F7). You will return to the Math/Columns menu, ready to turn on Math mode as described in the next section. A [Math Def] hidden code that contains the settings you just specified will have been inserted into the text at the cursor position.

Each of the settings on the Math Definition screen is described in detail below.

Setting Column Type

The first setting is for the column type, which you choose from a menu at the bottom of the screen.

Formulas perform addition and other calculations across lines, instead of down columns. Type **0** (for a Calculation column) if the column will contain a formula. The cursor will move to the middle of the screen, where you can enter the formula for the column. You can have only four Calculation columns per math area. (See "Calculating Across Lines" later in this chapter for a discussion of formulas.)

Type **1** to define a Text column if you will have a label or other text in the middle of a math area. For example, you may want to produce a table of sales figures with salespeople's initials in the fourth column. Specifying a Text column will prevent the column's entries from being included in any totals or formulas, even if you enter a number into the column. (WordPerfect will not, however, prevent you from entering, in a Calculation column, a formula containing a reference to a Text column. When the formula is calculated, it will treat the text in the column as having a value of zero.) Specifying a column as a Text column also tells WordPerfect to treat any characters you later type in that column as ordinary characters rather than as special math operators.

Type **2** (for a Numeric column) if the column will contain numbers. You can also place *math operators* in a numeric column to perform subtotals, totals, and grand totals. These operators are displayed on the screen but are not printed.

Type **3** (for a Total column) if the column will contain *offset totals*. This special type of total is derived from the numbers that are in the column to the *left* of the Total column, instead of from the Total column itself. Offset totals are frequently used in accounting reports.

Setting Negative Number Format

Next you select the format you want for negative numbers resulting from calculations. You can choose to have the numbers either enclosed in parentheses (the default) or preceded by a minus sign. Type a minus sign to change the format from the default setting.

Setting the Number of Digits After the Decimal

The last setting on the Math Definition screen allows you to select the number of digits you want after the decimal point in all calculations for each column. You can type any number from 0 to 4. Note that the Math function will format only the numbers that are calculated, not numbers that you enter. However, for consistency, you can enter numbers in the same format as the format you specify here for calculated numbers.

Turning Math Mode On and Off

After defining your columns, you enter Math mode to create a *math area* in your document. While in Math mode, you enter the text and numbers in the columns you previously defined. After pressing <Exit> to end Math column definition, type **1** for "Math On" to turn on Math mode. If you skipped the definition process, you will first need to press the

<Math/Columns> key (ALT+F7). The following message appears at the bottom of the screen:

Math

A hidden code, [Math On], is inserted into the document at the cursor position.

After you have entered the text and numbers for this math area (as described in the next section), you will press the <Math/Columns> key (ALT+F7) and type **1** for "Math Off." The "Math" message will disappear from the screen, and a hidden code, [Math Off], will be inserted into the document. Each math area is defined by these two hidden codes. When the cursor is positioned between them, you will see the "Math" message displayed at the bottom of the screen, indicating that Math mode is on.

USING THE MATH FUNCTION

After following the steps described in the previous section, you enter text, numbers, and math operators into the math area, and then you calculate the results.

Entering Text, Numbers, and Operators

Press the TAB key to move the cursor to the first Math column you want to use. If the column you tab to is defined as a Numeric, Calculation, or Total column, the TAB key will *automatically* perform the Tab Align function (and you will see the "Align Char = ." message at the bottom of the screen). That is because these columns usually contain numbers with decimal points that need to be aligned. The TAB key will function normally (that is, it will left align your text) when you tab to a Text column.

After positioning the cursor at the column you wish to use, enter the number, math operator, or text that you want to appear in the column. (Math operators are described in the section "Calculating Down Columns" later in this chapter.) Then, press TAB to move to the next column, or press ENTER to end the line.

If the column you tab to is a Calculation column, you will see an exclamation point (!) after you tab to the column. This indicates that the result of a formula will be placed at this point when the math area is calculated. (Since the Math function automatically performs the Tab Align function when you tab to a Calculation column, the decimal point of the result will be aligned at the column's tab position.) To continue, press the TAB key to move to the next column, or press ENTER to end the line. If you do not wish a result to be placed at this position, simply press BACKSPACE to erase the ! before continuing. You can separate the lines in the math area by any number of blank lines, if you wish.

Calculating a Math Area

When you want WordPerfect to calculate the numbers in a math area, you use the Calculate command. Make sure that the cursor is positioned within the math area (the "Math" message should be displayed at the bottom of the screen). Then press the <Math/Columns> key (ALT+F7) and type **2** for "Calculate." All formulas and totals in the current math area will be updated.

Subtotal, Total, and Grand Total operators will only add numbers that are within the math area in which the operators are located. For example, a Subtotal operator will not include in its result numbers that were entered in a previous math area.

If WordPerfect cannot evaluate one of your formulas, it will produce "??" in place of a result. Check the formula by positioning the cursor immediately after the [Math Def] code you generated earlier and repeating the Math column definition process.

CALCULATING DOWN COLUMNS

The characters +, =, t, T, and N all function as math operators when entered in Math mode. The operators are not printed, even though they appear on the screen. Because these characters function differently from the way they usually do (you can tell they are different because they are bold on the Reveal Codes screen), you cannot enter them into a normal document and then later add the [Math Def] and [Math On] codes. You must enter the operators while Math mode is turned on, or WordPerfect will not recognize them as math operators.

To insert one of the operators, you simply type the character, instead of or with a number, in a column. You can precede any math operator with a dollar sign or other symbol that you want to appear in front of the number when it is calculated.

Math Operators

Here are the math operators you can use and the function each performs:

+   *Subtotal*
This character adds all of the numbers above it that are in the same column. If you place the character in the document after another Subtotal operator, it will add all the numbers that appear *after* that operator.

=   *Total*
This character adds all of the subtotals above it that are in the same column. If you place the character in the document after another Total operator, then it will add all the subtotals that appear *after* that operator.

*   *Grand Total*
This character adds all of the totals above it that are in the same column. If you place the character in the document after another Grand Total operator, it will add all the totals that appear after that operator.

Figure 7-3 shows an example of a column of figures on the screen with a Subtotal operator at the bottom.

When you place one of these operators in a column that has been defined as a Total column (see "Setting Column Type" earlier in this chapter), the operator will perform its function on numbers and totals that appear in the column to its left, creating an offset total. This allows subtotals, totals, and grand totals to be broken out from the columns of numbers that they are adding. An example of an offset total is shown in Figure 7-4.

If there are no totals of the proper type in the previous column, then the function will work normally with numbers and totals from within the same column. For example, let's say you have a document with numbers in the third column, like the one shown in Figure 7-5.

In the fourth column (which you have defined as a Total column), you have periodic subtotals of the numbers in the third column. At the end of the report, you want a total of all the subtotals in the fourth column. You

```
Name              Sales        .

John              54,000
Mary              23,500
Julie             62,750
Frank             87,250
George            23,000
Paul             140,750
Mellissa          40,500
Ringo             35,250
Steve            125,000
Dale              96,500

Total:                        +

 -
```

Math   Doc 1   Pg 1   Ln 15   Pos 10

Figure 7-3.   Example of a math document with a Subtotal operator

can simply place the = operator in the fourth column; since there are no subtotals in the third column, it will add up the subtotals in the fourth column as it would if the column were not defined as a Total column.

Forced Total Operators

There are three other math operators that you can place in a Math column. You place the first two before a number to force the Math function to treat the number *as if it were* a calculated subtotal or total. The last is used to force a negative value.

t   *Subtotal Number*

When you type this character before a number in a Math column, the

```
Name                Sales

John                54,000
Mary                23,500
Julie               62,750
Frank               87,250
George              23,000
Paul               140,750
Mellissa            40,500
Ringo               35,250
Steve              125,000
Dale                96,500

Total Sales ------------>   688,500+
```

Math   Doc 1 Pg 1 Ln 15   Pos 10

Figure 7-4.   Example of a math document with an offset total

number is treated as if it had been calculated as a subtotal by the Math function. It will then be included in any subsequent total calculations.

T *Total Number*

When you type this character before a number in a Math column, the number is treated as if it had been calculated as a total by the Math function. It will then be included in any subsequent grand total calculations.

N *Negative Number*

When you type this character before a number or math operator in a Math column, the number (or result) is considered a negative value in subsequent subtotals, totals, and grand totals.

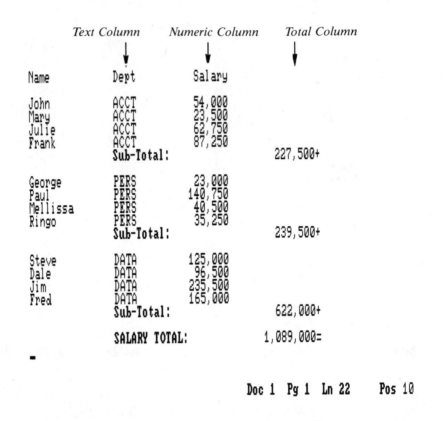

Figure 7-5.   Example of a math document with an offset column for totals

SOME PRACTICE EXAMPLES

Follow these steps to create a simple document that uses some of these special math operators. Make sure the screen is clear.

1. Press the <Screen> key (CTRL+F3) and type **1** for "Window."

2. Type **23** and press ENTER.

This sets the size of the current window to 23 lines, causing a ruler to appear at the bottom of the screen. The ruler is useful when you are using the Math function, since it displays the current tab settings.

3. Press the <Line Format> key (SHFT+F8) and type **1** for "Tabs."

4. Press the <Delete End-Of-Line> key (CTRL+END).

5. Type **35** and press ENTER.

6. Type **45**, press ENTER, and then press the <Exit> key (F7).

This sets tab stops at 35 and 45 for two Math columns. The ruler will reflect the two tab stops you have defined.

7. Press the <Tab Align> key (CTRL + F6).

8. Press the <Underline> key, type **Sales**, press the <Underline> key again, and press ENTER twice.

9. Press the <Math/Columns> key (ALT+F7) and type **2** for "Math Def."

For this exercise, column A needs to be defined as a Numeric column. Since this is the default setting, you can skip the entry.

10. Press RIGHT ARROW.

11. Type **3** to define column B as a total column.

12. Press DOWN ARROW twice, then press LEFT ARROW twice.

13. Type **0** and then **0** again to set a format of zero decimal places for calculated numbers in both columns.

14. Press the <Exit> key.

15. Type **1** to turn on Math mode.

You will see the message "Math" appear at the bottom of the screen. Now you are ready to enter labels and numbers in the math area.

16. Press the <Bold> key (F6), type **S.F. Office**, press the <Bold> key, and then press ENTER.

```
                   Sales

S.F. Office
John               54,000
Mary               23,500
Julie              62,750

Total                +


-
```

```
Math                          Doc 1  Pg 1  Ln 10     Pos 10
```

Figure 7-6.   Example of a math document with a Subtotal operator

17. Type **John**, press TAB, type **54,000**, and press ENTER.

18. Type **Mary**, press TAB, type **23,500**, and press ENTER.

19. Type **Julie**, press TAB, type **62,750**, and press ENTER twice.

20. Type **Total**, press TAB, type + (a plus sign), and press ENTER twice.

The plus sign indicates that you want the Math function to subtotal the numbers in the column above. Your screen will look like the one shown in Figure 7-6.

21. Press the <Math/Columns> key (ALT+F7).

Notice that choice 2 is "Math Def" when you are not in Math mode but "Calculate" when you are in Math mode. You must be in Math mode (when the cursor is in a math area) to perform calculations.

```
                        Sales

S.F. Office
John                    54,000
Mary                    23,500
Julie                   62,750

Total                  140,250+


-
```

```
Math                              Doc 1  Pg 1  Ln 10      Pos 10
```

Figure 7-7.   Example of a math document with a calculated Subtotal operator

22. Type **2** for "Calculate."

The screen will look like the one shown in Figure 7-7.

That's all there is to using the Math function to add a column of numbers. This example used the Subtotal operator; the next example uses the Total operator to add two subtotals. With the text from the previous exercise still on the screen, follow these steps:

1. Using the same procedure as in the previous exercise, enter the following text and numbers directly under the previous text:

```
L.A. Office
Bill              65,000
Frank             32,000
Linda             12,250

Total                +
```

```
                      Sales

S.F. Office
Julie                62,750
John                 54,000
Mary                 23,500

Total               140,250+

L.A. Office
Bill                 65,000
Frank                32,000
Linda                12,250

Total                    +_
```

Math   Doc 1 Pg 1 Ln 15   Pos 36

Figure 7-8.   Example of a math document with two Subtotal operators

Your screen should look like the one shown in Figure 7-8.

2. After typing + in the last line, press ENTER twice, press the <Bold> key, type **WEST COAST:**, and press the <Bold> key again.

3. Press TAB and type = (an equal sign).

   The equal sign indicates that you want the Math function to total the two subtotals that appear above it.

4. Press ENTER twice.

5. Press the <Math/Columns> key, and type **2** for "Calculate."

```
Total                140,250+

L.A. Office
Bill                  65,000
Frank                 32,000
Linda                 12,250

Total                109,250+

WEST COAST:          249,500=

-
```

Math   Doc 1 Pg 1 Ln 19   Pos 10

Figure 7-9.   Example of a math document with a Total operator

Your screen should look like the one shown in Figure 7-9.

This example used the Total operator to add two subtotals. The next exercise will use the Grand Total operator to add two totals.

Although you could place the Grand Total operator in the same column as the Total operators, in this exercise you will place it in the next column to the right, creating an offset total. This makes the number more noticeable. The number will calculate properly, since you defined column B (the second column) as a Total column.

1. Following the same steps as in the first exercise, enter the following text and numbers below the previous text:

```
Bill                65,000
Frank               32,000
Linda               12,250

Total              109,250+

WEST COAST:        249,500=


N.Y. Office
Rachelle            87,000
Alphonzo            54,250
Jim                 31,000

Total:                    +

Boston Office
Skippy              92,500
Biff                42,250
Muffy               39,750

Total:                    +

EAST COAST:               =
Math
```

              Doc 1 Pg 1 Ln 34   Pos 36

Figure 7-10. Example of a math document with two Total operators

```
N.Y. Office
Rachelle            87,000
Alphonzo            54,250
Jim                 31,000

Total                     +

Boston Office
Skippy              92,500
Biff                42,250
Muffy               39,750

Total                     +

EAST COAST:               =
```

Your screen should look like the one shown in Figure 7-10.

2. After typing = in the last line, press ENTER three times, press the <Bold> key, and type **TOTAL COMPANY SALES:**

3. Press the TAB key *twice* and type ✱

4. Press ENTER.

5. Press the <Math/Columns> key and type **2** for "Calculate."

The number 596,250 will appear as the grand total for all of the sales figures you entered. The next exercise uses the Total Number operator to enter a sales total that is not actually calculated by the Math function.

1. Move the cursor to the line below the line that starts "EAST COAST."

2. Press ENTER, press the <Bold> key, type **EUROPE:**, and press the <Bold> key again.

3. Press the TAB key and type **T154,000**

4. Press ENTER.

5. Press the <Math/Columns> key and type **2** for "Calculate."

6. Press the <Math/Columns> key and type **1** for "Math Off."

Notice that the "Total Company Sales" now reflects the sales from the European Division.

CALCULATING ACROSS LINES

The math operators described in the previous section total numbers only down columns. To total numbers and perform other calculations across lines, WordPerfect uses math formulas that you enter during the Math column definition process. When you enter a formula for a column, it applies to every line in that column. You cannot use different formulas for individual lines in a single column without turning off Math mode and redefining the Math columns.

You can use formulas to calculate tax and commission amounts, as well as averages and totals of numbers (or other totals) on the same line.

Using Formulas

To use a formula for a column entry in a line, type **0** for the column type on the Math Definition screen. (See "Defining Math Columns" earlier in this chapter.) The cursor will move to the middle of the screen, where you enter the formula. You can enter formulas for up to four columns in each math area.

Formulas can contain numbers, letters identifying other column entries on the same line, and common math operators. You cannot use values from other lines in a formula. (The math operators used in a formula are different from the math operators used to subtotal, total, and grand total columns of numbers.) Column letters can be either uppercase or lowercase. Here is a list of math operators you can use in a formula:

Operator	Function
+	Addition
-	Subtraction
*	Multiplication
/	Division

Math formulas are usually calculated from left to right. You can use parentheses to affect the order of calculation, but you cannot *nest* them. That is, you cannot use a set of parentheses within another set. The numbers and operators in parentheses are evaluated before the rest of the formula.

To enter a negative number into a formula, type a minus sign (−) and then the number. To use a positive column value as a negative number, or vice versa, type a minus sign (−) and then the column letter.

Following are some examples of formulas and their results. Let's assume that in one line, column A contains the number 350 and, in the same line, column B contains the number 52.

Column C Formula	Result
A*.03	10.50
2+A*.5	176.00
2+(A*.5)	177.00
A/B	6.73
-A-5	(355.00)

Special Formula Operators

Several special operators are used by themselves as the entire formula. These special operators must be entered without any numbers, column letters, or other math operators. They perform functions on numbers or totals across lines. Here is a list of the special operators you can use, as well as which function each operator performs:

+   *Line Total—Numeric Columns*
When this character is entered by itself as a formula, the result will be the total of all the numbers on each line that appear in Numeric columns (whether calculated or entered).

=   *Line Total—Total Columns*
When this character is entered by itself as a formula, the result will be the total of all the numbers on each line that appear in Total columns (whether calculated or entered).

+/   *Line Average—Numeric Columns*
When these characters are entered by themselves as a formula, the result will be the average of all the numbers on each line that appear in Numeric columns (whether calculated or entered).

=/   *Line Average—Total Columns*
When these characters are entered by themselves as a formula, the result will be the average of all the numbers on each line that are in Total columns (whether calculated or entered).

Some Practice Examples

Follow these steps to create a math document that calculates across lines using formulas. Make sure the screen is clear.

1. Press the <Line Format> key (SHFT+F8) and type **1** for "Tabs."

2. Press the <Delete End-Of-Line> key (CTRL+END).

3. Type **35** and press ENTER.

4. Type **45** and press ENTER.

5. Type **55**, press ENTER, and then press the <Exit> key (F7).

This sets tab stops at 35, 45, and 55, for three Math columns.

6. Press TAB, and then press the <Center> key (SHFT+F6).
   This will center the text over the tab stop.

7. Type **Cost**, press TAB, and press the <Center> key.

8. Type **Markup**, press TAB, and press the <Center> key.

9. Type **Price** and press ENTER twice.

10. Press the <Math/Columns> key (ALT+F7) and type **2** for "Math Def."

11. Press RIGHT ARROW to accept the default setting (Numeric column) for column A.

12. Type **0** to define column B as a Calculation column.

13. Type **A*.45** and press ENTER.

14. Type **0** to define column C as a Calculation column.

```
                        Cost    Markup    Price

Rubber Gloves          23.65      !        !
Rubber Cement           4.32      !        !
Rubber Ball             6.32      !        !
-




Math                                    Doc 1  Pg 1  Ln 6      Pos 10
```

Figure 7-11. Example of a math document with formulas

15. Type **A+B** and press ENTER.

16. Press the <Exit> key.

17. Type **1** to turn on Math mode.

18. Type **Rubber Gloves**, press TAB, type **23.65**, press TAB twice, and press ENTER.

19. Type **Rubber Cement**, press TAB, type **4.32**, press TAB twice, and press ENTER.

20. Type **Rubber Ball**, press TAB, type **6.32**, press TAB twice, and press ENTER.

    The screen should look like the one shown in Figure 7-11.

21. Press the <Math/Columns> key (ALT+F7) and type **2** for "Calculate."

22. Press the <Math/Columns> key and type **1** for "Math Off."

    The screen should look like the one shown in Figure 7-12.

	Cost	Markup	Price
Rubber Gloves	23.65	7.10!	30.75!
Rubber Cement	4.32	1.30!	5.62!
Rubber Ball	6.32	1.90!	8.22!

Doc 1 Pg 1 Ln 6   Pos 10

Figure 7-12. Example of a math document with calculated formulas

Follow these steps to create a document that uses one of the special math operators. Make sure the screen is clear.

1. Press the <Line Format> key (SHFT+F8) and type **1** for "Tabs."

2. Press the <Delete End-Of-Line> key (CTRL+END).

3. Type **25** and press ENTER.

4. Type **35** and press ENTER.

5. Type **45** and press ENTER.

6. Type **55**, press ENTER, and then press the <Exit> key (F7).

This sets tab stops at 25, 35, 45, and 55, for four Math columns.

7. Press the <Tab Align> key (CTRL+F6) and type **Jan**

    The Tab Align function will right align your column labels.

8. Press the <Tab Align> key and type **Feb**

9. Press the <Tab Align> key and type **Mar**

10. Press the <Tab Align> key and type **Avg**

11. Press ENTER twice.

12. Press the <Math/Columns> key and type **2** for "Math Def."

13. Press RIGHT ARROW three times to accept the default settings for columns A, B, and C.

14. Type **0** to define column D as a Calculation column.

15. Type **+/** and press ENTER.

    This formula will produce the average of the numbers on each line.

16. Press DOWN ARROW twice and press LEFT ARROW four times.

17. Type **0** four times to set all four columns for no decimal places.

18. Press the <Exit> key (F7).

19. Type **1** for "Math On."

20. Type **Harry**, press TAB, type **87**, press TAB, type **45**, press TAB, type **23**, press TAB, and press ENTER.

```
            Jan     Feb     Mar     Avg

Harry       87      45      23      52!
George      45      98      23      55!
Britt       12       9      12      11!

Total      144+    152+    58+     118!
-
```

Doc 1 Pg 1 Ln 8   Pos 10

Figure 7-13. Example of a math document with a special operator

21. Type **George**, press TAB, type **45**, press TAB, type **98**, press TAB, type **23**, press TAB, and press ENTER.

22. Type **Britt**, press TAB, type **12**, press TAB, type **9**, press TAB, type **12**, press TAB, and press ENTER twice.

23. Type **Total**, press TAB, type +, press TAB, type +, press TAB, type +, press TAB, and press ENTER.

24. Press the <Math/Columns> key and type **2** for "Calculate."

25. Press the <Math/Columns> key and type **1** for "Math Off."

The Math function calculates the average sales level for each salesperson, totals each month's sales, then calculates the average sales level for all of the months. The screen should look like the one shown in Figure 7-13.

8 INTEGRATION WITH OTHER PRODUCTS

WordPerfect is well equipped to interact with files from other programs. It can read and write ASCII text files directly and can translate other types of files to and from WordPerfect format. With WordPerfect, you can also write macros to aid in file translation.

This chapter will discuss each program individually, describing the best procedures for transferring files to and from WordPerfect for each one. Some information will be duplicated in the various sections, but each section will describe the entire procedure necessary for the transfer.

In this chapter, the term *importing a file* means transferring a file from another program into WordPerfect format. The term *exporting a file* means transferring a WordPerfect file to another program.

The material in this chapter may seem somewhat technical to you. However, you will always be provided with explicit directions for making the integration between WordPerfect and the program you are working with.

DEALING WITH ASCII FILES

What is an ASCII file? ASCII stands for American Standard Code for Information Interchange. This code was established as a standard means of communication between computers, as well as between computers and peripherals such as printers.

In the ASCII environment, each character (letter, number, or punctuation mark) is identified by a number, called the character's *ASCII code.* ASCII codes 1 through 31 are considered *control codes.* Instead of producing characters, these codes usually control a function, such as clearing the screen or positioning the cursor. Many of the control codes were originally intended for use with line printers (like daisy wheel printers).

As originally defined, the ASCII codes range from 0 to 127. However, most computers have an extended ASCII character set that contains 256 characters and control codes. In the IBM Extended Character Set, the extra 128 codes consist of graphic characters, foreign letters, and special symbols. Some programs use these extra codes to designate formatting commands.

The terms "ASCII file" and "DOS text file" refer to files that contain very few, if any, control codes and no codes at all higher than the original 128. Therefore, ASCII files consist primarily of ASCII codes 32 through 127. Since most word processing programs insert control codes to add formatting commands like boldfacing and underlining, files produced by these programs are not considered ASCII files.

The most rudimentary method of transferring a document from another word processor into WordPerfect is to convert it first to an ASCII file from within the other program and then to retrieve it into WordPerfect using the Text In/Out function. Use this method only when no other transfer method is available. Since the ASCII file will not contain any control codes, all formatting will usually be lost with this method.

When you receive data by modem, it is commonly stored on disk in an ASCII file. You can use WordPerfect to edit the file by importing it with the Text In/Out function.

To see WordPerfect's functions for dealing with ASCII files, press the <Text In/Out> key (CTRL+F5). The Document Conversion, Summary and Comments screen will appear, as shown in Figure 8-1. Menu choices 1, 2, 3, and 6 are used to import and export ASCII files.

Importing ASCII Files

There are basically two types of ASCII files, those in a "streaming" format which have Hard Returns only at the end of each paragraph, and those with a Hard Return at the end of every line. In WordPerfect, you have two choices for retrieving ASCII files: direct, or with Hard Return

```
Document Conversion, Summary and Comments

    DOS Text File Format
         1 - Save
         2 - Retrieve  (CR/LF becomes [HRt])
         3 - Retrieve  (CR/LF in H-Zone becomes [SRt])

    Locked Document Format
         4 - Save
         5 - Retrieve

    Other Word Processor Formats
         6 - Save in a generic word processor format
         7 - Save in WordPerfect 4.1 format

    Document Summary and Comments
         A - Create/Edit Summary
         B - Create Comment
         C - Edit Comment
         D - Display Summary and Comments




    Selection: █
```

Figure 8-1.   Document Conversion, Summary and Comments screen

conversion. Retrieve streaming ASCII files directly with choice 2 from the Document conversion menu. ASCII files with a Hard Return at the end of every line can either be retrieved directly (with choice 2) or with Hard Return conversion (choice 3).

Retrieving ASCII Files Directly

You should retrieve streaming ASCII files directly—as they require no converting—as well as spreadsheet or database "print-to-disk" reports, program files, or other files with non-paragraph form text. If a file was formatted with longer lines than WordPerfect's default margins allow, the program will insert Soft Returns in the text. In this case, you must widen WordPerfect's margins to accommodate the ASCII file.

To retrieve an ASCII file directly, type **2** for "Retrieve" from the Document Conversion, Summary and Comments menu, type the name of the ASCII file, and press ENTER. Alternatively, you can use the List Files function to highlight the file you want to retrieve, and then type **5** for "Text In." The ASCII file will be inserted at the cursor position.

Retrieving ASCII Files
With Hard Return Conversion

You should retrieve ASCII files which contain paragraph-form text, and are not in the streaming format, with Hard Return Conversion. This function converts Hard Returns to Soft Returns, so that WordPerfect will be able to reformat the text when you begin editing, or when you use margins, tabs, indents, or other formatting functions.

Hard Returns convert to Soft Returns using these guidelines:

- Any occurrence of two Hard Returns in a row are left intact. This is usually an indication of the end of a paragraph and a following blank line, so the Hard Returns are not converted.

- An occurrence of a Hard Return that falls within the Hyphenation Hot Zone is converted to a Soft Return. The Hot Zone is initially set to extend from seven characters in from the right margin to the right margin itself. So, any Hard Returns which are located near the end of a line will be converted.

By following these rules, WordPerfect will normally convert all of the unnecessary Hard Returns. However, it may miss some of them, or convert ones that shouldn't be converted. Look out for these problems as you edit the file. If you are in doubt, check the Reveal Codes screen to see if a line ends with a Soft or Hard Return. You may also need to change the margin settings to reflect the format of the ASCII file *before* retrieving the file.

Tab Settings

ASCII files sometimes contain tab codes. A tab code is one of the few control codes that are included in an ASCII file. A tab code (ASCII code 9) is considered a control code because it is assigned to one of the first 32 codes of the ASCII character set.

You know that you can change the tab settings in your documents at any time, but in the ASCII environment, tabs are usually 8 spaces apart.

Because of this, you might want to set a tab stop every 8 spaces in the WordPerfect document so that the text will be formatted correctly.

Use the incremental method of specifying tab stops to place them 8 spaces apart. (See the section "Line Formatting" in Chapter 1 for a discussion of setting tabs with the incremental method.)

Editing ASCII Files

If you frequently work with ASCII files which are formatted with a particular line length or with tabs set for every 8 spaces, you might want to create a macro that inserts these codes for you. This way, you can execute the macro before retrieving the ASCII file, and the file will be formatted correctly.

If you do a lot of work with ASCII files, you may want to work the other way around. That is, you could change WordPerfect's Initial Settings so that the margins and tabs are set to work with ASCII files; whenever you wanted to work with a normal WordPerfect file, you would restore the original settings in the document.

P-Edit (a *program editor* that comes with WordPerfect Library) is a better tool for working with large ASCII files than is WordPerfect. Most importantly, it will retrieve and save them much faster than WordPerfect, since it does not have to take the time to format the text within margins and pages. For a complete description of WordPerfect Library, see Appendix D, "WordPerfect Library."

Exporting ASCII Files

You can save any WordPerfect document as an ASCII file, either in a DOS Text format with a Hard Return at the end of every line, or in a Generic Word Processing "streaming" format with a Hard Return only at the end of each paragraph. In either case, none of WordPerfect's codes are saved in the resulting file.

However, many positioning functions will be converted to spaces to "fill" the area that would normally be blank on the WordPerfect screen. For example, centered lines will have spaces inserted in place of the Center code, so that the line *looks* centered. In the same way, other codes are converted to simulate the effect they produce on the WordPerfect screen, including indent and flush right codes.

To see the options for saving ASCII files, press the <Text In/Out> key (CTRL+F5).

Saving in DOS Text Format

This format is very useful for creating documents which you plan to send as messages through remote bulletin boards and electronic mail services. It is also used for saving DOS files such as batch files, or program files.

Tabs are converted to spaces with this function. This means the text will look correctly formatted, no matter how it is viewed, or with which word processing program. However, it also means that the format cannot be easily changed, as it could be if the tabs were left intact. To create a file with the tab codes intact, use the Generic Word Processing format.

To save a file in the DOS Text format, type **1** from the Document Conversion, Summary and Comments screen, type the name of the file, and press ENTER.

Saving in Generic Word Processing Format

This format is used to save a WordPerfect document in a form that will be most easily readable by another word processing program. If you cannot find a direct conversion between WordPerfect and another program (see the next section, "Using Convert"), this is the best way to transfer the file.

In this format, Hard Returns are placed only at the end of each paragraph, instead of at the end of each line. In this way, the word processing program that will import the file will be able to easily reformat the text.

In addition, [TAB] codes are retained. However, since tab settings are not saved, the file will not appear properly formatted in the other word processing program unless the tab stops are reinstated to their original settings. Hard Page Breaks are also retained.

To save a document in the Generic Word Processing format, type **6** from the Document Conversion, Summary and Comments screen, enter the desired name for the file, and press ENTER.

Hard Return Codes

Each Hard Return used in the file formats described above actually consists of two ASCII codes: a code 13 (which is a carriage return) and a code 10 (which is a line feed). The reason that two codes are used for this simple function dates back to the early days of teletype printers. For the purposes of this book, it is sufficient to say that this is considered standard for ASCII files in the MS-DOS environment.

In some situations, one of the two codes may not be needed. For example, programs on the Apple Macintosh use only a code 13 (carriage return) at the end of each paragraph. If you retrieve a file that you have saved as an ASCII file from WordPerfect into a Macintosh word processing program, you will see a small box (indicating an unprintable character) at the beginning of every line. This character is the code 10 (line feed) that is found after each code 13.

Following is a BASIC program that removes line feeds from a text file. (To use the program to remove carriage returns instead of line feeds, change the "13" in line 130 to "10".)

```
10 CLEAR:CLS:KEY OFF
20 PRINT "Program to strip LF's from text files":PRINT
30 PRINT "Hit RETURN to quit":PRINT
40 INPUT "Input file name";INF$
50 IF INF$="" THEN 200
60 INPUT "Output file name";OUTF$
70 OPEN "i",1,INF$
80 OPEN "o",2,OUTF$
90 LNFL=LOF(1)
100 CLS
110 LINE INPUT#1,LIN$
120 IF EOF(1) THEN 190
130 PRINT#2,LIN$;CHR$(13);
140 POSFL=POSFL+LEN(LIN$)+2
150 DONE=INT(POSFL/LNFL*100)
160 DONE$=RIGHT$(STR$(DONE),LEN(STR$(DONE))-1)
170 LOCATE 1,1:PRINT "Processing file: ";
        INF$;" - ";DONE$;"% complete."
180 GOTO 110
190 CLOSE:GOTO 10
200 CLOSE
```

USING CONVERT

Convert is a general conversion utility that is distributed with WordPerfect, on the Learning Disk. It provides a way to share files with a variety of other major programs.

Although the program you want to communicate with may not appear on Convert's menu, you can frequently find a format to act as an intermediary. That is, the program you want to communicate with may have a conversion utility of its own that has on its menu a choice that also appears on Convert's menu. You could then transfer the file from WordPerfect format to the intermediary format and then from the intermediary format to the format of the program you want to work with.

Convert works with two types of files: document files and database files. With document files, the program translates as many of the formatting codes as it can from one file format to another. With database files, the program mainly arranges the data in different ways, with a variety of field and record delimiters. (A delimiter is a character or set of characters that marks the end of a field or record.)

Document Files

Here are the types of document files that Convert can work with:

WordPerfect This is the standard WordPerfect document format.

Revisable-Form-Text (DCA) This is a format that IBM established as a standard for transferring documents between different word processing systems on IBM mainframe computers and microcomputers. While you may never have an opportunity to use an IBM mainframe, this format can often be a good intermediary link between two programs, since it retains such formatting commands as margin changes and underlining. Many major word processing programs have recently added the DCA to those formats it can translate to and from.

WordStar Use this format for transferring files between WordPerfect and WordStar. Although almost all word processing programs can translate to and from this format, it is *not* the best one to use as an intermediary between two programs. This is because WordStar itself has many intrinsic limitations that manifest themselves in your document files. For example, when you press the TAB key in WordStar, the program inserts spaces instead of a tab code. Therefore, when you translate a file to WordStar, all tabs are translated to the appropriate number of spaces. This makes it more difficult to reformat the document after you have imported it into another program like WordPerfect.

MultiMate   Use this format for standard MultiMate documents, which have a .DOC extension.

Seven-bit transfer format   WordPerfect files contain a variety of control codes that are only understood by WordPerfect. If you were to view these files with another program, or from DOS with the Type command, you would see these codes as a lot of unintelligible graphic characters. In simple terms, these codes use 8 bits, which means that their ASCII codes are higher than 127. All normal, readable characters (like letters, numbers, and punctuation marks) use 7 bits, which means their ASCII codes are all lower than 127.

In order to transfer a document with 8-bit control codes over a telephone modem, you would need to use a communications program that has a file transfer protocol (the most common one is called XMODEM). However, you can transfer 7-bit files without this protocol. The Seven-bit transfer format provides a way to translate a WordPerfect document temporarily into a 7-bit file so that it can be sent by modem without a transfer protocol. After the file has been received, it can be translated back to the original WordPerfect format with *all* control codes intact. The Seven-bit transfer format is not very frequently used because most communication programs provide a file transfer protocol. Obviously, this is the best way to transfer WordPerfect documents, since they do not have to be converted at all.

Navy DIF   This is a special version of DIF (Data Interchange Format) that was developed and is mainly used by the Navy as a standard format for transferring documents between various word processing systems. If you are in the Navy, you probably already know everything you need to about this format; if you are not in the Navy, you probably still know everything you need to about this format.

Database Files

The Convert program also translates database files to and from Word-Perfect's secondary merge format. (See the section "Secondary Merge Files" in Chapter 3, "Merge," for a description of the secondary merge file format.) This capability allows data that is stored and manipulated in a database program to be transferred to WordPerfect for mailmerge purposes. You can also transfer data in a secondary file to a database or spreadsheet program for high-power manipulation.

Here are the types of database files that Convert can work with:

WordPerfect Secondary Merge   This is a WordPerfect document with fields of data that end with a ^R [HRt] sequence and records that end with a ^E [HRt] sequence. Documents in this format can be used by WordPerfect's Merge function to create form letters and other merged documents.

Mail Merge   This is a format that can be customized according to the type of input document you have. When you choose this format, the program will ask you for a *field delimiter*, a *record delimiter*, and any characters that should be stripped from the file. The most common format for this type of file to have is a comma as a field delimiter and a Hard Return as a record delimiter.

WordStar MailMerge files use this format, and most databases and programming languages can output a file into the MailMerge format. In fact, it is among the most common of data formats for microcomputers.

When entering the characters that separate fields and records and that should be stripped from the file, you can either enter the characters directly or enter their ASCII codes between curly brackets. For example, to indicate that records end with a Hard Return you would type {**13**}{**10**}, since these ASCII codes produce a Hard Return. Sometimes the data file will have quotation marks around text fields. These quotation marks are an example of characters that you would have Convert strip out for you.

Spreadsheet DIF   DIF (Data Interchange Format) is a format that was developed by VisiCorp for transferring data between the pioneer spreadsheet VisiCalc and other VisiCorp products. It has since become a common format for transferring any data formatted into rows and columns.

You can use the DIF format for transferring data between WordPerfect and popular spreadsheet programs like Lotus 1-2-3 and between WordPerfect and many database programs. It can also be useful in situations where database files cannot be translated into MailMerge format. One disadvantage of this method is that a database or spreadsheet program often includes data in the file that is unnecessary in WordPerfect, such as field titles. To rectify this situation, retrieve the converted file into WordPerfect and delete the first record, which contains the field names.

Running Convert

To run Convert, you must be in DOS and not in WordPerfect.

On a floppy-based system, insert the Learning Disk in drive A and the disk with the files you want to convert in drive B. Type **b**: and press ENTER to make drive B the default drive. Then type **a:convert** and press ENTER to run the conversion program.

On a hard disk system, the Convert program should be loaded into your WordPerfect directory. If you are running DOS Version 2.XX, make the WordPerfect directory your default directory. Then, type **convert** and press ENTER. If you are running DOS Version 3.XX, make your current directory the one that contains the files you want to convert. Then type the name of your WordPerfect directory followed by "convert" and press ENTER. For example, you would type **\wp\convert** and press ENTER if your WordPerfect directory were named \wp.

After you have entered the command to run Convert, the program will prompt you for an input file name and an output file name. These file names cannot be the same. If you are running DOS Version 2.XX on a hard disk, you will need to precede the file name with a directory path (for example, \wp\data\input.fil). The program will then prompt you for the input file's format type, as shown in Figure 8-2.

The type of input file you select will determine the type of output file that will be created. If you type 1 for an input type (WordPerfect's document format), you will be presented with a list of the other document formats from which to choose an output file type, as shown in Figure 8-3.

If you type a number between 2 and 6 as the input type (the other document formats), the program will automatically convert the output file to normal WordPerfect document format.

If you type 7 or 9 for an input type (MailMerge or Spreadsheet DIF), the program will automatically make the output file a secondary merge document. For choice 7 (MailMerge), the program will prompt you for the characters that are used to separate fields in the file, the characters that are used to separate records in the file, and any characters

```
Name of Input File? input.fil
Name of Output File? output.fil


1 WordPerfect to another format
2 Revisable-Form-Text (IBM DCA Format) to WordPerfect
3 Navy DIF Standard to WordPerfect
4 WordStar 3.3 to WordPerfect
5 MultiMate 3.22 to WordPerfect
6 Seven-bit transfer format to WordPerfect
7 Mail Merge to WordPerfect Secondary Merge
8 WordPerfect Secondary Merge to Spreadsheet DIF
9 Spreadsheet DIF to WordPerfect Secondary Merge

Enter number of Conversion desired _
```

Figure 8-2.   Convert program input choices

```
Name of Input File? input.fil
Name of Output File? output.fil


1 WordPerfect to another format
2 Revisable-Form-Text (IBM DCA Format) to WordPerfect
3 Navy DIF Standard to WordPerfect
4 WordStar 3.3 to WordPerfect
5 MultiMate 3.22 to WordPerfect
6 Seven-bit transfer format to WordPerfect
7 Mail Merge to WordPerfect Secondary Merge
8 WordPerfect Secondary Merge to Spreadsheet DIF
9 Spreadsheet DIF to WordPerfect Secondary Merge

Enter number of Conversion desired 1

1 Revisable-Form-Text (IBM DCA Format)
2 Final-Form-Text (IBM DCA Format)
3 Navy DIF Standard
4 WordStar 3.3
5 MultiMate 3.22
6 Seven-bit transfer format

Enter number of output file format desired _
```

Figure 8-3.   Convert program document output choices

that you would like to strip from the file. For any of these, you can simply type the character, or you can enter its ASCII code between curly brackets. For example, you would type {13}{10} for the record delimiter if each record ends with a Hard Return (carriage return + line feed).

If you type 8 for an input type (secondary merge), the program will generate a DIF file as the output.

Unfortunately, the fact that these selections are made automatically means that the Convert program cannot be used to translate between some formats (for example, from DIF to MailMerge). However, a macro might help you effect such transfers. See Chapter 10, "Macro Library," for a variety of macros that can help with converting files.

SIDEKICK

SideKick, from Borland International, is a popular RAM-resident program that provides instant access to several useful functions. (A RAM-resident program loads once when you turn on your computer and then remains "resident" in memory. The program can then be called up instantly while you are running another program.) One of the most important of SideKick's functions is its Notepad, which is essentially a limited word processing program.

SideKick is especially useful for taking notes while running other programs. You might be working on a spreadsheet or even typing a letter in WordPerfect when you suddenly want to type a note to yourself. In this way, SideKick can be a useful adjunct to WordPerfect. Typically, you would type text into SideKick on the spur of the moment and then transfer it into WordPerfect for editing, formatting, and embellishment.

Importing SideKick Files

SideKick produces standard ASCII files, so to retrieve a file into Word-Perfect that was created in SideKick, use the Text In function described in "Dealing With ASCII Files" earlier in this chapter.

If you will be using SideKick and WordPerfect together on a frequent basis, it helps to have a strategy in mind when you create your SideKick files. Text transfer will be easier if you limit what you type into SideKick. Enter just simple paragraphs that are separated with one space; leave any fancy formatting until you are editing the text in WordPerfect. This ensures that you will not have a lot of work fixing up the file after you import it into WordPerfect.

SideKick, like WordStar and many other programs, does not generate a [TAB] code when you press the TAB key. Instead, it inserts spaces to fill the area between the cursor position when you press the TAB key and the place the cursor ends up. Also, SideKick does not paginate its text, so it has no equivalent to a Hard Page Break. Because of this, SideKick files usually do not contain any control codes at all.

Exporting Files to SideKick

To save a WordPerfect document in a format that can be read by SideKick, simply use the "Saving a DOS Text File" function as described in "Dealing With ASCII Files" earlier in this chapter.

You may want to be able to view part of a WordPerfect document while running another program. Saving the document as an ASCII file and then retrieving it into SideKick allows you to view it from within any program.

NOTEBOOK

Notebook is a simple file management program that helps you work with WordPerfect's secondary merge files. It comes as part of a collection of programs called WordPerfect Library. Notebook retrieves and saves secondary merge files directly—there is no need to first translate them with the Convert program. Notebook allows you to view your data either in a row-and-column format (like a spreadsheet) or in a record format (like a traditional database program).

When you save a file from Notebook, it is saved as a normal Word-Perfect secondary merge document that can then be used in a merge operation. Notebook inserts a *header record* into the file with special information about your data. You can retrieve this file into WordPerfect and use the Line Draw function to make a fancy record entry/edit screen.

Notebook Header Record

When you load into WordPerfect a file saved by Notebook, you will see that the first record contains a variety of settings for the file, like field names, sizes, and placements within the record format, as well as the record format layout itself. This is the special header record that Notebook inserted. The first thing that appears in each field of this record is the Merge code ^N. You will recall from Chapter 3 that the ^N code indicates to the Merge function that it should move to the next record. In this way, the Merge function never tries to merge the data that is in this header document; it will advance to the second record whenever a field is requested from the first record. In essence, it is a record that WordPerfect will ignore when merging but that contains vital data for Notebook.

Header Record Fields

The header record is divided into fields, just as a normal record is. Each field contains a different type of information that Notebook needs to keep track of the data. (^R Merge code marks the end of each field, as in normal records.) Following is a list of the first four fields in the header record and the type of data each contains. Notebook will add more fields at the end of the header record if it needs to, so that the record has as many fields as the first record of data in the file.

Field 1:   *Field names and definitions*
The field names appear in boldface. You may only edit the names of the fields. Be careful not to delete the Bold codes, which Notebook uses to mark the beginning and end of each actual field name.

Field 2: *Notebook display definition*
This one-line field contains settings that Notebook uses to place the fields in the list display. Do not edit this field.

Field 3: *Record layout background text*
This field contains the record layout that Notebook will use when you enter and edit data. It is best to first edit this field with WordPerfect. Include any line drawing you want. You can also use boldface to emphasize text (for example, field names) in the layout. With these functions you can make your entry screen more understandable and easier to work with. After you have created the record format in WordPerfect, use Notebook's Record Display Setup function to place the fields in the correct locations.

Field 4: *Date format definition*
Although you can edit this field from WordPerfect, it doesn't make much sense to do so. Use the Date Format function in Notebook to change it if you need to.

Using WordPerfect Secondary Files With Notebook

To use your existing secondary merge documents with Notebook, follow these steps:

1. Retrieve the file into Notebook.

2. Use the Record display Setup function to enter field names: Press SHFT+F8, type **2** for "Record display," and type a name for the first field. Press CTRL+END to delete the default field name. Then press ENTER twice to end the field name. Type a name for each of the remaining fields, pressing CTRL+END and then ENTER twice after each one. When you are done, press the <Exit> key.

3. Save the file, and then retrieve it into WordPerfect.

4. Use the Line Draw function with WordPerfect's other editing commands to create a record layout in the third field of the header record. Be sure to make enough room above the ^R code before using the Line

```
^N
First 2,13,2,23,
Last 2,25,2,51,D
Address 4,13,4,45,
City, ST 6,13,6,32,
Zip 6,40,6,49,
No. 10,13,10,15,D
Comments 8,18,10,51,
^R
^N
1,12 0,1 2,12 0,1 3,26 0,1 4,26 0,1 5,12 0,1 6,12 0,1
^R
^N
```

Name:	
Address:	
City, ST:	Zip:
Comments:	
No:	

Doc 1 Pg 1 Ln 1   Pos 10

Figure 8-4.   Example of a record layout

Draw function. Figure 8-5 shows an example of a record layout that was created with the Line Draw function.

5. Save the file, and then retrieve it into Notebook.

6. Use the Record Setup function to size and position the fields to fit the record format you designed.

7. Save the file.

Now your secondary file is prepared for use with Notebook. You can use Notebook to enter and edit your data, and then use WordPerfect to merge the data into reports and form letters.

Using Notebook Secondary Files
With WordPerfect

If you want to use WordPerfect's Sort and Select functions to manipulate data in a Notebook secondary document, you need to take steps to ensure that you do not accidentally alter the header record. You can either define all of your data *except* for the header record as a block, or you can use the Cut function to temporarily remove the header record and then "paste" it into a safe place. The former method is faster if you will be performing the Sort/Select function once or twice, but the latter method makes more sense if you will be using the function several times.

To use the block definition method, follow these steps:

1. Retrieve the file into WordPerfect.

2. Define the second and subsequent records as a block: Move the cursor to the beginning of the second record (the first record of actual data), turn Block on by pressing the <Block> key (ALT+F4), and move the cursor to the bottom of the document.

3. Start the Sort/Select function by pressing the <Merge/Sort> key (CTRL+F9).

To use the Cut/Paste method, follow these steps:

1. Retrieve the file into WordPerfect.

2. Define the entire header record as a block: Move the cursor to the top of the document, press the <Block> key (ALT+F4), press the <Search> key (F2), press the <Merge E> key (SHFT+F9), press ENTER, and then press ESC.

3. Use the Cut function to remove the record from the document: Press the <Move> key (CTRL+F4) and type **1** for "Cut Block."

4. Press the <Switch> key (SHFT+F3) to switch to Document 2.

5. Retrieve the header record by pressing the <Move> key and typing **5** for "Retrieve Text."

6. Press the <Switch> key to switch back to Document 1.

7. Perform the desired Sort/Select function.

8. Move to the top of the document and "paste" the header record back: Press the <Move> key and type **5** for "Retrieve Text."

If you can no longer retrieve the header (because you used the Copy or Cut function again), you can get a copy of the header from the one you placed in Document 2.

By taking one of these precautions, you avoid repositioning or removing the header record during a sort or select procedure. Always make sure that the header record is not unintentionally disturbed when you are editing a Notebook secondary document with WordPerfect.

INCORPORATING REPORTS

Many spreadsheet and database management programs, such as Lotus 1-2-3 and dBASE III, have the ability to "print to disk." This means that these programs can save their files in an ASCII format that you can import directly into WordPerfect. Because of this feature, it is possible to use WordPerfect to format and print reports generated by these programs. The principles and techniques described in this section deal with Lotus 1-2-3 and dBASE III, but they can also be applied to many other programs.

First, let's define what is meant by "print to disk." Normally, when you print a Lotus or dBASE III file, the information goes directly to the printer. Sometimes it is what you see on the screen and at other times it has been formatted by the program's report mechanisms. With both programs (and with many others), it is also possible to send the output to a file on the disk, rather than to the printer. The images that would normally appear on paper are instead written to a standard ASCII file that can then be imported into WordPerfect for editing or included as part of a larger report.

There are a number of reasons you might want to do this. One is to overcome the limitations associated with the original program's print functions. You might, for instance, want to use WordPerfect's print enhancements, such as boldface and underlining, or some of WordPerfect's many format options.

Another, and perhaps more important, reason to import such files is so that they can be used as part of larger WordPerfect documents. Imagine that you are writing a 100-page report and need to include several spreadsheets as part of the report. You could, of course, retype the data in WordPerfect. Another alternative would be to print the spreadsheet using Lotus 1-2-3 and hand-insert it into the WordPerfect report after it is printed. This is not only inconvenient, it also throws off the page breaks and page numbering of the WordPerfect document.

A better alternative is to use the ability of 1-2-3 or dBASE to "print to disk" and import that file directly into the WordPerfect report. Then you can use WordPerfect to enhance the report and ensure that all of your page numbers, headers, and other formatting standards are used for your entire document—including data generated by the other program.

In the following sections you will see how to print to disk in both 1-2-3 and dBASE. It is assumed that you already know how to use the programs. Even if you do not use one of those programs, the spreadsheet and database management programs you do use probably have similar capacities to generate ASCII print files.

Lotus 1-2-3

To print a report to disk in 1-2-3, follow the same basic steps that you would use to print it on paper. By specifying that you want the output to go to a file instead of to the printer, you create a file that can be incorporated into a WordPerfect document.

Printing to a File

The command to print a 1-2-3 file is / P. The default sends the output to the printer, but if you select "File" (by moving the cursor to the right and pressing ENTER or by typing an F), any cells that you print will be output to a file instead of to the printer. The program asks you to enter your "print file name" and displays any other "print files" that already exist on the disk. Lotus 1-2-3, by default, adds the extension .PRN to the end of any file name you give. (With 1-2-3 Release 2, you can override that default by including your own extension on the file name or by adding a period to the end of the file name to indicate that there is no extension.)

On a hard disk system, 1-2-3 will save the print file in the 1-2-3 default data directory. To override this default in 1-2-3 Release 2, press ESC twice and replace the suggested data directory with any other directory, including one normally used to store WordPerfect files. With 1-2-3 Release 1A, you will need to issue the / File Directory command before issuing the / Print File command in order to change the default directory. If there is already a file with the name you choose, 1-2-3 will ask if you wish to replace that file.

Once this is done, 1-2-3's normal print menu is displayed. As you generally do when printing in 1-2-3, first select Range to indicate the range (or portion) of the worksheet you wish to print.

Specifying Unformatted Printing

When 1-2-3 prints to disk, it does so exactly as it prints to paper. It provides the same default margins, including margins on the top and bottom of the page. When 1-2-3 comes to what it thinks is a new page, it indicates a page break by inserting blank lines. When you tell it to "go," it creates an ASCII file with the same spacing as would normally appear when you use the printer. This formatting can create problems when you import the file into WordPerfect. Therefore, you want the 1-2-3 print file to be totally *unformatted* so that WordPerfect can provide the page breaks, margins, and other necessary formatting.

To create an unformatted print file, type **O** for "Options"; then type **O** again for "Other." This brings up another menu from which you type **U** for "Unformatted."

At this juncture you type **Q** for "Quit" to return to 1-2-3's main print menu and then type **G** for "Go" to print the file to disk. When this is done, you must type **Q** for "Quit," as this completes the printing and closes the file.

Checking the File Before
Leaving Lotus 1-2-3

There is a way to see what the file will look like prior to leaving 1-2-3. This is done with the program's File Import command.

First, you clear the worksheet by typing **/WEY**. Then you type **/FI** for "File Import" followed by **T** for "Text" and then the name of the print file you just created. You can also highlight the file name and simply press ENTER. (If you are using 1-2-3 Release 2 and you overrode either the .PRN extension or the directory for storing the file, you may have to designate the path, file name, or extension.)

Once you select the file name, the file will load into 1-2-3, and what you see on your screen is exactly what you will see when you later retrieve the file into WordPerfect.

dBASE III

To print to disk in dBASE III, use the Report command. After you have made a database active with the Use command, type the following line at the dot prompt to save a report as a file:

```
REPORT FORM reportname TO FILE filename
```

where "reportname" is the name of a report form you have previously defined and "filename" is the name of a file that will contain the printed report. Precede the file name with a path specification if you wish to store the file in a directory other than the current directory. If you do not specify an extension with the file name, dBASE adds .TXT to the end of the name you provide.

If, for example, you type **REPORT FORM cshflow TO FILE report**, dBASE will generate a file called REPORT.TXT in the default directory that contains the dBASE III report called CSHFLOW.

Importing Reports Into WordPerfect

Once you have created an ASCII print file, the next step is to exit 1-2-3 or dBASE III and enter WordPerfect so that you can retrieve the file.

First, move to the location within your WordPerfect file where you want the report to appear. If you are not sure where you want it to be placed, you can position the cursor anywhere and move the report later.

Next you need to reset the margins to leave enough room for the width of the report. Usually this means setting the margins to 0 and 80. If you have printed a report wider than 65 columns, and you don't reset the WordPerfect margins, the lines from the 1-2-3 or dBASE III print file will not fit within WordPerfect's default margins. This would result in text being wrapped around and not being very readable.

The next step is to press the <Text In/Out> key (CTRL+F5); then type **2** to retrieve the file as a DOS text file. Type the file name and press ENTER. (Remember that for 1-2-3 files, unless you designated a dot or another extension, the file will end in .PRN. For dBASE III, the file will end in .TXT. And, unless you designated a directory, the file will reside on the data directory that was active at the time the file was saved.)

After you enter the file name, the report will appear on your screen at the cursor location in the current document.

CONVERTING dBASE AND 1-2-3 DATA TO SECONDARY MERGE FILES

In the previous discussion, you saw how 1-2-3 and dBASE print files could be integrated into WordPerfect reports. It is also possible to use data from either of the programs to create a WordPerfect secondary merge file. This enables you to take advantage of the data entry, edit, and search abilities of dBASE or 1-2-3 while also using the merge capacity of WordPerfect. Just as with the print files, the principles here apply to other spreadsheet and database management programs.

Lotus 1-2-3, dBASE III, and many other programs can translate their files into one or more standard file structures that can be converted by WordPerfect's Convert utility into a WordPerfect secondary merge file. dBASE can create files that WordPerfect's Convert utility translates as MailMerge files. Lotus can translate worksheet files into DIF files that can in turn be converted into secondary merge files by WordPerfect's Convert program.

Converting either a dBASE or a 1-2-3 data file into a WordPerfect secondary merge file is a two-step process, the first step in dBASE or 1-2-3, and the second with WordPerfect's Convert program.

Lotus 1-2-3

To convert a 1-2-3 file, you must first make sure that the information you want to convert (usually a database) starts in the upper-left corner of the spreadsheet (cell A1). This reduces the amount of excess data that would otherwise be carried through the conversion process. You might want to save a separate copy of your worksheet for conversion purposes so that you can maintain the worksheet in its original layout for use within 1-2-3.

After you have prepared the worksheet, use Lotus's Translate program (available from the Lotus Access menu) to translate your spreadsheet into a DIF file. Then use WordPerfect's Convert program to convert the DIF file into a secondary merge file. (See "Using Convert" in this chapter for a description of the Convert program.) After conversion, you may need to retrieve the resulting file into WordPerfect and manually delete the first few records of the data, depending on the condition of your original worksheet.

dBASE III

To convert a dBASE III file, you use dBASE's Copy command to convert the dBASE file into a standard data file. This is done by typing the following line at the dBASE dot prompt:

```
COPY TO filename DELIMITED
```

where "filename" is the name of the file that will contain the data. You can precede the file name with a path specification if you wish to store the file in a directory other than the current directory. If you do not specify an extension with the file name, dBASE adds .TXT to the end of the name you provide.

You can now use the Convert program to translate the file into a WordPerfect secondary merge file. (See "Using Convert" for general instructions on running Convert.)

When you run Convert, specify "Mail Merge" as the input file type. The program will then prompt you for three things: the field delimiter, the record delimiter, and any characters that should be stripped (removed) from the resulting file. The dBASE III file is formatted with character fields surrounded by quotes, fields separated by commas, and a Hard Return (ASCII code 13 *and* code 10) after each record. Therefore, at the prompt for a "field delimiter," type a comma (,) and press ENTER. At the prompt for a "record delimiter," type {**13**}{**10**} and press ENTER. At the prompt for characters to be stripped, type a quotation mark (") and press ENTER. The file will be properly translated.

dBASE III's Copy command outputs date fields with the four digits of the year, followed immediately by the two digits of the month, and then by the two digits of the day. For example, the date May 2, 1963, would be output as 19630502. Since this would not be very meaningful in a WordPerfect merged document, you might want to convert this date to a more standard format. (See Chapter 10, "Macro Library," for a macro that can perform this function.)

USING WORDPERFECT WITH DESQVIEW

It is possible, with certain software, to run more than one program at a time on your PC. The process generally involves using a program that not only allows you to run multiple programs, but also allows those programs to run within a "window" on your PC's screen. The most popular of these programs include Windows from Microsoft Corporation, GEM from Digital Research, and DesqView from QuarterDeck Office Systems. This section discusses topics relating to the use of WordPerfect with DesqView.

It should be noted that, although more limited in its abilities, Word-Perfect Corporation's Shell (see Appendix D, "WordPerfect Library") provides a more stable environment that most of the programs mentioned previously, especially when used with other WordPerfect Corporation products.

Hardware Considerations

To take full advantage of DesqView, you should equip your PC with an expanded memory board. Such a board provides the PC with up to two megabytes of additional RAM, in addition to the 640K that may already be available. This additional RAM is essential if you want to run a number of programs at once. With 640K of RAM, you can run Word-Perfect simultaneously with Lotus 1-2-3, but there is virtually no room left over to run additional programs. With two megabytes of RAM, you have room enough to run several programs simultaneously.

If you install DesqView on a hard disk (it is not copy protected), it checks to see what application programs it can recognize on your system and automatically adds those to its menu of available programs. You can later add programs to or delete programs from the menu. WordPerfect 4.1 is among the popular programs handled by DesqView's automatic installation procedure.

With DesqView, more than one program at a time can process data. You can edit a WordPerfect file and, at the same time, use a communications program to transfer information from your computer to another computer via modem. Simultaneously, a program like dBASE III can be sorting a large database in the background.

This so-called multi-tasking comes at a cost, especially if your computer is equipped with an 8088 CPU (like the standard PC and XT) rather than a faster CPU like the 8086 or the 80286 that comes with the AT. Programs can be very sluggish when they are running consecutively with other programs. Even WordPerfect slows down a little when another program is running in the background. Likewise, if WordPerfect is running in the background, it will slow down another program running in the foreground.

Fortunately, there is a way to minimize this speed loss. You can use DesqView's Change Program option to keep specified programs inactive while they are operating in a background window. Those programs are still instantly available, but they do not process data until they are brought to the foreground.

By default, DesqView installs the WordPerfect program (and most other application programs) to run in both the foreground and background. However, there are very few situations in which it is useful to run a word processor in the background. One case is when you are printing a long document. WordPerfect has a built-in print spooler that allows it to print while you are editing. The spooler is inoperable, though, if WordPerfect is not running. Thus, if you wish to print WordPerfect files while running other programs under DesqView, you need to keep the default and allow WordPerfect to run in both the background and foreground.

Transfer Data

Earlier in this chapter you saw how you could transfer data from 1-2-3, dBASE, and other programs into a WordPerfect file. If you are using DesqView, there is an easier route to a similar end. That is because DesqView allows you to transfer what is on the screen in one program to another program running in a different window. You do this by marking the section of the screen as a block and transferring that block to another program.

DesqView Macros

DesqView also allows you to create keyboard macros that are similar to those used in WordPerfect. However, in DesqView you can define any CTRL key, function key, or virtually any other key as a macro. That, plus WordPerfect's built-in macro processing capabilities, lets you use many more keys for macros. With a few exceptions, DesqView's macro capabilities are similar to what is available with ProKey, a program for creating macros.

Multiple WordPerfects

DesqView also makes it possible to run two or more copies of the same program at the same time. As you know, WordPerfect can normally edit up to two documents at a time. Using DesqView, you can extend that limit by running WordPerfect in more than one window at a time. Each window that contains WordPerfect is then capable of handling up to two files. It is like having a window processor within a window processor.

The only problem with running WordPerfect in more than one window is that you must watch out for the overflow files that WordPerfect creates while it is editing. WordPerfect automatically deletes these files when you exit normally. If you open WordPerfect in a second window, the overflow files created by the copy in the first window are going to be present. When you open WordPerfect in a second window, the program asks, "Are other copies of WordPerfect currently running?" Type **y**, and the message "Directory in use. New WP Dictionary:" is displayed. Type any directory name other than the WordPerfect system directory, and press ENTER. By using a directory different from the one currently in use, you can run WordPerfect in as many windows as you have directories and memory to run it in. Each "copy" of WordPerfect that you are running requires a minimum of about 200K of memory.

9 USING PRINTERS

Printers are often a source of frustration to computer users. In fact, printers sometimes seem to have minds of their own. Text mysteriously does not print in bold (although it shows as bold on the screen), lines are not centered, and paper and mailing labels get jammed behind the platen.

The first step in reducing printer anxiety is to configure your software properly to work with your printer. This chapter leads you through that process and then helps you find ways to use your printer's various capabilities. The chapter first teaches you how to install your printer; then it shows you how to send control codes to your printer and how to change fonts and pitch settings for a particular print job. Finally, it describes how to use special characters, both on the screen and on the printer.

INSTALLING PRINTERS

As it is shipped, WordPerfect supports over 100 printers. This section discusses the process of selecting which of these printers you will be using on your system, which ports you will have them connected to, and what type of paper feed you will be using.

Printer Numbers

In WordPerfect, you can have up to six *printer numbers,* each of which defines a specific combination of a printer (using a printer definition from a list of printers), a *printer port,* and a *paper feed type.* Once defined, these printer numbers are used in the Print Options menus to specify where a print job should be directed and which printer control codes should be used to control your printer. This allows you tremendous flexibility in setting up the various printer combinations you will be using on your system.

For example, you might want to define the dot matrix printer attached to port 1 as Printer 1 and your letter-quality printer on port 2 as Printer 2. Simply changing the printer number on the Print Options menu lets WordPerfect know where to direct the print job.

You can also define two printer numbers for the same printer. For example, you might specify Printer 1 as your letter-quality printer when you want continuous form-feed paper and Printer 2 as the same printer when you want cut-sheet forms for letterhead. By changing the printer number, you could then control whether WordPerfect would stop for you to insert a new sheet of paper at the end of each page.

Printer Definitions

The printer definitions are found on two separate numbered lists: the *main printer list*, and the *currently active* printer list.

The *main printer list* shows all of the printers that the program supports. This list is stored in the files WPRINT1.ALL, WPFONT1.ALL, WPRINT2.ALL, and WPFONT2.ALL. These files are on the two Printer Disks.

The *currently active printer list* contains definitions for all of the printers that you will be working with and is stored in the WPRINTER.FIL and WPFONT.FIL files, which are found on the WordPerfect system disk or directory. When you select your printer from the main list, its definition is copied to the currently active list of printers.

The Printer Installation Process

To install printers in WordPerfect, you need to know three things:

- The name and model of each printer on your system.

- The interface ports your printer(s) will use, such as LPT1: for the first parallel port on your system or COM1: for the first serial port. Most printers are parallel, but if yours is serial, you will also need to know the printer's baud rate and other communication parameters.

- The types of paper feed your printer(s) will use (single sheet, tractor feed, or an automatic sheet feeder).

Starting the Installation Process

To select the printer(s) that you will be working with in WordPerfect, press the <Print> key (SHFT+F7), type **4** for "Printer Control," and then type **3** for "Select Printers." The currently active list of printers will appear, as shown in Figure 9-1.

Printer Definitions in C:\WP\WPRINTER.FIL

   1 Standard Printer   2 DOS Text Printer

PgDn for Additional Printer Definitions
Exit when Done
Printer 1   Cancel to Ignore Changes
Using Definition: **1**   Arrow Keys To Change Printer Number

---

Figure 9-1.   The currently active printer list

If you are selecting printers for the first time, you will see only two printers on the menu: "Standard Printer" and "DOS Text Printer." (If you do not see any printers listed, you have installed WordPerfect incorrectly. See Appendix A, "Installation," for instructions.)

Selecting a Printer Number

At the bottom of the screen is a message that indicates you are installing "Printer 1." Printer 1 is the printer that text will be sent to by default, unless you modify WordPerfect's Initial Settings. Therefore, you should install Printer 1 for the printer, printer port, and paper feed type that you will use most often. (To increment the printer number at the bottom of the screen, press the UP ARROW key; to decrement the number, press the DOWN ARROW key.)

Selecting a Printer Definition

To select a printer from the main list of printers for the current printer number (in this case, for Printer 1), press the PGDN key. If you are using a floppy disk system, insert Printer Disk 1 in drive B and type **B**. If you are using a hard disk system, insert Printer Disk 1 in drive A and type **A**.

The first screen of the main printer list will appear, similar to the one shown in Figure 9-2. (The printer definitions are updated by WordPerfect Corporation on a regular basis, so your screen may have definitions somewhat different from the ones shown.)

You can scroll down this list with the PGDN key to see additional printers and scroll back up with the PGUP key. The list is numbered sequentially and is in alphabetic order by printer name. Printers that WordPerfect Corporation has fully tested appear first on the list; printers that have not been fully tested appear last. Those printers that have not been fully tested are marked with an asterisk for "Limited Telephone Support." When you reach the last page of the list, pressing the PGDN key returns you to the beginning.

If you cannot locate your printer in the list, press the <Cancel> key (F1) to return to the Printer Control screen, remove Printer Disk 1, insert Printer Disk 2, and repeat the process.

When you have found the printer definition that most closely matches the printer you want to install, type its number from the list and press

```
Printer Definitions in A:WPRINT1.ALL
     1  AMT Office Printer (Diablo)      2  AMT Office Ptr (IBM Color)
     3  AST TurboLaser Dutch PS          4  AST TurboLaser Landscape
     5  AST TurboLaser Portrait          6  AST TurboLaser Swiss PS
     7  Alps P2000                       8  Apple Imagewriter/DMP
     9  Brother HR-1                    10  Brother HR-15/20/Dynax DX-15
    11  C.Itoh 8510 Prowriter           12  C.Itoh C310EP
    13  C.Itoh D10-40                   14  C.Itoh Starwriter/Printmaster
    15  Canon A1 Courier 10 N           16  Canon A1 Courier 10 N/R
    17  Canon A1 Courier 10 R           18  Canon A1 Elite 12 N
    19  Canon A1 Elite 12 N/R           20  Canon A1 Elite 12 R
    21  Canon A1 Garland PS N           22  Canon A1 Garland PS R
    23  Canon A1 Line Printer N/R       24  Canon A1 Pica 10 N
    25  Canon A1 Pica 10 N/R            26  Canon A1 Pica 10 R
    27  Centronics 351                  28  Cordata LP300X Bookman PS
    29  Cordata LP300X Courier          30  Cordata LP300X Karena PS
    31  Cordata LP300X Swiss PS         32  Cordata LP300X Taylor


                                   PgDn for Additional Printer Definitions
                                   Exit when Done
Printer 1                          Cancel to Ignore Changes
Using Definition: _                Arrow Keys to Change Printer Number
```

Figure 9-2.   The main printer list

ENTER. The program copies the printer definition from the main list to the currently active list.

Selecting a Printer Port

After you select a printer definition, the screen clears and you are prompted for a printer port specification. Enter the number that corresponds to the printer port on which you have attached the printer you wish to install. The most common selection is 0 for LPT1:, the primary parallel port.

If you enter a number that corresponds to a serial port (4 through 7), the program asks you for four additional settings: baud rate, parity, number of stop bits, and character length (number of data bits). If you do not know these settings, you should either consult your printer manual or contact your dealer.

Selecting a Paper Feed Type

After you have selected the correct port for the printer, you are prompted for the "Type of Forms." Type **1** for "Continuous" if you will be using tractor-fed paper (or just press ENTER since it is the default); type **2** for "Hand Fed" if you will be using single sheets of paper (like letterhead); or type **3** to choose "Sheet Feeder" if your printer is equipped with an automatic sheet feeder.

If you select "Sheet Feeder," the program asks you for four additional settings: the number of lines to generate between pages (sometimes necessary in order to eject the pages properly), the column position of the left edge of the paper (since many sheet feeders center pages on the platen rather than aligning them on the left), the number of bins your sheet feeder has, and, finally, the name and model of the sheet feeder. The sheet feeder manual usually does not state what these values should be, so you may need to find the right settings by trial and error.

Ending the Installation Process

After you have selected a printer definition number (from the main printer list), a printer port, and a method for paper feed, you are returned to the Printer Definition screen. The printer you just selected now appears at the bottom of the list.

At the bottom of the screen is a message indicating that you are now installing Printer 2. You can repeat the process to select up to six printer/port/feed combinations (using printer definitions from either the currently active list of printers or the main list).

When you are finished, press the <Exit> key (F7) to return to the Printer Control screen. From this screen, you can type **2** for "Display Printers and Fonts" to verify that you have installed your printers correctly.

Printing to Disk

To direct your output to a disk file instead of to a printer, choose **8** for "Device or File Pathname" as your port specification when you are defining your printer number. After you type **8**, the cursor will move to the right of the prompt. Enter the file name that you want to use for the output. Precede the file name with a path specification if you do not want the file to be stored in the default directory.

The file that will be created when you generate a print job using this printer number will contain all of the special control codes for the printer definition that you selected, even though you are only storing the output in a file at this point. You can later send this file to a printer by entering this line at the DOS prompt:

```
COPY filename device_name
```

where "filename" is the name you just specified and "device—name" is the name of the printer port that your printer is attached to (for example, LPT1: for a parallel port or COM1: for a serial port).

The ability to print to disk is useful if you are writing documents at one location and planning to print them at another location. Normally, you would have to take a WordPerfect system disk with you and hope that the hardware setup is compatible with your copy of the program. With the print-to-disk feature, you could format and output the document to disk and then simply take the disk containing the formatted file with you to the system that has the printer. Just make sure that you use the correct printer definition when you define the printer number for printing to disk.

FONTS, CONTROL CODES, AND PITCH

WordPerfect has several ways to affect the look of your printed document. Which ones you use will depend on the type of printer you have. Some printers use a combination of pitch settings and fonts, while others use only one or the other.

Traditionally, the term *pitch* refers to the width of the characters, and the term *font* refers to a particular style or look of the characters. In WordPerfect, these definitions hold when you work with a daisy wheel printer. With this type of printer, changing the pitch will result in altered character spacing, while changing to a different font will cause the program to pause for you to insert a different print wheel (for a different print style).

However, the traditional definitions of pitch and font do not exactly apply when you work with a dot matrix printer. This type of printer has more options than a daisy wheel printer for producing various styles and sizes of text. Changing the pitch often causes a dot matrix printer to alter the *size* of the characters, rather than the spacing. Generally, though, WordPerfect uses a font change to indicate a change in either character size or print style on a dot matrix printer.

Fonts

WordPerfect has up to eight fonts defined for each printer definition. When you change to a new font in a document, you tell WordPerfect that you want to start printing with a different print wheel, font cartridge, or print style. Each type of printer uses these fonts in a different way.

A *daisy wheel* printer uses different print wheels to print a variety of typefaces. With this type of printer, when the program encounters the code for a font change in your document, you will hear a beep and printing will stop. You must replace the print wheel in the printer with the one you want to use and then tell WordPerfect to continue with the new wheel.

A *dot matrix* printer generally uses different fonts to change the look of the text. Each printer has its own combination of built-in features, such as emphasized, italic, condensed, and elongated print. Many will also have a near-letter-quality mode that produces high quality output.

Some dot matrix printers use font cartridges to produce different typefaces. Often these printers can have several font cartridges installed at one time. In this case, font changes switch you among the available cartridges and let you use special characters that are available only in specific cartridges.

Character Tables

Besides indicating a specific print style or typeface, each font is also associated with a *character table*. Each print wheel, font cartridge, or internal dot matrix character set has a limited number of available characters. These characters may also vary in width. WordPerfect needs to know which characters are available for each font (and the ASCII codes for each character), as well as the width of each character. This information is stored in character tables.

Relationship Between Fonts
And Character Tables

After you have installed your printer as described in the section "The Printer Installation Process," you can see which character tables have been assigned to the eight available fonts by pressing the <Print> key (SHFT+F7), typing **4** for "Printer Control," and typing **2** for "Display Printers and Fonts." The first three printer numbers are displayed. Each printer number is followed by the name of the printer definition you have selected for it. If you have not selected a printer definition for a printer number, it will default to the "Standard Printer" definition. Next to the definition name, you will see the type of paper feed you selected. The default setting for this is "Continuous." Finally, there is a list of the character tables assigned to each of the eight fonts for the printer definition selected.

On a daisy wheel printer, the character tables listed refer to the different print wheels you can use with your printer. For most print wheels, you can use Font 1, unless your print wheel has a special character set (like the Greek alphabet) or uses proportional spacing (usually indicated with a PS somewhere in the wheel's name).

Proportional spacing means that each character is spaced according to its particular width. This gives a very clean, "typeset" look to the text. To use a proportional spacing print wheel, or one with a special character set, you will need to specify the correct font number on the Print Format screen (as described later in this chapter in the section "Selecting a Font"). That way, the appropriate character table will be used with the print wheel. You will also need to set the correct pitch (as described later in this chapter in the section "Setting Pitch").

On a dot matrix printer, unlike on a daisy wheel printer, you will not be able to tell from the "Display Printers and Fonts" screen what each font will do, since there will usually be only one or two character tables defined for the printer definition. (On a dot matrix printer, fonts can change the size, style, or enhancement of the text—the character table usually remains the same.) To see the effect each defined font will have, you need to print out some sample text using each one. You can do this by retrieving the file PRINTER.TST from the Learning Disk (or from the WordPerfect system directory on a hard disk system) and printing it.

When you do this, you will see at the bottom of the page a sample of the print style invoked by each defined font.

With dot matrix printers that use font cartridges, the font numbers listed are sometimes assigned a *combination* of a style change and a specific character table. With some printers, the font numbers are also associated with *specific sockets* in the printer. If, for example, a font is assigned a character table for a Modern PS font cartridge in the third socket on the printer, you must insert that cartridge only in that socket.

Since there are so many possible combinations of fonts, print wheels, font cartridges, and character tables, there is no way that they can all be documented here. Therefore, you will have to experiment with each of the fonts that work with your printer to learn about its available styles, print wheels, and special characters.

If you want to change the preset combinations of fonts and character tables, you will need to learn about the Printer program (see the section "Modifying Printer Definitions" later in this chapter).

When you are finished examining the defined font numbers for the first three printer numbers, press any key to display the next three printer numbers. Press another key to return to the Printer Control screen. Then press SPACE to return to the document.

Changing Fonts

To change to a different font within a document, first move the cursor to the point where you want the new font to take effect. Then press the <Print Format> key (CTRL+F8). You will see the Print Format screen, as shown in Figure 9-3.

The font number at the top of the screen shows the font currently in effect. (When you change to a different font, as with other formatting commands, the new font remains in effect until WordPerfect encounters another font change.) Type **1** for the pitch and font settings, and press ENTER to bypass the pitch setting (you can also enter a new pitch setting, if desired). Then type the font number you wish to use and press ENTER. Press ENTER again to clear the Print Format screen. A [Font Change:] code is inserted into the text at the cursor position.

When the program encounters the font change hidden code, it will send any control codes specified in the printer definition for your printer. With a daisy wheel printer, it will switch to a different character table and then beep and wait for you to change the print wheel. With a dot matrix

```
Print Format

    1 - Pitch                          10
        Font                           1

    2 - Lines per Inch                 6

  Right Justification                  Off
    3 - Turn off
    4 - Turn on

  Underline Style                      5
    5 - Non-continuous Single
    6 - Non-continuous Double
    7 - Continuous Single
    8 - Continuous Double

    9 - Sheet Feeder Bin Number        1

    A - Insert Printer Command

    B - Line Numbering                 Off

Selection: A
```

Figure 9-3.   The Print Format screen

printer, the program will send control codes to change the print style. With a dot matrix printer that uses font cartridges, the program will send control codes to change the print style, change to a different character table, change to a different font cartridge, or perform any combination of the three.

Sending Printer Codes

WordPerfect sends most control codes to the printer automatically, usually because of a formatting command that you inserted into your text. However, you can manually send control codes at any point in the document. This allows you to use printer functions that do not correspond to WordPerfect functions.

To send control codes manually, you must first find out the ASCII control codes that the printer uses to initiate the desired function. These codes are usually listed in the printer's manual. The codes can be shown in the manual in many ways, but a code that represents a letter, number, or punctuation mark is usually shown as the character itself, while a control code is usually indicated either by its ASCII control code number or by a description of the code.

For example, you may want to have your printer use ultra-condensed (very small) print, and there is no WordPerfect font set up to use this type style. Upon looking in your printer manual, you find that the printer command to initiate this print style is "ESCAPE Q". You might also see a notation that the control code ESCAPE is assigned to ASCII code 27. (Most printer code sequences start with the ESCAPE control code. This code basically signals the printer to "Look out, here comes a special function." The characters that follow the ESCAPE indicate which function to initiate.) Since Q is a printable character, it is unnecessary to use its ASCII code. Therefore, to use this function you will need to send the printer an ASCII code 27, followed by the letter Q. (Since uppercase letters have different ASCII codes from lowercase letters, it is very important that you type the *exact* letter indicated in the manual.)

Sending a Code

To send the code sequence to the printer from within a document, first move the cursor to the point where you want the new style to start. Then press the <Print Format> key (CTRL+F8) and type **A** for "Insert Printer Command." At the bottom of the screen is a prompt asking for a "Cmnd." At this point, you can enter any *printable* character simply by typing it. To enter a control code, you must enter its ASCII code surrounded by angle brackets (less-than and greater-than signs).

To enter the example for ultra-condensed print, type **<27>** (this sends the ASCII control code 27, which is ESCAPE), followed by **Q**. When you are finished entering the codes, press ENTER. Press ENTER again to clear the Print Format screen. You can use Reveal Codes to see that the function inserted a [Cmnd:] hidden code at the cursor position that contains the codes you entered. When the program encounters this hidden code while printing, the printer codes will be sent to the printer just as you entered them.

Sending Many Codes

Some printers require long strings of codes to invoke various features. Also, some dot matrix printers allow you to transfer a *custom character set* into the printer's memory. (This allows you to create your own special characters.) This process is called "downloading a font" and also requires long strings of control codes to be sent to the printer.

You can create a file on disk that contains these code sequences and have WordPerfect send them to the printer for you. You can create this file using a program written in BASIC or with a text editor. To have WordPerfect send the file, first move the cursor to the place in your document where you want the program to send the file. Then press the <Print Format> key (CTRL+F8), type **A** for "Printer Command," press the <Retrieve Text> key (SHFT+F10), type the file name (including any drive letter or path specification necessary), and press ENTER. Press ENTER to clear the Print Format screen. A hidden code is placed in the text at the cursor position.

You can use Reveal Codes to see the code. You will see that the [Cmnd:] code contains <126> followed by the name of the file you specified. When WordPerfect encounters this code during printing, the control codes in the specified file will be sent to the printer. The <126> code is WordPerfect's internal code for the Retrieve Text function. However, you cannot enter the <126> code directly at the "Printer Command" prompt.

Changing Pitch

The pitch of your text is defined as the number of characters that fall in a one-inch space across the page. For example, if there are 10 characters per inch across a printed page, the text is printed in 10 pitch. If the characters are either smaller or spaced more closely together so that there are 12 characters per inch across the page, the text is printed in 12 pitch. Therefore, the higher the pitch, the smaller (or more tightly spaced) the text will be printed.

For most dot matrix printers, WordPerfect uses the pitch setting on the Print Options screen to change the width of the characters. Only pitch settings of 10, 12, and 15 will have any effect. To get characters of other sizes, you must change to a different font number.

On daisy wheel printers, the pitch setting affects the amount of space between characters. Therefore, if you are using a print wheel with small characters, you may want to change the pitch setting to bring the characters closer together. Usually, the size of the print wheel will be stated on its box as well as on the wheel itself. Some print wheels can produce text that looks good in more than one pitch.

Most daisy wheel printers (and some dot matrix printers) adjust the character spacing using HMI (Horizontal Motion Index). This allows them to modify the character spacing in very small increments because the actual spacing is determined by a formula based on the requested pitch. Because of this, you can usually try a variety of settings for the pitch to see which looks best.

To set the pitch, first move the cursor to the place in your document where you want the new pitch setting to take effect. Then press the <Print Format> key (CTRL+F8); the Print Format screen will appear. The pitch setting at the top of the screen will display the current setting, according to the cursor position in the document. Type **1** to get to the font and pitch settings, type in a new pitch value, and press ENTER. You can also enter a font number at this point, if you like, or you can press ENTER again to use the current setting. Then press ENTER to clear the Print Format screen. A hidden code [Font Change:] will be inserted into the text at the cursor position. The new pitch font settings will remain active until the program encounters another such hidden code.

Since entering a new pitch setting changes the amount of printed text on each line, you should be sure to reset your margins each time the setting is changed. Because the left and right margins of a document are specified by a certain number of character spaces, when you change to a higher pitch setting (more characters per inch), the actual width of the left margin will be smaller. Also, since more text is printed per inch, the text will not stretch as far across the page as with the wider setting, so the right margin will appear larger. When you increase the pitch setting, then, you will probably also want to increase your left and right margin settings. When you decrease the pitch setting, you will probably want to decrease your left and right margin settings.

Proportional Spacing

To use proportional spacing, you must

- Have a printer capable of proportional spacing (most daisy wheel and laser printers are, as well as some dot matrix printers).

- Have a proportional spacing print wheel, font cartridge, or internal character set.

- Make sure that the print wheel or font cartridge you are using is listed as one of the fonts defined for your printer on the "Display Printers and Fonts" screen.

- On a daisy wheel printer, set the switches (if any) for a proportional spacing wheel and for a 10-pitch font.

- Specify in the document, when you insert the [Font Change:] code, the font number that corresponds to the appropriate print wheel or font cartridge.

- Specify in the document, when you insert the [Font Change:] code, a pitch setting that ends with an asterisk (*). (For example, a typical setting is 13*. This indicates that the pitch is approximately 13, although the actual number of characters per inch will vary. You may need to experiment with other pitch values.)

You must satisfy all of the above criteria before WordPerfect can line up tables, justify paragraphs, and otherwise align proportionally spaced text. You can use non-supported proportional spacing print wheels with WordPerfect, but you will have problems with functions like tabs, centering, and paragraph justification. Generally, the text will simply not line up properly.

USING SPECIAL CHARACTERS

As discussed in the section "Dealing With ASCII Files" in Chapter 8, "Integration With Other Products," the only characters that the computer industry can agree upon are the letters, numbers, and punctuation marks on your keyboard. Almost every computer and printer, though, has many other characters defined. These characters are usually a combination of symbols, foreign letters, and graphics characters.

Although both your screen and your printer may be able to produce some of these additional characters, you need to follow these steps before you can actually use them:

- Determine whether the desired printer character comes *predefined* (as described in the next section).

• Specify how the character will be generated on the screen.

• Instruct WordPerfect on how to produce the character on the printer, if necessary.

If you determine that the character you wish to use comes predefined for your printer, you can skip the last step entirely. In this case, to print the character you only need to find out which special screen character represents it and then specify how you will produce the screen character on the screen.

Two powerful tools are provided to help you use special characters:

• CONTROL or ALT key mapping (which allows you to use the CONTROL and ALT keys in conjunction with letters to display special characters on the screen).

• Printer character tables (which, among other things, allow you to specify any combination of characters and ASCII codes to print the characters shown on the screen).

Determining Predefined Special Characters

You can determine which special characters, if any, have been predefined for your printer definition and character table combination by performing a simple test: First make sure that the screen is clear. Then retrieve the file FONT.TST from the Learning Disk. (On a hard disk system, this file should be located in the WordPerfect system directory.) FONT.TST contains a map of all of the ASCII characters. After you have retrieved the file, print it by using the <Print> key. (You may first want to insert a [Font Change:] code to select the correct font.

When printed, each ASCII code is translated according to the defined character table into the appropriate printer character. When a character has not been predefined, it will usually translate to a blank space. The table contains both normal and special characters that have been assigned to screen characters. If you see the special character you want on this printout, note the ASCII code of the screen character that produced it by taking the number that appears at the left edge of the row and adding to it the number that appears at the top of the column. (The numbers at the top range from 0 to 19, although the numbers 11 through

19 do not show the first digit.) You should use this number as the value for the CONTROL or ALT key mapping that you will be performing in the next section.

If you cannot locate the character you want on the printout, it is *not* predefined, and you will need to modify the character table after defining the CONTROL or ALT key mapping. This procedure is described later in this chapter, in the section "Modifying a Character Table."

Producing Special Characters on the Screen

To produce a special character on the screen, you assign the character to a CONTROL or ALT key combination. When you do this, your cursor can be located anywhere in any document, since the function does not generate a hidden code. Rather, the changes you make are stored in a file on disk when you exit WordPerfect. (The file's name is {WP}SYS.FIL, and it is the same file in which your printer selection *number* choices, not the actual definitions, are stored.)

To map a special character to a CONTROL or ALT key, press the <Screen> key (CTRL+F3), and type **3** for "Ctrl/Alt keys." The Key Mapping screen will appear, as shown in Figure 9-4.

At the top of the screen, there are four columns of ALT and CONTROL keys, each key with an associated value. The value of each is 0, since no characters have yet been mapped. At the bottom of the screen are five rows of special characters. The positions between 32 and 126 are blank since these are the standard letters and numbers of the character set. The rest are specific to the IBM Extended Character Set. You can see that there is quite a selection of characters for you to choose from.

The section symbol is a popular special character; it is frequently used in legal documents. (A section symbol looks like two interlocked S's, on top of each other.) Let's go through the process of first defining a CONTROL key combination for the section symbol and then, in the next section, instructing WordPerfect how to print the character.

First, press the key combination you wish to define. In this case, let's use CTRL+S (the S will remind you of "section").

Note: Any ALT keys that you use for producing special characters will be *unavailable* for macro names. Because of this, you should try to use the CONTROL key definitions first.

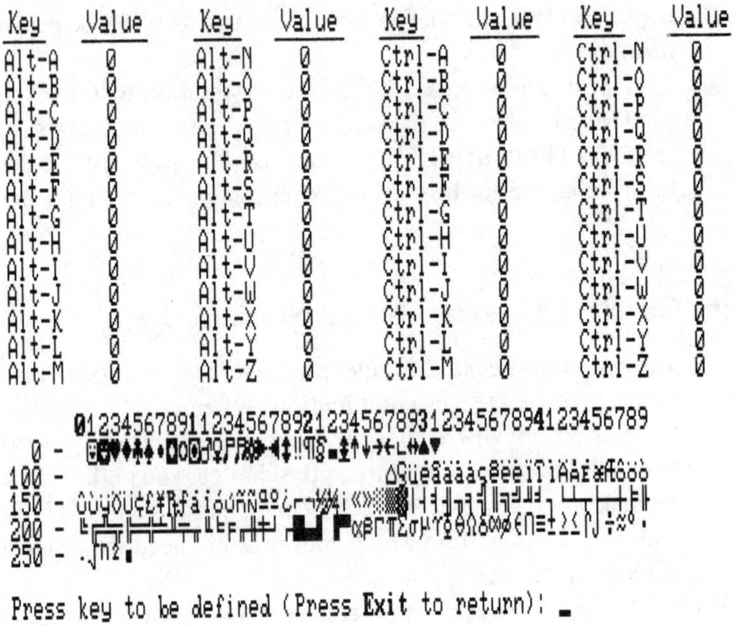

```
Key    Value    Key    Value    Key    Value    Key    Value
Alt-A    0      Alt-N    0      Ctrl-A   0      Ctrl-N   0
Alt-B    0      Alt-O    0      Ctrl-B   0      Ctrl-O   0
Alt-C    0      Alt-P    0      Ctrl-C   0      Ctrl-P   0
Alt-D    0      Alt-Q    0      Ctrl-D   0      Ctrl-Q   0
Alt-E    0      Alt-R    0      Ctrl-E   0      Ctrl-R   0
Alt-F    0      Alt-S    0      Ctrl-F   0      Ctrl-S   0
Alt-G    0      Alt-T    0      Ctrl-G   0      Ctrl-T   0
Alt-H    0      Alt-U    0      Ctrl-H   0      Ctrl-U   0
Alt-I    0      Alt-V    0      Ctrl-I   0      Ctrl-V   0
Alt-J    0      Alt-W    0      Ctrl-J   0      Ctrl-W   0
Alt-K    0      Alt-X    0      Ctrl-K   0      Ctrl-X   0
Alt-L    0      Alt-Y    0      Ctrl-L   0      Ctrl-Y   0
Alt-M    0      Alt-Z    0      Ctrl-M   0      Ctrl-Z   0
```

Press key to be defined (Press **Exit** to return): ▮

Figure 9-4.   The Key Mapping screen

After you press CTRL+S, the cursor will move next to the key name. At this point, you need to type the ASCII code value of the character you wish to assign to the specified key combination. If the printer character you want is predefined, enter the number from the printed FONT.TST file. Otherwise, locate the character you wish to use in the table at the bottom of the screen, and then determine its ASCII code by adding the number at the left edge of the row to the number at the top of the column (bold numbers indicate increments of 10). Enter this ASCII code and press ENTER.

For the example, you can see that the section sign has the ASCII code of 21. Therefore, type **21** and press ENTER. The section sign appears to the right of the "Ctrl-S" prompt. Press the <Exit> key to leave the Key Mapping screen.

From now on, whenever you want a section sign in a document, press the CTRL+S key combination where you want the sign to appear. You can use it in any document, in the same way as you would any other character. (Note that, if your printer can print a special character that is not available on the screen, you can use some other character on the screen to represent the desired printer character.)

Producing Special Characters on the Printer

After you have defined a key combination that will produce your special character on the screen, you need to determine how to produce this character on your printer and to instruct WordPerfect accordingly.

There are basically two ways that a special character can be produced on the printer: either the printer has the character in its character set, in which case you will need to determine its ASCII code, or you can create the character by using a combination of other characters.

Determining a Character's ASCII Code

Most dot matrix printers list in their manuals all of the characters they can produce, together with ASCII codes for each character. In this case, find the character you want to print on this list and note its ASCII code.

On daisy wheel printers, each print wheel has a different set of characters that it can print. Therefore, unless the print wheel came with an ASCII code listing, you will need to determine the desired character's ASCII code yourself.

First, look at the actual characters on the print wheel. If you can't find the character you want, you know you will have to do without it, buy a print wheel that has it, or else create it using other characters. If you do find the character, you need to determine its ASCII code.

To do this, you might try working with the FONT.TST file. When you printed it using WordPerfect's Print command (as previously described in "Determining Predefined Special Characters"), the program translated each code according to the current character table. But if the character you desire did not come predefined, it printed as a space on the printout. However, you can use this file in a different way.

By using the computer's Print Screen function (which prints the contents of the screen to the printer at any time), you can print the same document *without* translation. In that case, each character you see in the printout will correspond to the screen character with the *same ASCII code.* If you find the right character in the printout, you can use the numbers along the side of the table to determine the ASCII code of the printer character. Then you can use this number when modifying the printer's character table, as described in the next section.

To print the FONT.TST file with the Print Screen function, first make sure the screen is clear, and then retrieve the FONT.TST file from the Learning Disk. Press the <Replace> key (ALT+F2), type **N** for "No Confirm," press ENTER twice, press ESC, press ENTER once, and press ESC. Then move the cursor back to the top of the document. You will have taken out the double spacing in the document so that all of the characters are together on one screen.Now press SHFT+PRTSC (which invokes the Print Screen function).

One problem with this method is that some of the first 32 ASCII codes in the table may cause the printer to do strange things when you print the screen (like spit out paper).To avoid this, try deleting the first two rows of characters, and then press SHFT+PRTSC again.

Also, the printer may be able to print the character only after switching to an *alternate character set.* This lets the print wheel use more special characters than would normally be allowed in the limited space of the ASCII character set. Generally, there is a control code that you can send to the printer to cause it to start using the alternate character set. To send the code to the printer directly, press the <Print> key (SHFT+F7), type **5** for "Type-thru," type **1** for "by line," press the <Print Format> key, and enter the control code just as with the Insert Printer Command function described in the section "Sending Printer Codes" earlier in this chapter. Then press ENTER twice to send the command immediately to the printer. Press the <Exit> key to continue working with the FONT.TST file.

Before you go on, you should have done one of the following:

- Found the correct ASCII code for the desired character in the printer's manual.

- Determined the correct ASCII code using the procedure just described.

- Determined that the character will need to be created by combining other characters.

Modifying a Character Table

First, you must determine which character table you need to modify in order to print the desired character. Refer to the subsection "Character Tables" in the previous section to find out which table you will be using. (You should already have selected your printer before continuing with this process. See "Installing Printers" earlier in this chapter.)

For the purposes of the section symbol example, let's assume that you are working with XYZ dot matrix printer definition, with the XYZ character table. The section symbol has the ASCII code of 156 on this printer.

To modify the character table, you need to run the PRINTER program. To do this, you must exit WordPerfect so that you are at the DOS prompt, which is usually A>, B>, or C>.

On a floppy disk system, place the Learning Disk in drive B. Make sure that the A drive is the default drive by typing **A:** and pressing ENTER. Then, with the WordPerfect system disk still in drive A, type **B:PRINTER** and press ENTER.

On a hard disk system, the PRINTER program should already be loaded onto your hard disk. Make the WordPerfect system directory (usually \wp or \word) your default directory, and then type **PRINTER** and press ENTER.

After you have entered the PRINTER program, follow these steps:

1. Type **4** for "Character Tables (Examine, Change)."

2. Type the number representing the character table that you want to modify, and press ENTER.

The character table is displayed on the screen. Note that there are four columns of characters across the screen. In each column are four items: the screen character, the screen character's ASCII code, the code that is sent to the printer (an asterisk [*] indicates that more than one code is sent), and some adjustment numbers. The numbers go across all four columns and then to the next row. As the cursor is moved to the different characters (with the arrow keys as well as many WordPerfect cursor positioning keys like <Screen Up> or <Screen Down>), information for each is shown at the bottom of the screen.

3. Position the bar cursor at the screen character you defined earlier. For the example, position the cursor at the screen character for ASCII code 21 (second column, sixth row).

4. To change the setting for the string to be sent to the printer, type **A**. The cursor will move to the bottom of the screen. Delete the existing string and type the string that should be sent to the printer whenever WordPerfect encounters this screen character.

Enter the string in the same way as described in the section "Sending Printer Codes" earlier in this chapter. In the PRINTER program, however, you can simply press the ESC key to generate the <27> code and the SPACE key to generate code <32>, the ASCII code for a space.

You can enter a string that will create a new character out of two existing characters. Most printers will perform a backspace when they encounter an <8> (for ASCII code 8). This lets you *overprint* two characters to create the new character. For example, you can create a French "c cedilla" by entering a "c", then an <8> to perform the backspace, and then a comma (,).

Also, some printers must be prepared before they can print a desired character. For example, to enter the code for a character that requires the *alternate character set* on a daisy wheel printer, first enter the <A> code and then a single character (or ASCII code). WordPerfect will automatically send the control codes to switch to the alternate character set, print the specified character, and then switch back to the normal character set.

Similarly, some dot matrix printers need to switch to a foreign character set to print certain foreign characters. You can find out from the printer manual which codes you need to send to do this. Enter the codes to switch to the foreign character set, then the codes (or letter) needed to print the desired character, and then the codes to switch back to the normal character set.

For the XYZ printer, you would press the <Delete-End-of-Line> key (CTRL+END) to delete the old code, type <156> to insert the correct string for the section symbol, and then press ENTER.

5. Type **E** to exit the Character Table editing screen.

6. Press ENTER twice to exit the PRINTER program.

The changes you made are stored in the WPFONT.FIL file, which stores all of the information for the fonts and character tables.

You can now use the screen character anywhere in your document using the CONTROL or ALT key you defined earlier. It will print out on your printer when you print your file as long as you have specified the correct font number for the modified character table in your document.

MODIFYING PRINTER DEFINITIONS

A WordPerfect printer definition is simply a list of codes that the program uses to make the printer perform special functions like underlining, boldfacing, and superscript. With the PRINTER program (found on the Learning Disk), you can enter and change these codes to create or modify printer definitions, using a series of menus. For an understanding of the process of creating and modifying WordPerfect's printer definitions, read the manual "Defining a Printer Driver," which comes with WordPerfect.

Chapter

10 MACRO LIBRARY

This chapter contains a collection of useful macro applications that range from simple one-command macros to detailed procedures that require several macros working together.

Implementing many of WordPerfect's features requires the use of either long sequences of keystrokes or key combinations that can sometimes be difficult to find. You can use macros like the ones in this chapter to facilitate the use of often-used functions, as well as for less frequently used advanced features.

You can also use WordPerfect's macros to create *routines* that perform specific tasks. For example, you can create macros that generate letters, translate files, or scroll two documents simultaneously.

Note: Before using the macros in this chapter, you should work through Chapter 2, "Macros," unless you have had substantial previous experience using WordPerfect's macros.

The steps of each macro are fully explained so that you will understand the logic well enough to duplicate the procedure in your own macros. The keystrokes are indicated in the macro listings with the same conventions that have been used throughout this book, except that WordPerfect keys (like <Bold> and <Print>) are not followed by the actual corresponding keystrokes (like F6 and SHFT+F7). To find the correct keystrokes, you should refer either to the keyboard template or to the Quick Reference Card included with this book.

The names given to most of the macros in this chapter are merely suggestions. Since you are likely to have a unique collection of macros that you use on a regular basis, you may want to use your own macro names to avoid conflicts with other macro names. In general, you should use ALT Key macros for features that you use frequently and named macros for features that you only use occasionally.

You might also want to create macros with names like DRAW, DATE, and SPELL, which invoke functions suggested by their names. Even though you may not save on keystrokes with this method, you might find it helpful since you won't have to remember or look up the individual keystrokes.

IMPLEMENTING WORDPERFECT FEATURES

Below are some examples of ways that you can use macros to make common WordPerfect tasks simpler. You should be able to construct your own time-saving procedures using the examples given here as a guide.

Quick Move—Delete and Undelete

The normal way to move a block of text is to mark the block and use the <Move> key. This requires quite a few keystrokes. Another way to accomplish the same thing is to delete the text and then, with the <Cancel> key, undelete it. That, too, requires several keystrokes, but you can automate the process with a macro.

Macro Details

Let's name the Delete macro ALT+D and the Undelete macro ALT+U. First, mark the block of text you want to move. Then execute the ALT+D macro, which deletes the text. Move to the position where you want the text to be placed and execute the ALT+U macro, which undeletes the text.

ALTD.MAC—Delete marked block
  Delete block and confirm
  DEL **y**

ALTU.MAC—Undelete previously deleted text
  Undelete and choose most recent deletion
  <Cancel> **1**

Strange as it seems, this is also an easy way to copy text. You can delete the text, immediately undelete, move to where you want to copy it, and undelete again.

Mark a Line

You may want to mark an entire line as a block—for example, to underline a title or mark text for a table of contents. A simple macro can make the process quick and easy. Naming the macro ALT+L will remind you that it marks a line.

ALTL.MAC—Mark an entire line as a block
1. *Move to left edge of line (before all codes)*
   HOME, HOME, HOME, LEFT ARROW
2. *Turn Block on*
   <Block>
3. *Move to right edge of line*
   HOME, HOME, RIGHT ARROW

Save and Resume

It is important that you save your document frequently to minimize the risk of losing text. You can use an ALT Key macro (for example, ALT+S) to simplify the saving process.

ALTS.MAC—Save document and resume
Save, confirming overwrite of old file
<Save> ENTER **y**

Printer Commands

You can automate many common printer commands with macros. For example, you can have the ALT+P macro start a print job:

ALTP.MAC—Start a print job
Full print
<Print> **1**

Then you can have another macro, ALT+G, send a "Go" to restart the printer after a printer pause.

ALTG.MAC — Send the printer a "Go" for next sheet or print wheel
  Send printer a "Go"
  <Print> **4 g** <Cancel>

If you have a printer that uses single sheets of paper, you need to perform two steps to start printing a document: generate a print job, *and* send the first "Go" (assuming that you have already loaded the first sheet of paper). In this case, you might want your ALT+P macro to perform both of these steps. You would then use the ALT+G macro to continue the print job for each page.

Note: WordPerfect requires a pause of about a half a second after you generate a print job and before you issue the "Go" command. This is because the macro executes so quickly that it would otherwise issue the "Go" before the program had registered that the print job was ready. Therefore, you would have to manually issue the "Go" to start the print job after the macro executes. (See the section "Timed Pause" in Chapter 2, "Macros," for a description of this process.)

Everyone who uses a word processor has had the experience of wanting to abort a printout in midstream. WordPerfect has a set of commands for stopping the printer, but the time you need them most is when you are least likely to remember the sequence. You can use a Stop macro to stop the printer and cancel a print job entirely:

STOP.MAC — Stop the printer and cancel current print job
  1. *Stop the printer*
     <Print> **4 s**
  2. *Cancel the current print job*
     c ENTER
  3. *Restart printer and return to document*
     g <Cancel>

Purge Hidden Codes

Sometimes WordPerfect's hidden codes can pose a problem when you are trying to reformat a document. For example, you cannot change the margins for the entire document if you have scattered [Margin Set:] codes throughout the document. Reformatting problems can also occur with Line Spacing codes and Printer Font and Pitch codes.

One solution is to maintain a series of macros that will purge a document of specified hidden codes. That is, they will delete *all* of the specified codes found in the current document. You can then reformat the entire document with just one hidden code.

For example, let's say that you have a document in which you have inserted several different margin settings. You decide to reformat the entire document with margins of 15 left and 65 right. You can make a macro like this one to purge the document of [Margin Set:] codes:

DELMARG.MAC — Delete all [Margin Set:] codes from document

1. *Go to top of document*
   HOME, HOME, UP ARROW
2. *Replace all [Margin Set] codes with nothing*
   <Replace> **n** <Line Format> **3** ESC, ESC
3. *Go to top of document*
   HOME, HOME, UP ARROW

Now you can reformat all of the text by inserting a new [Margin Set:] code at the top of the document.

Generating a Table of Contents

There are several keystrokes involved in the generation of a table of contents but here again, you can automate the process with a macro.

Macro Details

The macro removes any [U] hidden underlining and [B] hidden bold codes from the titles in the table of contents, since titles are commonly underlined or boldfaced in the text but not in the table of contents. This step can be omitted if you want these enhancements in the table of contents or if they are not used in the document. You can use the same process to strip any other unwanted codes from the table of contents.

Step 1 of the macro generates the table of contents. Steps 2, 3, and 4 delete all underline codes from the table of contents. Steps 5, 6, and 7 delete all bold codes from the table of contents. Step 8 positions the cursor at the top of the document.

Here is the macro listing:

TOC.MAC — Table of contents generation
1. *Generate TOC*
   \<Mark Text\> **6 8 Y**
2. *Move to beginning of TOC*
   \<Reverse Search\> \<Mark Text\> **7** ESC
3. *Mark TOC as block*
   \<Block\> \<Search\> \<Mark Text\> **8** ESC
4. *Delete underlines*
   \<Replace\> **n** \<Underline\> ESC, ESC
5. *Move to beginning of TOC*
   \<Reverse Search\> \<Mark Text\> **7** ESC
6. *Mark TOC as block*
   \<Block\> \<Search\> \<Mark Text\> **8** ESC
7. *Delete bold*
   \<Replace\> **n** \<Bold\> ESC, ESC
8. *Return to top of document*
   HOME, HOME, UP ARROW

WINDOWS

WordPerfect's windowing function allows you to view two separate documents on the screen simultaneously. (See "Windows" in Chapter 1, "Basics Refresher," for a description of the Window function.) Although you can create many different combinations of window sizes, you will probably only use a few different configurations. Macros can set up your most common window layouts with a single keystroke. You can also use macros to help scroll text in the windows.

Single Document Split-Screen

Basically, there are two distinct uses for windows in word processing programs:

- To view two separate documents simultaneously

- To view two sections of the same document simultaneously.

Since WordPerfect's windows are essentially an extension of the dual-document editing feature, they do not provide the latter ability. While you *can* have the same document loaded into two windows, you *cannot* have the program automatically incorporate changes made to one into the other. Each window's document is treated as a completely separate, unrelated file.

However, you can perform an equivalent function by using the macro described next. This macro copies the entire contents of Document 1 into Document 2 and then returns to Document 1. Document 1 is then used as the "work document" and Document 2 as the "view document." Changes are made only to the work document and never to the view document. Whenever a sufficient number of changes have been made, you can use the same macro to update the view document.

Macro Details

To use this procedure, follow this sequence:

1. Split the screen manually (or with one of the window setup macros in this chapter).

2. Use the macro listed below to copy Document 1 to Document 2.

3. Switch back and forth as necessary to scroll both windows (or use one of the window scrolling macros in this chapter).

4. Type or make changes only in Document 1.

5. When a significant number of changes have been made in Document 1, use the macro listed here to update Document 2:

DUP.MAC — Duplicate document in second window
  1. *Go to top of document*
     HOME, HOME, UP ARROW
  2. *Mark entire document as a block*
     <Block> HOME, HOME, DOWN ARROW
  3. *Copy text*
     <Move> **2**
  4. *Switch to Document 2, clear screen, retrieve text*
     <Switch> <Exit> **n n** <Move> **5**
  5. *Return to Document 1 and go to top of document*
     <Switch> HOME, HOME, UP ARROW

Dual-Document Scrolling

Do you ever need to compare two documents that are practically identical? Perhaps one is a little bigger than the other or has a more recent date. It can often be difficult to remember which one to delete and which to retain.

You can use some simple macros to simultaneously scroll both documents, which allows them to be compared more easily.

Macro Details

The macros listed next make the assumption that you have loaded one document into Document 1 and another into Document 2 and that you have split the screen evenly. (Eleven lines per window is exactly even.)

To name these macros, you can use whichever ALT keys are available that make sense to you. One suggestion is to borrow the "diamond pattern" on the left side of the keyboard that WordStar uses for scrolling. For example, since WordStar uses CTRL+R to scroll up and CTRL+C to scroll down, you can use ALT+R and ALT+C as names for the WordPerfect macros that scroll the two documents up and down. These macros are shown here:

Scroll both windows down
<Screen Down> <Switch> <Screen Down> <Switch>
Scroll both windows up
<Screen Up> <Switch> <Screen Up> <Switch>

Miscellaneous Window Controls

You can create several other macros that are useful for window control. Here are two macros that enable you to alter the current window size:

Make current window half-size
<Screen> **1 11** ENTER
Make current window full-size
<Screen> **1 24** ENTER

Macro Details

You might also want to define a macro named ALT+S to switch windows. Although this function normally takes only one key (SHFT+F3), ALT+S is easier to remember.

Another set of window scrolling macros allows you to scroll Document 2 up and down while keeping the cursor in Document 1. This can be useful if, for example, you are writing a document in Document 1 but need to refer to another document in Document 2. While keeping your place visually on the screen, you can scroll through your second document to find the desired text. Here are the macros:

Scroll other window up
<Switch> <Screen Up> <Switch>
Scroll other window down
<Switch> <Screen Down> <Switch>

FILE CONVERSIONS

WordPerfect's Convert program can perform many types of file translations. (See "Using Convert" in Chapter 8, "Integration With Other Products," for a description of the Convert program.) Macros, however, provide an easy way for you to customize your own translation routines.

Following are several macros that will convert a document (or merge file) into a different format. If you follow the steps in each macro, you should be able to understand the logic well enough to create routines that will fit your own needs.

Tab Regeneration

A file with [TAB] codes is much easier to reformat in WordPerfect than a file in which indentation has been achieved with spaces. You can easily reposition columns that have been formatted with tabs by setting new tab stops. Also, you can copy and move columns separated by tabs with the Cut/Copy Column function. However, ASCII files (and files that have been imported from some word processing programs) sometimes contain spaces where [TAB] codes would be more appropriate. You can use the macros listed next to replace spaces with [TAB] codes.

A common use for this routine would be to aid in the conversion of WordStar files, since WordStar has no code designating a Tab function. (When the Tab or Center Line command is used in WordStar, spaces are simply inserted to indent the text. Therefore, the Convert program has no way to recognize these spaces as a Tab or Center Line command.)

The macros work best if you know (or can deduce) the tab stop interval that was used when the file was created. WordStar's default ruler has tab stops set five spaces apart.

Macro Details

This routine consists of two separate macros. The first macro replaces all occurrences of the specified number of spaces with a [TAB] code. The second macro then strips excess spaces after the [TAB] codes to make the file easier to edit.

After the first macro issues the Replace command, it pauses at the "Search" prompt for you to enter the proper number of spaces to search for. For example, if the document was prepared with tab stops at five-space intervals, press SPACE five times when the macro pauses, and then press ENTER. Every occurrence of five consecutive spaces in the document will be replaced with a single [TAB] code.

These macros are not completely reliable. For example, there may be times when there are not enough spaces between the position where the TAB key was pressed in the original document and the position of the next tab stop for the spaces to be found by the replace routine. However, the routine should be able to do most of the work, leaving you to perform a minor tune-up rather than a major overhaul.

The macros for this routine follow. (The sequence CTRL+PGUP, ENTER, ENTER in the first macro is the <Pause> command, which is described in the section "The Pause That Refreshes" in Chapter 2, "Macros.")

SPC2TAB.MAC — Spaces to tabs, part 1
1. *Go to top of document*
   HOME, HOME, UP ARROW
2. *Pause for number of spaces, replace with [TAB]'s*
   <Replace> **n** CTRL+PGUP, ENTER, ENTER, ESC
   TAB, ESC

3. *Go to top of document to prepare for next routine*
   HOME, HOME, UP ARROW

4. *Branch to second macro*
   <Macro> **spc2tab2** ENTER

SPC2TAB2.MAC — Spaces to tabs, part 2

1. *Search for [TAB] with trailing space*
   <Search> TAB, SPACE, ESC

2. *Delete space*
   BACKSPACE

3. *Go to beginning of line*
   HOME, HOME, LEFT ARROW

4. *Repeat macro until search fails*
   <Macro> **spc2tab2** ENTER

Secondary Merge to Mailmerge

WordPerfect's Convert program can convert files from a mailmerge format (commas between fields and a Hard Return after each record) into a secondary merge format. However, it cannot convert files in the other direction — from a secondary merge format to a mailmerge format. You can use a macro to perform this translation.

With the secondary merge document, each field ends with an ^R [HRt] sequence, and each record ends with an ^E[HRt] sequence. With the mailmerge format, each field ends with a comma (except for the last field) and is usually enclosed in quotes. Each record ends with a Hard Return.

Here is a sample secondary merge record:

```
John D. Franken^R
766 Maple St.^R
San Francisco^R
CA^R
95463^R
^E
```

Here is the same record in mailmerge format:

```
"John D. Franken","766 Maple St.","San Francisco","CA","95463"
```

Double quotes are necessary for *text* fields because some will contain a comma, which would incorrectly signal the end of the field. By enclosing fields in double quotes, you ensure that each is considered as a single field, regardless of internal commas.

However, you do not want to place double quotes around a *numeric* field. (A numeric field is one that contains numbers that you might use for calculation. A salary, for example, is a numeric field whereas a ZIP code is not.) The first macro that follows will place double quotes around every field in the secondary merge file; if the file contains any numeric fields, you will need to remove them with a macro like the second one.

Depending on the program into which you will be importing the mailmerge file, *date* fields may require special formatting and may also need the double quotes removed.

Macro Details

First, clear the screen and retrieve a secondary merge file. (While defining the macro, you will be translating this file.) The macro uses the Replace command to replace the merge codes with the comma-double quote delimiters.

Steps 1, 4, and 7 of the macro (see the listing that follows) move the cursor to the top of the document in preparation for the Replace command.

Step 2 formats the file with the widest possible margins. This is because WordPerfect's Text In/Out function automatically inserts a Hard Return at the end of each line when it is saved, and the length of each line is determined by the current margin settings. Since a Hard Return marks the end of a record in the mailmerge format, this would cause problems. Therefore, you cannot use this procedure with lines longer than 250 characters, since this is the widest margin you can set in WordPerfect.

Step 3 replaces all of the ^R [HRt] field merge codes with a double quote (to end the previous field), a comma (to separate the fields), and another double quote (to begin the next field).

Step 5 takes off the comma and double quote that step 3 erroneously placed at the end of each line (record), as well as the ^E and [HRt] that were originally at the end of each record. These codes are all replaced with an [HRt] code and a double quote to start the first field of the next record.

The last problem with the file is addressed in steps 6 and 8. Since there is no first field after the last record, step 6 deletes the extra double quote generated by step 5, and since there is no [HRt] before the first record, step 8 adds a double quote to begin its first field.

Step 9 causes the program to beep and pause for you to press ENTER, confirming that the file looks correct. (You can omit this step, if desired.) Step 10 proceeds to the Text In/Out screen. The backspace causes the program to beep again (and to erase the default file name). The macro ends at the file name prompt. Here is the complete macro listing:

SFTOMM.MAC — Secondary file to mailmerge format

1. *Go to top of document*
   HOME, HOME, UP ARROW

2. *Insert wide margin set*
   <Line Format> **3 0** SPACE **250** ENTER

3. *Replace ^R codes with quotes and comma*
   <Replace> **n** <Merge R> ENTER, ESC *","* ESC

4. *Go back to top of document*
   HOME, HOME, UP ARROW

5. *Replace extraneous comma/quote/^E/[HRt] sequence with [Hrt]/quote*
   <Replace> **n** *,"* <Merge E> ENTER, ESC, ENTER *"* ESC

6. *Delete extra quote from end of file*
   DEL

7. *Go to top of document*
   HOME, HOME, UP ARROW

8. *Add missing quote to top of file*
   "

9. *Pause for visual check*
   CTRL+PGUP, ENTER, ENTER

10. *Start Save DOS Text File command*
    <Text In/Out> **1** BACKSPACE

If you have any numeric fields in your newly created mailmerge file, you will need to remove the double quotes from those fields in every record. To do this, use a macro to search for a delimiter as many times as necessary to get to the beginning of the numeric field, delete the leading double quote, search for the next delimiter, delete the trailing double quote, and then repeat the macro.

For example, let's assume that you have a file created with the previous macro that has records formatted like this:

```
"John Hawkins","Marketing","54000","Single"
```

In this case, the record consists of three text fields (name, division, and marital status) and one numeric field (salary). The numeric field is the third one in the record. The macro listed next removes the double quotes from the field to identify it properly as a numeric field.

After you understand how the macro feels its way around a record by searching for delimiters (like the double quote-comma-double quote combination or the double quote-[HRt] combination), you will be able to customize this macro for your own files:

MMNUM.MAC — Mailmerge numeric field conversion

1. *Go to top of document*
   HOME, HOME, UP ARROW
2. *Search for first delimiter*
   <Search> "," ESC
3. *Search for second delimiter*
   <Search> ESC
4. *Delete unwanted quote*
   BACKSPACE
5. *Search for third delimiter*
   <Search> ESC
6. *Position cursor to delete quote*
   LEFT ARROW, LEFT ARROW
7. *Delete unwanted quote*
   BACKSPACE
8. *Go to beginning of next record*
   <Search> ENTER, ESC
9. *Restart macro*
   <Macro> **mmnum** ENTER

dBASE III Date Conversion

As mentioned in Chapter 8, "Integration With Other Products," when you output dBASE III data to an ASCII delimited (mailmerge) file, dBASE formats dates like this:

```
YYYYMMDD
```

where "YYYY" is the year, "MM" is the month, and "DD" is the day.

For example, here is a record created with the dBASE Copy To command that contains a text field (name), a date field (birthdate), and a numeric field (salary):

```
"Frank Sarconi",19541021,34000
```

The record contains the information that Frank Sarconi was born on October 21, 1954. After WordPerfect's Convert program is used to translate the mailmerge format file into the secondary merge format, the same record will look like this:

```
Frank Sarconi^R
19541021^R
34000^E
```

You can write a macro that will go through a file with records in this format and convert the dates to a more readable form.

Macro Details

The macro uses the Undelete function to quickly reposition the numbers of the date.

Step 1 searches for the ^R [HRt] sequence at the end of the first field, positioning the cursor at the beginning of the second field (the date field, in our example). When you create this macro for your own files, repeat this step as many times as necessary to position the cursor at the beginning of the date field you want to convert.

Step 2 deletes the four digits of the year. Steps 3 and 4 position the cursor and then place a slash between the month digits and the day digits. Steps 5 and 6 position the cursor and then place a slash after the day digits. Step 7 restores the four digits of the year at the cursor position. Steps 8 and 9 position the cursor before the last two digits of the year and delete the first two digits (the "19"):

Step 10 searches for the end of the record, positioning the cursor at the beginning of the next record in preparation for the next execution of the macro. Step 11 repeats the procedure on all of the records until the search in step 1 fails (no more fields are located).

When the macro has completed execution, the records should be formatted like this one:

```
Frank Sarconi^R
10/21/54^R
36000^E
```

The macro is listed here:

DB3DATE.MAC — DBASE III date field conversion

1. *Search for the end of the first field (can be repeated)*
   <Search> <Merge R> ENTER, ESC

2. *Delete year*
   DEL, DEL, DEL, DEL

3. *Move past month*
   RIGHT ARROW, RIGHT ARROW

4. *Enter slash between month and day*
   /

5. *Move past day*
   RIGHT ARROW, RIGHT ARROW

6. *Enter slash after day*
   /

7. *Undelete year*
   <Cancel> **1**

8. *Move past last two digits*
   LEFT ARROW, LEFT ARROW

9. *Delete "19"*
   BACKSPACE, BACKSPACE

10. *Search for end of record*
    <Search> <Merge E> ENTER, ESC

11. *Restart macro*
    <Macro> **db3date** ENTER

Formatting Articles for Newspapers and Magazines

Many newspaper and magazine publishers have in-house news editing systems that interface with typesetting computers. These systems usually have a stringent set of rules dictating the format of your text, whether it is submitted on disk or via telephone modem. You can have a macro properly format a WordPerfect document to prepare it for these systems.

You can use similar macros to format WordPerfect documents for a variety of other systems. For example, many commercial typesetters will now accept a file directly from your word processor (normally as an ASCII file). This file is then edited by the typesetter to include the many formatting commands that the typesetting computer uses to produce your text. Again, you can have WordPerfect perform much of this formatting and avoid editing charges.

The macros listed next are used by one of the authors, who submits articles to a major newspaper that uses the SII System 55 news editing system. This system requires that quoted items start with two double quotes and end with two single quotes. (This is because, unlike computers, typesetting systems use different characters for opening quotation marks and for ending quotation marks.) Also, this system expects paragraphs to be separated with a less-than symbol, a Hard Return, and then a three-space indent for the next paragraph, rather than with a blank space (that is, two Hard Returns).

Following are two macros that perform these format changes. (Be sure to save your document before executing either macro, in case something goes wrong.) The first macro, QUOTE.MAC, inserts the proper characters for quoted text. After executing this macro, look over your document to make sure that the quotes were translated properly. If you did not include a closing double quote somewhere, it will throw off the macro's Search commands and you will have to reload the original document and try again.

After you are satisfied that the quotes were translated properly, execute the second macro, SEND.MAC. This one inserts the characters necessary to separate paragraphs. Then it saves the file as an ASCII file with the name of SEND.ASC. You could then exit WordPerfect and run a communications program to send the file SEND.ASC by modem to the publication. See the section "Automatic Control Transfer" following this section for a description of how to fully automate this process.

Macro Details

In the first macro, QUOTE.MAC, step 1 searches for the first double quote in the document, which would be an opening quote. Step 2 then inserts an additional double quote directly after the first one.

Step 3 searches for the next double quote, which would be a closing quote. Step 4 deletes this and inserts in its place two single quotes. Step 5 restarts the macro, which will repeat until step 1 can no longer find a double quote.

In the second macro, SEND.MAC, step 1 replaces all occurrences of two consecutive Hard Returns with a single Hard Return. If the original document did not have paragraphs separated with a blank space, this step will have no effect.

Step 2 uses the <Goto> <Goto> key sequence to return the cursor to the location it had before the Replace command was issued. You can then start the macro at any point in the document; the macro will only affect text that follows the cursor position. This is useful if your document has some header information (like a title or byline) that you do not want formatted.

Step 3 replaces all Hard Returns with a less-than symbol, a Hard Return to end the paragraph, and three spaces as an indent for the next paragraph. Step 4 again returns the cursor to its original position.

Step 5 saves the file as SEND.ASC. This is useful if you will be performing this procedure frequently. Normally, you will have already saved the document in its original form as a WordPerfect document so that you can later retrieve and edit it. Therefore, you will not need to save the formatted ASCII file that you send to the publication. To make things simpler, then, you can use the same file name whenever you send a document, replacing the text each time with the new document.

Here are the macro listings:

QUOTE.MAC — Translate quotes for magazine/newspaper submission
1. *Search for a double quote*
   <Search> " ESC
2. *Enter additional double quote*
   "
3. *Search for second double quote*
   <Search> " ESC
4. *Delete second double quote and enter two single quotes*
   BACKSPACE ' '
5. *Restart macro*
   <Macro> **quote** ENTER

SEND.MAC — Formats a document for publication, saves it as SEND.ASC
1. *Replace two Hard Returns with one Hard Return*
   <Replace> **n** ENTER, ENTER, ESC, ENTER, ESC
2. *Go back to original cursor position*
   CTRL+HOME, CTRL+HOME
3. *Replace Hard Returns with <, Hard Return, and three spaces*
   <Replace> **n** ENTER, ESC < ENTER, SPACE, SPACE, SPACE, ESC

4. *Go back to original cursor position*
   CTRL+HOME, CTRL+HOME
5. *Save file as SEND.ASC, confirming overwrite*
   <Text In/Out> **1 send.asc** ENTER **y**

Automatic Control Transfer

You can perform some neat tricks with WordPerfect macros and DOS batch files that will automate the steps of sending documents via modem. In fact, you could use the concept described here to automate a variety of other tasks.

Note: This advanced procedure assumes that you have a hard disk and know how to write a DOS batch file.

As an example, let's assume that you have WordPerfect loaded on your hard disk in the \WP directory, that you store your documents in a directory called \WP\DATA, and that you use PC-Talk as your communications program, loaded in the \PC-TALK directory. Also, it is assumed that you store batch files in the root directory.

Procedure Notes

This procedure uses the DOS batch file command IF EXIST to test whether the file SEND.ASC exists in your data directory when you exit WordPerfect. If it does, PC-Talk will be executed (so you can transfer your document), and then you are returned to WordPerfect. If it doesn't, you exit to DOS as usual.

Assuming that your regular batch file looks like this,

```
cd \wp\data
\wp\wp
cd \
```

here is a batch file that performs the control transfer procedure to PC-Talk and back:

```
cd \wp\data
if exist send.asc del send.asc
\wp\wp
if exist send.asc goto send
```

```
goto end
:send
cd \pc-talk
pc-talk
cd \
wpgo
:end
cd \
```

Create this batch file in your root directory and call it WPGO.BAT. Use it whenever you want to run WordPerfect. Note that you can use a different name, as long as you change the self-referential line in the batch file (third from the last) accordingly. (See Appendix A, "Installation," for suggestions on hard disk setups.)

Here is a line-by-line explanation of this batch file listing:

cd \wp \data
Changes the current directory to your data directory so that files will automatically be stored there from within WordPerfect.

if exist send.asc del send.asc
Checks to see if the file SEND.ASC exists in the data directory, and deletes it if it does.

\wp \wp
Executes WordPerfect, which is loaded in the \WP directory. This method is only possible with DOS 3.XX. With DOS 2.XX, this line should read simply "wp". (See Appendix A, "Installation.") While in WordPerfect, you would use the SEND.MAC macro given previously to create the file SEND.ASC.

if exist send.asc goto send
Executed when you exit from WordPerfect, it checks for the existence of SEND.ASC (created by the macro SEND.MAC in the previous section). If it exists, the batch file branches to :SEND. If it does not exist, it continues with the next step.

goto end
If the file SEND.ASC does not exist, branch to :END (the end of the batch file) and exit normally.

:send
Marks this as the start of the SEND routine.

cd \pc-talk
Changes the default directory to the PC-TALK directory. (This can

be the directory of whichever communications program you are using.) If your communications program does not support subdirectories, you could first use COPY to put a copy of the file SEND.ASC into the proper directory. Just be sure to delete the file after you exit the communications program.

pc-talk
Executes the program PC-Talk (or any designated communications program). You would then dial a number and transfer the document. Some communications programs can be programmed for certain tasks, much like WordPerfect's macros. You might use this ability to send your document automatically.

*cd *
Changes the default directory to the root directory.

wpgo
Starts this batch file over again, which will delete the SEND.ASC file and return you to WordPerfect.

:end
Marks this as the start of the END routine, the end of the batch file.

*cd *
Changes the default directory to the root directory.

To use this procedure, you need to make two modifications to the SEND.MAC macro given previously:

5. Save file as SEND.ASC, no confirm necessary
   <Text In/Out> **1 send.asc** ENTER
6. *Exit WordPerfect without saving document*
   <Exit> **n y**

Now follow these steps:

• Write your document and save it in the usual fashion

• Execute QUOTE.MAC, if necessary (from the previous section)

• Check the document

• Execute SEND.MAC (from the previous section).

The macro formats and saves the file as SEND.ASC. Then it exits

WordPerfect, and the WPGO.BAT batch file you used to start the program picks up where it left off. It checks for the existence of the file SEND.ASC, and when it finds the file, it executes your communications program.

- Dial the phone number and transfer the SEND.ASC file

- Exit the communications program.

After you exit the communications program, the batch file again picks up where it left off. It restarts itself, deleting the SEND.ASC file and running WordPerfect. You can then continue with your work.

USING WORDPERFECT WITH EXTERNAL MACRO PROGRAMS

For most purposes, WordPerfect's macro function makes it unnecessary to use an external macro program such as ProKey, SuperKey, or Key-Works. However, WordPerfect's macro function has some limitations that external macro programs do not.

The major limitation is that the only single key sequences that can be used to implement a macro are single letters with the ALT key. Although this provides many choices, you may eventually run out of suitable ALT key combinations. Most other macro programs allow you to use the CTRL key (as well as the ALT key) in combination with almost any other key for macro definition.

There are several reasons why this might be desirable. First, it greatly increases the number of keys available for macros. Second, it makes it possible for WordPerfect to be configured so that it emulates another program, or the way you have chosen to redefine the keys on another program.

Using an external macro processor, you can create a common interface for all of your programs. Using ProKey, for example, you can create macros for WordPerfect, Lotus 1-2-3, dBASE III, and several other programs so that the same commands perform similar functions in all of the programs.

It is possible, for example, to always use ALT+R to retrieve a file, regardless of what program you are using. ALT+S can be used to save a file and resume work, CTRL+P to print a file, ALT+E to erase a range (or block) of text, and ALT+D to insert the current date. While you can create some (but not all) of these commands using WordPerfect's own macro processor, it may not be possible to do so with all programs you run.

Note: The techniques presented here have been tested with ProKey and the macro processor built into DesqView, a multitasking program described in Chapter 8, "Integration With Other Products." As far as we know, these techniques will work with all macro processors on the market, but before buying a macro program to work with WordPerfect, check that it meets your needs.

Making WordPerfect Like WordStar

Prior to using WordPerfect, one of the authors used WordStar as his primary word processing program. He switched to WordPerfect because of its many additional features, yet remained wedded to WordStar's keyboard interface. (WordStar uses CTRL keys for most functions, including moving around the document.) Without debating the wisdom of the WordStar interface, it is clear that it is very popular, not only among current and former WordStar users, but among many users of dBASE II, dBASE III, and other programs that use such WordStar key sequences as CTRL+E for UP ARROW, CTRL+X for DOWN ARROW, CTRL+S for LEFT ARROW, and CTRL+D for RIGHT ARROW.

Admittedly, this interface is a throwback to the days when many computers had no arrow keys (WordStar, first published in 1979, worked on old Apple II systems and all CP/M machines), but the interface has merit because it is possible for touch typists to move the cursor around the screen without having to move their hands off the home row of keys or their eyes off the screen. By examining the pattern of the keys, as shown in Figure 10-1, you can see the logic of the layout.

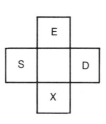

Figure 10-1. The WordStar control diamond

With ProKey or one of the other macro programs, it is possible to make WordPerfect emulate WordStar not only for these commands, but for many others as well. For example, you can make CTRL+G delete a character, CTRL+Y delete a line, and CTRL+B mark the start of a block (WordStar actually uses CTRL+KB, but we have taken liberties).

Where the WordStar command is a single CTRL key used with another key, you just use a macro program that defines that combination as performing the equivalent WordPerfect procedure. In some cases, however, WordStar requires two CTRL keys. This takes a little more forethought. For example, to go to the top of a file, WordStar requires you to press CTRL+QR. In WordPerfect, that command is HOME, HOME, UP ARROW. So, you need to define CTRL+Q as HOME and CTRL+R as HOME, UP ARROW.

By defining CTRL+Q as HOME, you can also cause WordPerfect to emulate WordStar's command for quick beginning and quick end of line movements. WordStar's CTRL+QD is the same as WordPerfect's HOME, HOME, RIGHT ARROW; and CTRL+QS equals HOME, HOME, LEFT ARROW.

Although you cannot emulate *all* of WordStar's commands using a macro program, you can certainly produce the important ones.

OFFICE AUTOMATION

WordPerfect's macros can be used to automate a variety of office tasks. You might not instantly recognize these tasks as candidates for macro procedures. However, macros can help ease the drudgery of these repetitive chores.

Letter Generation

You can have WordPerfect automatically date and address a letter for you. By combining macros with the Merge function, you can create a procedure that will take a name and address at the cursor location and place this information into a merge document for a letter.

Macro Details

The macro assumes that your names and addresses are stored in a secondary merge file with the data entered as shown next.

Syntax:

```
Fname^R
Lname^R
Address^R
City, ST^R
Zip^R
^E
```

Example:

```
Frank^R
Henderson^R
435 Maple Corner^R
Guerneville, CA^R
95446^R
^E
```

If you have a secondary merge document that is not formatted like this, you will need to modify the primary document and the macro to work properly with your format. You might want to experiment with a record formatted like the preceding one before making the modifications.

The procedure also requires a primary document to create the letter. Although you can modify the format in any way, follow these steps to create a sample letter. (See the section "The Primary Document" in Chapter 3, "Merge," for a description of primary documents.) Make sure the screen is clear.

1. Press the <Line Format> key (SHFT+F8).

2. Type **1** for "Tabs" and then press the <Delete End-of-Line> key (CTRL+END).

3. Type **45** and press ENTER and then the <Exit> key (F7).

4. Press TAB and then the <Merge Codes> key (ALT+F9), and type **D** to insert the merge code for the current date.

When a letter is actually generated, the current date will appear at the location of the ^D merge code.

5. Press ENTER twice.

6. Press the <Merge Codes> key, type **F** and then **1**, and press ENTER.

The code ^F1^ should appear at the cursor location.

7. Press SPACE and then the <Merge Codes> key, type **F** and then **2**, and press ENTER twice.

8. Press the <Merge Codes> key, type **F** and then **3**, and press ENTER twice.

9. Press the <Merge Codes> key, type **F** and then **4**, and press ENTER.

10. Press SPACE and then the <Merge Codes> key, type **F** and then **5**, and press ENTER.

11. Press ENTER twice.

12. Type **Dear**, press SPACE and then the <Merge Codes> key, type **F** and then **1**, and press ENTER.

13. Type **,** and press ENTER twice.

14. Press the <Merge Codes> key, type **G** and then **LETTER2**, press the <Merge Codes> key, and type **G**

This step causes the Merge function to execute the macro LETTER2 when the merge is complete. This macro deletes the LETTER.ADD file, which was temporary.

15. Press the <Save> key (F10), type **LETTER.FMT**, and press ENTER.

Your screen will look like the one shown in Figure 10-2 (except that the date will be different).

To use this procedure, first retrieve the secondary document that contains your names and addresses, and then find the name of the person (using the Search function if necessary) to whom you want to send a letter. Execute the macro, which clears the screen and inserts the current date, the person's name and address, and "Dear *fname*," at the top of the file. You can then write the text of the letter.

Here is the macro listing:

LETTER.MAC — Create a letter from address record
1. *Go to left edge of line*
   HOME, HOME, LEFT ARROW
2. *Mark record as a block*
   <Block> <Search> <Merge E> ESC, RIGHT ARROW
3. *Save block as LETTER.ADD*
   <Save> **letter.add** ENTER

   4. *Turn Block off*
      <Block>
   5. *Clear secondary document from screen*
      <Exit> **n n**
   6. *Execute merge with LETTER.FMT as primary document*
      <Merge/Sort> **1 letter.fmt** ENTER
   7. *Specify LETTER.ADD as secondary document*
      letter.add ENTER

LETTER2.MAC — Delete LETTER.ADD after LETTER.MAC is done
   1. *Highlight document in List Files*
      <List Files> **letter.add** ENTER, DOWN ARROW
   2. *Delete file*
      2 y <Cancel>

---

                                        ^D

```
^F1^ ^F2^
^F3^
^F4^ ^F5^

Dear ^F1^,

^GLETTER2^G_
```


                        Doc 1 Pg 1 Ln 9   Pos 21

Figure 10-2.   The letter format document — LETTER.FMT

Printing Envelopes

The following macro prints on an envelope the name and address appearing at the top of a letter.

Note: Before creating this macro, you must create a file called ENV.FMT that contains all the commands you normally type when you print an envelope. It might include, for example, setting the left margin to 40 and the top margin to 0.

The macro copies the contents of ENV.FMT to a file called ENV.PRT and then appends the recipient's name and address to that file. Finally, it prints the name and address on the envelope.

Each time you invoke the macro you must first place an envelope in your printer and make sure that the printer is turned on. Then move the cursor to the beginning of the recipient's name and address in the letter.

The macro listing is shown here:

ENV.MAC — Print address at cursor on envelope
1. *Copy ENV.FMT to ENV.PRT*
   <List Files> **env.fmt** ENTER, DOWN ARROW **8 env.prt** ENTER <Cancel>
2. *Move to beginning of line*
   HOME, HOME, LEFT ARROW
3. *Mark address as block*
   <Block> <Search> ENTER, ENTER, ESC
4. *Append address to ENV.PRT file*
   UP ARROW <Move> **3 env.prt** ENTER
5. *Print ENV.PRT file*
   <List Files> **env.prt** ENTER, DOWN ARROW **4**
6. *Pause half second for print to start*
   CTRL+PGUP **5** ENTER, CTRL+PGUP **0** ENTER
7. *Delete ENV.PRT and return to document*
   2 y <Cancel>

Letter Archive

Another useful office automation tool is the Letter Archive macro, which maintains an archive document containing all your letters. Each letter is separated by a Hard Page Break. When the file gets too large, you can rename the file and then restart the process with a new archive document. The biggest advantage to this type of system is that you do not have to come up with a unique file name for every letter you write.

Macro Details

Step 1 of the macro (see the listing that follows) positions the cursor at the top of the document.

Step 2 generates a Hard Page Break at the top of the page so that, when the file is appended to the LETTER.ARC file, the letter will start on a new page. This makes it easier to find a particular letter when you are browsing through the archive document. It also makes it easier to print the letter later (using the Page Print command).

Step 3 marks the entire document as a block, and step 4 appends the block to the file LETTER.ARC. Note that you cannot append to a document that does not exist, so be sure to save your first letter manually (using the <Save> key) as LETTER.ARC. Then, for your second and subsequent letters, you can use the macro to append your letters to the LETTER.ARC file.

Step 5 positions the cursor at the top of the document, and step 6 deletes the added Hard Page Break code. After the macro is complete, you can then go ahead and print the document, or simply clear the screen and start working with a new document.

When the LETTER.ARC gets large or out of date, you can rename it LETTER.OLD (or use some sort of date-naming convention like MARCH.ARC for all letters archived in the month of March). Then create a new LETTER.ARC file manually with the next letter you write, and you will be able to continue using the ARC.MAC macro for subsequent letters.

The macro listing is as follows:

ARC.MAC — Letter archive procedure

1. *Go to top of document*
   HOME, HOME, UP ARROW

2. *Generate Hard Page Break*
   CTRL+ENTER, LEFT ARROW

3. *Mark document as a block*
   <Block> HOME, HOME, DOWN ARROW

4. *Append block to file LETTER.ARC*
   <Move> **3 letter.arc** ENTER

5. *Go to top of document*
   HOME, HOME, UP ARROW

6. *Delete Hard Page Break*
   DEL

Document Assembly

The WordPerfect manual describes how to use the Merge function to perform a *document assembly* operation. Document assembly means that you build a document using any combination of standard paragraphs, along with customized text. You can insert as many paragraphs as you want into your document, and they can be inserted anywhere you want. You can use macros to create an easier and more flexible document assembly procedure.

This procedure uses three separate macros, along with WordPerfect's Dual Document Editing and Window functions. Since Document 2 is used in the procedure, do not use it for other purposes while performing the document assembly operation. (During the course of the procedure, the text in Document 2 is cleared.)

To begin with, you need to create a document that will contain all of your standard paragraphs. Follow the steps below to create this document. Make sure the screen is clear.

1. Press the <Center> key (SHFT+F6).

2. Type **Type a paragraph number and press ENTER**.

3. Press ENTER.

4. Press the <Center> key.

5. Type **Type**

6. Press SPACE and then the <Bold> key, type **0**, press the <Bold> key again, and then press SPACE.

7. Type **and press ENTER to end.**

8. Press ENTER and then press the Hard Page key (CTRL+ENTER).

Your screen should look like the one shown in Figure 10-3.

The screen message will be a prompt for you when you are entering the paragraph numbers later. Now you need to type the paragraphs themselves. Paragraphs should be numbered sequentially, so that you will later be able to print out this document for easy reference. You can use any sort of numbering system that you want for the paragraphs, although Arabic numbers are used in this procedure.

```
        Type a paragraph number and press ENTER.
          Type 0 and press ENTER to end.

================================================================================
-
```



```
                        Doc 1  Pg 2  Ln 1       Pos 10
```

Figure 10-3.   The standard paragraph document—PARA.STD

Follow these steps to create a few sample paragraphs.

9. Type **1.** and press the <Indent> key (F4).

10. Type

Now we are entering the text for the first paragraph. We could be typing some legal terms for this sample, but they would be hard to type. This should give us the idea.

11. Press ENTER twice.

12. Type **2.** and press the <Indent> key.

13. Type

Here we are typing the second paragraph. Again, we must let our minds roam free while we conjure up nonsense to type for the second paragraph.

14. Press ENTER twice.

15. Type **3.** and press the <Indent> key.

16. Type

Already we find ourselves typing the third paragraph. It seems hard to believe that just a few minutes ago, we hadn't even started typing the first paragraph.

17. Press ENTER twice.

If you like, go ahead and type a few more paragraphs like these. Be sure to start each paragraph with a number, a period, and the <Indent> function. Be sure to end each paragraph by pressing ENTER twice.

When you are finished, save the document as PARA.STD and clear the screen. Now you are ready to define the three macros.

Macro Details

There are three macros in this procedure: PARA.MAC, PARA2.MAC, and PARA3.MAC.

The first macro, PARA.MAC, starts the document assembly process. Step 1 of this macro (see the listing that follows) sizes the window for Document 1 to 20 lines, which leaves two lines visible in Document 2 for the prompt at the top of the PARA.STD file.

Step 2 switches to Document 2 and retrieves PARA.STD, the document that contains all of the standard paragraphs. The first two centered lines should appear in the small window at the bottom of the screen. Step 3 executes PARA2.MAC.

The second macro, PARA2.MAC, performs the actual process of copying the text of each selected paragraph from the standard paragraph document in Document 2 to the current document in Document 1, at the cursor position.

Step 1 of this macro specifies the fail macro, the macro that will be executed when the Search in step 2 fails. This happens when you enter a paragraph number that does not exist. Therefore, when you enter 0, the search will fail, and the macro PARA3.MAC will be executed. (See Chapter 2, "Macros," for a discussion of conditional branching macros.)

Step 2 issues the Search command. When you press the <Search> key, WordPerfect suggests the text that was used in the previous search operation. The BACKSPACE deletes this suggestion. The CTRL+PGUP, ENTER, ENTER sequence is a Pause for Input (which is described in the section "The Pause that Refreshes" in Chapter 2, "Macros").

Note: While defining this macro, you should press CTRL+PGUP and then ENTER, type **1**, and then press ENTER for this step. This way, you can proceed to define the rest of the macro as you would if a number had been entered at the pause. The 1 will not be recorded with the macro.

After the macro has paused for you to enter a number and to press ENTER, it adds a period and an Indent code to the Search string (to positively identify a paragraph number, and not a number within a paragraph). Then it starts the search.

Step 3 defines the paragraph (including a blank line at the end) as a block and then copies it. Step 4 returns the cursor to the top of the document so the prompt will display properly for the next execution. Step 5 switches to Document 1 and retrieves the paragraph at the cursor position.

Step 6 searches for two Hard Returns, to position the cursor after the retrieved paragraph. Step 7 switches back to Document 2 to repeat the selection process. Step 8 restarts the same macro, which prompts for a Search string again.

The third macro, PARA3.MAC, finishes the document assembly process. Step 1 of this macro clears the PARA.STD document from the screen so that you can use Document 2 for other purposes when you are not using it for document assembly. Step 2 switches back to Document 1. Step 3 restores Document 1's window to full size.

To use the document assembly macros, start with both documents blank. Then begin to type your document. When you want to insert a standard paragraph from the PARA.STD file, you invoke the macro PARA.MAC. The macro prompts you for a paragraph number. You type the number of the paragraph you want (keep a printed copy of the PARA.STD document for handy reference), and press ENTER. The paragraph is inserted into your document. You continue to enter paragraph numbers for other paragraphs you want inserted at the cursor position. When you are finished, you type **0** and press ENTER. You are then returned to your document.

To add, delete, and edit the standard paragraphs, simply retrieve the PARA.STD document, make the desired changes, and resave the document. Be sure to start each paragraph with a number (or other unique code) and with the Indent function, and to end each paragraph by pressing ENTER twice.

Here are the listings for the macros just described:

PARA.MAC — Starts document assembly procedure

1. *Set window for Document 1 to 20 lines*
   <Screen> **1 20** ENTER

2. *Switch to Document 2 and retrieve PARA.STD*
   <Switch><Retrieve> **para.std** ENTER

3. *Execute main routine, PARA2.MAC*
   <Macro> **para2** ENTER

PARA2.MAC — Main document assembly routine

1. *Indicate Fail Macro for conditional loop*
   <Macro> **para3** ENTER

2. *Start Search function pause for input*
   <Search> BACKSPACE, CTRL+PGUP, ENTER, ENTER . <Indent> ESC

3. *Copy paragraph at cursor position*
   <Block> ENTER, DOWN ARROW <Move> **2**

4. *Go to top of document*
   HOME, HOME, UP ARROW

5. *Switch to Document 1 and retrieve copied text*
   <Switch> <Move> **5**

6. *Position the cursor past the retrieved paragraph*
   <Search> ENTER, ENTER, ESC

7. *Switch back to Document 2*
   <Switch>

8. *Restart macro*
   <Macro> **para2** ENTER

PARA3.MAC — Complete document assembly procedure

1. *Clear PARA.STD from Document 2*
   <Exit> **n n**

2. *Switch back to Document 1*
   <Switch>

3. *Restore window to full size*
   <Screen> **1 24** ENTER

Appendix

A INSTALLATION

WordPerfect is distributed on five floppy disks:

- The System Disk

- Two Printer Disks

- The Learning Disk

- The Speller Disk

- The Thesaurus Disk.

The system disk contains the program files, which are *essential* for using the program. The files on the rest of the disks enhance the use of WordPerfect. For example, to use the special functions of your printer, you need the files on the Printer Disks. To access the Help system, to customize printer drives, or to load the tutorial documents, you need the files on the Learning Disk. To use the Spell-Check and Thesaurus functions of WordPerfect, you will need the files on the Speller and Thesaurus disks.

Before you can use WordPerfect, you must correctly install it for your particular hardware configuration. This appendix is divided into two major sections: "Floppy Disk Installation" and "Hard Disk Installation." To install WordPerfect, refer to the section appropriate for your equipment. A final section, "Using the Setup Menu," describes the process of using WordPerfect's Setup menu to set default parameters and backup options.

255

FLOPPY DISK INSTALLATION

The process of installing WordPerfect for use with a floppy disk system consists of these basic procedures:

- Copying the original Printer, Learning, Speller, and Thesaurus disks

- Copying the system disk to a bootable disk

- Writing an AUTOEXEC.BAT file for the bootable system disk

- Configuring the program for your printer

Note that if your computer system has 512K of RAM or more, you can improve WordPerfect's speed and convenience by letting the program use more memory than it normally would. See "Using More RAM" later in this section for details.

Copying the Original Disks

Before copying the disks, you should have five blank disks ready, as well as the DOS system disk that came with your computer. The blank disks do not need to be formatted. Label them "Printer Disk 1," "Printer Disk 2," "Learning Disk," "Speller Disk," and "Thesaurus Disk."

To copy the disks, follow these steps:

1. With your computer turned off, insert your DOS system disk into the A drive (typically the drive on the left or top).

2. Turn on your computer.

After your computer runs its diagnostic procedures, you will be prompted for a date and a time.

3. Type the current date in MM-DD-YY form (for example, 03-01-86) and press ENTER. Type the time in HH:MM form (for example, 14:20 for 2:20 P.M.) and press ENTER.

You will see the A> prompt.

4. Type **diskcopy a: b:** and press ENTER.

The program will prompt you to insert the source disk in drive A and the destination disk in drive B.

5. Place the original Printer Disk 1 in drive A and the blank disk labeled "Printer Disk 1" in drive B. Then press ENTER.

DOS will copy the entire Printer Disk 1 onto the new disk in drive B. When copying is complete, DOS will ask whether you want to copy another disk.

6. Type **y** (and press ENTER, if necessary).

Follow the same steps to copy the Printer Disk 2, Learning Disk, Speller Disk, and Thesaurus Disk.

When you have copied all five disks, indicate that you are finished by typing **n** (and pressing ENTER, if necessary) when asked about copying more disks.

Making a Bootable System Disk

The next step is to create a *bootable* disk for the WordPerfect working copy — a disk that has enough of the operating system on it to get your computer running. To do this, place the DOS system disk in drive A, and follow these steps:

1. Type **format b:/s** and press ENTER.

2. Insert a blank disk into the B drive and press ENTER.

The disk in drive B will be formatted. The /s option at the end of the FORMAT command indicates that you want to have the DOS system tracks installed on the disk. This makes the disk bootable, which means that you can start the computer without using the DOS disk.

3. When the format is complete, answer **n** to the prompt for formatting more disks. Press ENTER if necessary.

You will return to the A> prompt.

4. Remove the DOS system disk from drive A and replace it with the WordPerfect system disk (labeled simply "WordPerfect").

5. Type **copy *.* b:** and press ENTER.

DOS will copy the files from the WordPerfect system disk in drive A onto the formatted, bootable disk in drive B.

6. When all of the files have been copied, remove the original WordPerfect system disk from drive A. Remove the new copy from drive B, label it "WordPerfect — Working Copy," and place it in drive A.

You have now created a bootable copy of WordPerfect.

To start WordPerfect with this disk, insert it in drive A and turn on your computer. At the prompts, enter the date and time, then type **wp**, and press ENTER.

The next step is to create an AUTOEXEC.BAT file on the WordPerfect working copy disk that will automate the start-up sequence.

Creating an AUTOEXEC.BAT File

When you start your computer, DOS looks on the disk for a file named AUTOEXEC.BAT that contains a sequence of DOS commands. This file is called a *batch file*. (For a complete description of batch files, see your DOS manual.) If the file exists, DOS will execute the commands that it contains. If it does not exist, DOS will ask you for the date and time and then produce the A> prompt.

You create the AUTOEXEC.BAT file on the WordPerfect working copy disk. The batch file contains the commands needed to execute the WordPerfect program properly, as well as any other DOS commands that you want to have executed every time you start your computer. For example, your system might include a clock/calendar function that must be set with another program, or you might wish to install a memory-resident program (such as SideKick or ProKey) before running Word-Perfect. To do this, you need to put these programs on the WordPerfect working copy, and you need to insert the proper commands to execute them into the AUTOEXEC.BAT file. If there is not enough room on the WordPerfect working copy disk for these programs, you will have to start the computer with a different disk.

To use an AUTOEXEC.BAT file, you first use the DOS COPY command to copy onto the WordPerfect working copy any programs your batch file will be invoking. Then, with the WordPerfect working copy in the A drive and the A> prompt on the screen, follow these steps:

1. Type **wp** and press ENTER.

   You will see a prompt indicating that the WordPerfect system is using the A drive. Then an introductory screen will appear.

2. Press ENTER.

   The screen will clear, and the WordPerfect editing screen will appear.

At this point, type any commands that you want executed before WordPerfect is executed. Press ENTER after each one, just as if you were actually executing it in DOS. For example, you might type **astclock** and press ENTER to set the clock from multi-function boards made by AST Research. (Make sure you copied the file ASTCLOCK.COM from the disk that came with the board onto the WordPerfect working copy.)

After you create an AUTOEXEC.BAT file, DOS will *not* prompt you for the date and time upon start-up. Therefore, you must include the DOS commands DATE and TIME (on separate lines) if you want DOS to prompt you for them.

When you have entered all of the commands that you want executed before running WordPerfect, continue with step 3.

3. Type **b:** and press ENTER.

   This makes drive B the default drive, which forces WordPerfect, when it is executed, to use drive B for retrieving and saving documents.

4. Type **a:wp** and press ENTER.

   This executes the WordPerfect program that is on drive A, while keeping drive B as the default drive.

5. Type **a:** and press ENTER.

   This step reinstates the default drive as drive A after you exit Word-Perfect.

6. Press the <Text In/Out> key (CTRL+F5) and type **1**.

7. Type **autoexec.bat** and press ENTER.

   These steps save the current document as a DOS text file with the name AUTOEXEC.BAT on the current default disk, drive A.

You have now created an AUTOEXEC.BAT file that will automate the start-up sequence when you use the WordPerfect working copy disk.

Here is a simple AUTOEXEC.BAT file:

```
date
time
b:
a:wp
a:
```

Now exit WordPerfect and test the AUTOEXEC.BAT file you created.

8. Press the <Exit> key (F7) and type **n** and then type **y**

After a few moments, you should see the DOS A> prompt.

9. Insert a blank formatted data disk in drive B for your data.

10. Press CTRL+ALT+DEL.

This step *reboots* (restarts) your computer.

You should now see DOS follow the steps you entered into the AUTOEXEC.BAT file. After executing the commands, the screen will pause at the introductory WordPerfect display you saw earlier. If your batch file does not work properly, check for these situations:

• Did you name the AUTOEXEC.BAT file incorrectly?

• Did you use the <Save> key (F10) to save the AUTOEXEC.BAT file from WordPerfect, instead of the <Text In/Out> key (CTRL+F5)? If so, run WordPerfect, retrieve the file using the <Retrieve> key (SHFT+F10), and then resave it using the <Text In/Out> key. Then exit and reboot the computer.

• Did you fail to include the proper steps in the file? Use the DOS command TYPE to view the contents of the AUTOEXEC.BAT file in order to verify that you entered the commands accurately. To do this, enter the following line at the A> prompt:

```
type autoexec.bat
```

The contents of the AUTOEXEC.BAT file will be displayed.

After correcting any problems you find, return to the DOS A> prompt, and then reboot the computer to test the AUTOEXEC.BAT file again.

Printer Installation

To install WordPerfect for the printer you will be using, refer to the section "Printer Installation" in Chapter 9, "Using Printers."

During printer installation, you press the PGDN key to access the main list of supported printers. WordPerfect will then indicate that it cannot find the printer files. Insert in drive B the copy of the Printer Disk you made earlier in this section, and type **B** (do not press ENTER). Then, when you select your printer, the program will copy the correct printer definitions from the Printer Disk in drive B to the WordPerfect working copy disk in drive A.

Using More RAM

If your computer is equipped with 384K of RAM or more, you can configure WordPerfect so that it uses more memory to make the program faster and more convenient.

Running WordPerfect Faster

Normally, when you start the program, only parts of WordPerfect are loaded from the disk into memory. The other parts of the program are loaded only when they are needed. This allows a large program like WordPerfect to work in a computer with a smaller amount of RAM. However, if you include the option / r when you are starting WordPerfect, the program will load completely into RAM. This way, you won't have to wait for another part to load while you are running the program.

Here is a typical AUTOEXEC.BAT file containing the proper command for WordPerfect to load all of its segments into memory at once:

```
date
time
b:
a:wp /r
a:
```

Removing the WordPerfect
Working Copy Disk

Normally, you must not remove the WordPerfect working copy disk from drive A while you are running WordPerfect, since the program needs the disk to load its various segments and to save temporary files. (Temporary files are created by WordPerfect for text editing purposes and are deleted automatically when you exit WordPerfect.) However, you can combine the /r option described above with the /d option for redirecting WordPerfect's temporary files to allow the working copy disk to be removed from the drive. You can then keep the Learning Disk (for the Help file), the Speller Disk, or the Thesaurus Disk in drive A instead of needing to swap one of these disks with your data disk in drive B.

There are three steps you must take to use this procedure:

- Use a RAM disk program to create a small (64K) RAM disk (or have at least 64K always available on a data disk in drive B).

- Copy the printer definition files WPRINTER.FIL and WPFONT.FIL and the program file {WP}SYS.FIL onto the RAM disk (or the data disk in drive B).

- Start WordPerfect with both the /r option described in the last section and the /d option to redirect the temporary files to the RAM disk (or the data disk in drive B).

To use this option, type **/d**, then a dash, and then the drive or directory you want to use for the temporary files. The starting command will look like this:

```
wp /r /d-c:
```

(The space between the options is not required.)

You create a RAM disk with a RAM disk program, which puts aside a designated amount of RAM memory to act as if it were a real disk drive. It is assigned a drive letter (usually C on a two disk drive system) and is used like any other drive. There are a variety of RAM disk programs available. Many memory boards come with one. DOS Versions 3.0 and higher come with a RAM disk program, so you do not need an external program.

Using a RAM disk for the printer and temporary files will greatly improve overall WordPerfect performance, since RAM disks operate much faster then normal disk drives. However, you will need more than 384K of memory to use one.

Normally, a RAM disk of 64K is sufficient for the printer and temporary files. The size of the RAM disk will, in part, determine how large your documents can be. If you later find that you cannot edit as

large a document as you want to, you can always increase the RAM disk
size. (However, you must leave at least 384K available for WordPerfect: 250K for the entire program, and 134K for DOS and editing space.)
It is generally not a good practice to create a document larger than about
64K as it becomes very bulky to deal with. Also, if for some reason your
file becomes damaged (DOS forbid), you would not want such a large
piece of work to be lost.

To use the RAM disk program that comes with DOS Versions 3.0
and higher, you must copy a file called VDISK.SYS from the DOS
system disk to the WordPerfect working copy disk, and you must create a
file called CONFIG.SYS. (The CONFIG.SYS file is very much like the
AUTOEXEC.BAT file—DOS will look at the CONFIG.SYS file and
then the AUTOEXEC.BAT file before doing anything else.) Here is an
example of a CONFIG.SYS file that creates a 64K RAM disk:

```
device=vdisk.sys 64
```

(See your DOS manual for a complete description of this program.)

When you use a RAM disk, you will need to copy the two printer
files, WPRINTER.FIL and WPFONT.FIL and the system file{WP}SYS.
FIL onto the RAM disk each time you start your computer. Modify the
AUTOEXEC.BAT file to include these steps.

Here is an example of an AUTOEXEC.BAT file that copies the
needed files to RAM disk drive C and then starts WordPerfect with the
temporary files redirected to the same RAM disk:

```
date
time
copy wprinter.fil c:
copy wpfont.fil c:
copy {wp}sys.fil c:
b:
a:wp /r /d-c:
a:
```

If you will be storing the temporary files on your data disk in drive B,
make sure that you always have at least 64K available on the disk.
Obviously, you need to copy the two printer files and the system file onto
the data disk only once, rather than each time you start the computer.
Whenever you work with another data disk, however, you will need to
recopy the files. If you will be working with several data disks at one time,
it might be a good idea to include steps for copying the printer and

system files to the data disk when you start WordPerfect by including the copy steps in the AUTOEXEC.BAT file.

Here is an AUTOEXEC.BAT file that starts WordPerfect with the temporary files redirected to the data disk in drive B. Make sure that you always have a disk with enough space available in drive B when you start your computer with this setup.

```
date
time
b:
a:wp /r /d-b:
a:
```

If you will be using drive A for the Speller and Thesaurus Disks, be sure to configure WordPerfect using the Setup menu so that it will know where to find the files. (See the section "Using the Setup Menu" later in this chapter for details.)

HARD DISK INSTALLATION

The process of installing WordPerfect for use with a hard disk system consists of these basic procedures:

- Creating subdirectories for the WordPerfect program files, the tutorial files, and your data files.

- Copying program files from the WordPerfect system, Learning, Speller, and Thesaurus Disks into the WordPerfect system directory.

- Copying tutorial files from the Learning Disk into the WordPerfect Learn directory.

- Modifying the AUTOEXEC.BAT file (if necessary) and creating a WP.BAT batch file to start WordPerfect.

- Installing WordPerfect for the system directory.

- Configuring the program for your printer.

Creating Subdirectories

The first step in hard disk installation of WordPerfect is to create the *subdirectories* that will contain the program and tutorial files, as well as your own data files. (For a complete description on the use of subdirectories, refer to your DOS manual.)

Note that there are many strategies for setting up subdirectories on a hard disk. The hierarchical (tree-like) nature of the operating system allows you to create many logical divisions for storing your data files. For example, you may want to maintain separate directories for home and business work. You may also want to further divide your business work into categories for letters, reports, and memos, or perhaps for specific projects. The DOS subdirectory system gives you tremendous flexibility in this area. You can always add new subdirectories to your hard disk, and WordPerfect's List Files function makes it easy to move your files from one subdirectory to another.

This section will lead you through the steps for setting up the directories essential for running WordPerfect: one for the program files, one for the learning files, and one (simply called DATA) for your document files. You can use your own names for the directories in these steps, if you like. Just be sure you are consistent.

Before you start this procedure, your hard disk should be formatted and bootable. You will know this is the case if, when you turn on the computer with no disk in the floppy disk drive, the computer prompts you for the date and time (or otherwise appears to be operating normally). You also should have a subdirectory named \DOS that contains all of the files from the DOS disk(s). Although this is not necessary for WordPerfect operation, you should always install the DOS files on a hard disk before you install any applications.

To begin creating subdirectories, you should be looking at the DOS prompt for your hard disk (usually C> or C: \>). Normally, you will get this prompt after the computer has booted. If the system first asks you for the date and time, type the current date in MM-DD-YY form (for example, 03-01-86) and press ENTER. Type the time in HH:MM form (for example, 14:20 for 2:20 P.M.) and press ENTER.

When the DOS prompt is on the screen, follow these steps to create the subdirectories for the WordPerfect program:

1. Type **md \wp** and press ENTER.

   This creates the subdirectory \WP, which is one level below the root (top) directory. This subdirectory is where the WordPerfect program files will be stored. If you receive absolutely no message at all after typing this command, DOS is telling you that everything is all right. It will only object if there is something wrong (for example, if the \WP directory already exists).

2. Type **md \wp\data** and press ENTER.

This creates the subdirectory \WP \DATA, which is below the \WP subdirectory and therefore two levels below the root directory. This is where all of your documents will be stored. You can later create other subdirectories, if you desire.

3. Type **md \wp\lrn** and press ENTER.

This creates the subdirectory \WP \LRN, which is also below the \WP subdirectory and therefore two levels below the root directory. This is where the tutorial files from the Learning Disk will be copied.

You have now created all the necessary subdirectories. Before you continue with the next step—copying the WordPerfect program and tutorial files—you need to make the \WP subdirectory your current directory.

4. Type **cd \wp** and press ENTER.

Now you are ready to copy the WordPerfect program and tutorial files onto the hard disk.

Copying the Program Files
Onto the Hard Disk

Have all of the WordPerfect disks available and the DOS prompt (usually C> or C: \WP>) on your screen. The \WP directory should be your current directory. Then follow these steps to copy the program files onto the hard disk:

1. Insert the WordPerfect system disk (usually labeled "WordPerfect") in drive A.

2. Type **copy a:*.*** and press ENTER.
   DOS copies all of the files from the disk in drive A.

3.   Insert the Speller Disk in drive A.

4.   Type **copy a:*.*** and press ENTER.

5.   Insert the Thesaurus Disk in drive A.

6.   Type **copy a:*.*** and press ENTER.

7.   Insert the Learning Disk in drive A.

      The Learning Disk contains both program files and tutorial files. The following steps copy just the program files from the Learning Disk into the \WP subdirectory.

8.   Type **copy a:*.fil** and press ENTER.

9.   Type **copy a:*.exe** and press ENTER.

10.   Type **copy a:*.tbl** and press ENTER.

11.   Type **copy a:*.mex** and press ENTER.

12.   Type **copy a:*.man** and press ENTER.

13.   Type **copy a:*.tst** and press ENTER.

14.   Type **copy a:*.com** and press ENTER.

Copying the Tutorial Files Onto the Hard Disk

This procedure copies the tutorial files onto the hard disk.

1.   Type **cd \wp \lrn** and press ENTER.

      This step makes the \WP \LRN subdirectory your current directory.

2.   Be sure that the Learning Disk is in drive A.

3.   Type **copy a:*.*** and press ENTER.

WordPerfect comes with two types of tutorials. First, the TUTOR program leads you through learning various word processing tasks on the screen. Second, the manual contains a tutorial that uses documents located in the \WP\LRN directory.

To use the TUTOR program, type **cd \wp\lrn** at the DOS prompt, and press ENTER. Then, type **path c:\wp** and press ENTER. Finally, type **tutor** and press ENTER. When you are finished using the tutorial program, exit to the DOS prompt, and then restart the computer with CTRL+ALT+DEL to reset the proper PATH.

To use the tutorial files, start WordPerfect in the usual way, then press the <List Files> key (F5), type = and then **\wp\lrn**, and press ENTER. Follow the tutorial in the manual.

Creating Batch Files

You can create a batch file to make your data directory, \WP\DATA, your current directory before starting WordPerfect. WordPerfect will then use the \WP\DATA directory for loading and saving your data files. If you start WordPerfect in this way, however, you must tell DOS where to find the WordPerfect program, since the \WP WordPerfect system directory will *not* be the current directory.

Exactly how you tell DOS to locate the WordPerfect program depends on which version of DOS your computer is using—2.XX (2.0 or higher, but lower than 3.0) or 3.XX (3.0 or higher).

Note: If at any point in the following procedures WordPerfect pauses before it starts and displays the message "Can't find correct copy of WP.EXE," type **c:\wp\wp.exe** and press ENTER.

Batch Files for DOS 2.XX

With DOS 2.XX, starting WordPerfect when the \WP WordPerfect system directory is not your current directory requires that a PATH statement that includes the \WP directory be placed in the AUTOEXEC. BAT file on your hard disk.

The AUTOEXEC.BAT file is a text file in the root directory of your hard disk containing a series of DOS commands that your computer will automatically execute each time you boot it up.

The PATH statement tells DOS where to look for programs that it cannot find in the current directory — for example, if you want to run the DOS programs CHKDSK and FORMAT without having to make the \DOS subdirectory the current directory. (For more specific information on the AUTOEXEC.BAT file and the PATH statement, see your DOS manual.)

Once you have modified the AUTOEXEC.BAT file so that the PATH statement includes the \WP subdirectory, DOS will be able to find the WordPerfect program when you type **wp**, even if your current directory is \WP\DATA.

The first step is to see if an AUTOEXEC.BAT file already exists on your hard disk, and if it does, to see whether it contains a PATH statement. To check for the AUTOEXEC.BAT file and PATH statement, begin at the DOS prompt (usually C> or C: \>), and then follow these steps:

1. Type **cd \wp** and press ENTER.

   Since you have not yet set the DOS PATH to include the \WP subdirectory, this step makes the \WP directory the current directory before you run WordPerfect.

2. Type **wp** and press ENTER.

   You will see an introductory screen about WordPerfect.

3. Press any key to continue.

   You will see the WordPerfect editing screen.

4. Press the <Text In/Out> key (CTRL+F5).

5. Type **2** for "Retrieve a DOS text file."

6. Type **\autoexec.bat** and press ENTER.

If the message "ERROR: File not found" appears at the bottom of the screen and you are returned to the Document Conversion, Summary and Comments screen, you do not have an AUTOEXEC.BAT file on your hard disk. You will need to create one that includes the PATH statement.

If you are returned to the editing screen and a document appears, you do have an AUTOEXEC.BAT file. Then you need to find the PATH statement, if one exists, and modify it to include the \WP subdirectory. If a PATH statement does not exist, you need to type one.

Since hardware and software configurations can vary greatly, there is no single PATH statement for all systems. However, this is the general PATH statement syntax:

```
PATH dir;dir;dir...
```

where "dir" is the name of a subdirectory that you want included in the PATH. A typical PATH might look like this:

```
PATH c:\;c:\dos
```

This PATH indicates that if a program cannot be found in the current directory, DOS should look in the root directory for it (c: \ ), and then in the c: \dos directory.

The same PATH statement modified for WordPerfect looks like this:

```
PATH c:\wp;c:\;c:\dos
```

Note that it is important for the \WP directory to be placed first in the PATH statement, before any other directories. Now let's look at the three possible situations you might have.

If you do not have an AUTOEXEC.BAT file, you must create one and then enter a PATH statement into it. To begin, make sure that you are at the editing screen by pressing the <Cancel> key (F1) to clear the Document Conversion, Summary and Comments screen. Then type a PATH statement like the preceding one that includes the \WP subdirectory and press ENTER. If you wish, you may also enter any other DOS commands that you want executed whenever you start your computer. For example, the existence of the AUTOEXEC.BAT file will cause DOS to skip the DATE and TIME prompts, so if you still want to enter these, type **date**, press ENTER, type **time**, and press ENTER again.

If you have an AUTOEXEC.BAT file but it does not contain a PATH statement, at the beginning of the file type a new PATH statement that includes the \WP subdirectory, and press ENTER. The PATH statement should then be on its own line.

If you have an AUTOEXEC.BAT file that contains a PATH statement, position the cursor at the first subdirectory name in the statement, and type **c:\wp;** so that the \WP subdirectory is specified first.

When you are finished entering or modifying the PATH statement, you need to save the AUTOEXEC.BAT file. Follow these steps:

1. Press the <Text In/Out> key (CTRL+F5).

2. Type **1** for "Save current document as a DOS text file."

3. Type **\autoexec.bat** and press ENTER.

   If WordPerfect asks you whether to replace the existing file, type **y** to confirm the replacement.

4. Clear the screen by pressing the <Exit> key (F7), typing **n** in response to the "Save Document?" prompt, and typing **n** in response to the "Exit WP?" prompt.

Now you need to create a second batch file that will start WordPerfect and make \WP\DATA the current directory. Follow these steps:

1. Type **cd \wp \data** and press ENTER.

2. Type **wp %1** and press ENTER.

   The "%1" in this line allows you to enter a parameter when you start the batch file that will be passed to WordPerfect. For example, you will be able to type "wp *filename*" where *filename* is the name of a document that you want to edit, or "wp /s" to use the WordPerfect Setup menu. (See the section "Using the Setup Menu" later in this chapter.)

3. Type **cd ** and press ENTER.

   This step will return you to the root (top) directory when you exit WordPerfect.

4. Press the <Text In/Out> key (CTRL+F5) and type **1**.

5. Type **\wp.bat** and press ENTER.

6. Press the <Exit> key (F7), type **n**, and then type **y**.

   You should now see the DOS prompt (usually C> or C: \WP).

The next step is to test the WP.BAT batch file. First, you need to reboot your computer, since the new PATH statement in your AUTO-EXEC.BAT file has not yet been activated. Make sure there is no disk in drive A.

1. Press CTRL+ALT+DEL.

This step reboots your computer. The screen will clear, and you will see the prompts that appear every time your computer is turned on.

You should then see the DOS prompt on the screen (usually C> or C: \>).

2. Type **wp /s** and press ENTER.

This step executes the WP.BAT batch file. The "/s" indicates that you want WordPerfect to display the Setup menu before starting the program. You should see the batch file automatically change the current directory to \WP\DATA and then execute the WordPerfect program. The introductory screen will appear.

3. Press any key.

The Setup menu will appear.

See the section "Using the Setup Menu" later in this chapter for a description of the setup process.

Batch Files for DOS 3.XX

With DOS 3.XX, you do not need to modify the AUTOEXEC.BAT file to start WordPerfect properly. This is because DOS 3.XX has a feature that allows you to precede a program name with a subdirectory name. You can therefore tell DOS exactly where on the hard disk the program is located when you *start* WordPerfect.

To create a batch file that will make \WP\DATA the current directory and will start WordPerfect for you, first make sure that you are seeing the DOS prompt (usually C> or C: \>) on the screen. Then follow these steps:

1. Type **cd \wp** and press ENTER.

2. Type **wp** and press ENTER.

You will see an introductory screen about WordPerfect.

3. Press any key to continue.

You will see the WordPerfect editing screen.

4. Type **cd \wp\data** and press ENTER.

5. Type **\wp\wp %1** and press ENTER.

In this statement, the " \wp \" indicates that the "wp" program is located in the \WP directory. This way, DOS will know where to find WordPerfect.

The "%1" allows you to enter a parameter when you execute the batch file that will be passed to WordPerfect. For example, you will be able to type "wp *filename*" where *filename* is the name of a file that you want to edit, or "wp /s" to use the WordPerfect Setup menu. (See the section "Using the Setup Menu" later in this chapter.)

6. Type **cd ** and press ENTER.

   This step will return you to the root (top) directory when you exit WordPerfect.

7. Press the <Text In/Out> key (CTRL+F5) and type **1**.

8. Type **\wp.bat** and press ENTER.

   Now you need to exit WordPerfect and try out the batch file.

9. Press the <Exit> key (F7), type **n**, and then type **y**.

   You should see the DOS prompt (usually C> or C: \WP>) on the screen.

10. Type **cd ** and press ENTER.

11. Type **wp /s** and press ENTER.

    This step executes the WP.BAT batch file. The "/s" indicates that you want WordPerfect to display the Setup menu before starting the program. You should see the batch file automatically change the current directory to \WP \ DATA and then execute the WordPerfect program. The introductory screen will appear.

12. Press any key.

    The Setup menu will appear.

See the section "Using the Setup Menu" later in this chapter for a description of the Setup process.

Printer Installation

To install WordPerfect for the printer you will be using, refer to the section "Printer Installation" in Chapter 9, "Using Printers."

Since the printer files have already been loaded onto the hard disk, the program should not prompt you for the Printer Disk during the printer installation process.

When WordPerfect indicates that it cannot find the printer files, insert the Printer Disk in drive A and type **A** (do not press ENTER). When you select your printer, the program will copy the correct printer drivers from the Printer Disk in drive A to the WordPerfect system directory on the hard disk.

USING THE SETUP MENU

You can use WordPerfect's Setup menu to indicate the subdirectory or drive where the Speller and Thesaurus files are located. You can also use the Setup menu to configure the program for the format settings you use most frequently and to tell WordPerfect whether or not to make an automatic backup of your document and how often. Once you have done this, you can also specify in which subdirectory the backup file should be placed.

To reach the Setup menu, type **wp /s** at the DOS prompt, and press ENTER. (On a floppy disk-based computer, first make sure that you are seeing the A> prompt and that the WordPerfect working copy disk is in drive A.) If you have not yet installed your printer, you will first see an introductory screen. Press any key; the Setup menu will appear, as shown in Figure A-1.

Specifying Disks or Directories

WordPerfect will normally look for the Thesaurus, Spelling Dictionary, and Supplemental Dictionary files on the default disk or directory.

On a floppy disk-based computer system that is not configured to use more RAM (see the section "Removing the WordPerfect Working Copy Disk" earlier in this chapter), this configuration will work. This is because the default drive will be drive B, where the Speller and Thesaurus disks would normally be placed when you use those functions.

For all other configurations, however, you will need to tell WordPerfect where to find these files. To do this, type **1** from the Setup menu for

```
                              Set-up Menu

0 - End Set-up and enter WP

1 - Set Directories or Drives for Dictionary and Thesaurus Files
2 - Set Initial Settings
3 - Set Screen and Beep Options
4 - Set Backup Options

Selection: _

Press Cancel to ignore changes and return to DOS
```

Figure A-1.   The Setup Menu screen

"Set Directories or Drives for Dictionary and Thesaurus Files."

For a floppy-based computer system that is configured to use more RAM so that the WordPerfect working copy disk can be removed from drive A, press the RIGHT ARROW key, then the LEFT ARROW key, then type **A:** and press ENTER. Repeat this sequence for all three prompts. This tells WordPerfect to look in drive A: for the Speller and Thesaurus files.

For a hard disk system, press the RIGHT ARROW key, then the LEFT ARROW key, then type **C:\WP** and press ENTER. Repeat this sequence for all three prompts. This tells WordPerfect to look in the \WP directory (the WordPerfect system directory) for the Speller and Thesaurus files.

Changing Initial Settings

WordPerfect comes with certain default values for its formatting functions. For example, margins are set for 10 and 74, tabs are set every five spaces, and right justification is turned on. However, you can use the Setup menu to change these default settings if you will be frequently using other settings. For example, you can have your documents always formatted with double line spacing or with narrow margins.

While the ability to change the defaults is a useful feature of Word-Perfect, it can cause some problems. WordPerfect's tutorial documents (as well as documents you might receive from other WordPerfect users) were written using the default values that were shipped with the program. Because of this, specific formatting codes for many features were not included in these documents.

For example, since the default margins are set for 10 and 74, someone wanting to create a document with those same margins would have no reason to insert a [Margin Set:] code. When the same document is loaded into a version of WordPerfect whose Initial Settings have been modified so that the default margins are set, for example, at 12 and 60, the document would be completely reformatted.

You should consider this before modifying the Initial Settings. If you will be sharing files with people who are running different copies of WordPerfect, you might want to agree on a standard set of Initial Settings or agree not to modify the original settings. It is also a good idea to wait until you have worked through the tutorial, if you intend to do so, before modifying the Initial Settings.

To change WordPerfect's Initial Settings, type **2** for "Set Initial Settings." The Initial Settings screen will appear as shown in Figure A-2.

At this point, you can press any of WordPerfect's function keys to change the format options invoked by those keys. For example, to change the default margins, press the <Line Format> key (SHFT+F8), type **3** for "Margins," and then enter the desired margin settings. To turn right justification off, press the <Print Format> key, type **3**, and then press ENTER to clear the menu.

When you are finished changing the Initial Settings, press ENTER at the Change Initial Settings screen to return to the Setup menu.

Setting Backup Options

WordPerfect has two methods of protecting your document with backups. You can use either, both, or neither.

The first method, the Timed Backup option, automatically saves a copy of your document at prescribed intervals. Each time the document is saved, the previously saved file is erased. For example, if you set this function for 15 minutes, the program will pause every 15 minutes to make a copy of your current document. You will therefore never lose more than 15 minutes' worth of your work due to a power failure or

Change Initial Settings

Press any of the keys listed below to change initial settings

Key	Initial Settings
Line Format	Tabs, Margins, Spacing, Hyphenation, Align Character
Page Format	Page # Pos, Page Length, Top Margin, Page # Col Pos, W/O
Print Format	Pitch, Font, Lines/Inch, Right Just, Underlining, SF Bin #
Print	Printer, Copies, Binding Width
Date	Date Format
Insert/Typeover	Insert/Typeover Mode
Mark Text	Paragraph Number Definition, Table of Authorities Definition
Footnote	Footnote/Endnote Options
Escape	Set N
Screen	Set Auto-rewrite
Text In/Out	Set Insert Document Summary on Save/Exit

Selection: _

Press **Enter** to return to the Set-up Menu

Figure A-2.   The Change Initial Settings screen

system crash. The backup files are named {WP}BACK.1 for Document 1 and {WP}BACK.2 for Document 2. If you were to lose power, you could reboot and retrieve one of these files and then save the file with an appropriate name.

The second method, the Original Backup option, automatically saves the previous version of a document with a special name whenever you save a new version. This way, if you save a file and then later want to see the older version, you can retrieve the original backup that WordPerfect made for you. The disadvantage of this method is that you will always have two copies of every document you create (the new version and the old version). This can make your disk very cluttered.

WordPerfect is shipped with both of these options disabled. To enable one or both of them, type **4** from the Setup menu for "Set Backup Options." The Backup Options screen will appear, as shown in Figure A-3. This screen contains some details about both backup options.

Set Timed Backup

To safeguard against losing large amounts of text in the event of a power or machine failure, WordPerfect can automatically backup the document on your screen at a chosen time interval and to a chosen drive/directory (see Set-up in the WordPerfect Installation pamphlet). **REMEMBER--THIS IS ONLY IN CASE OF POWER OR MACHINE FAILURE. WORDPERFECT DELETES THE TIMED BACKUP FILES WHEN YOU EXIT NORMALLY FROM WORDPERFECT.** If you want the document saved as a file you need to say 'yes' when you exit WordPerfect normally.

Number of minutes between each backup: **0**

Set Original Backup

WordPerfect can rename the last copy of a document when a new version of the document is saved. The old copy has the same file name with an extension of ".BK!". Take note that the files named "letter.1" and "letter.2" have the same original backup file name of "letter.bk!". In this case the latest file saved will be backed up.

Backup the original document? (Y/N) **N**

Figure A-3.   The Backup Options screen

After you have read the information, type the number of minutes you would like as an interval between backups. Fifteen minutes is generally a good interval to start with. You might want a shorter interval if you live in an area that is especially prone to power failures or a longer interval if the backup procedure disturbs your writing process. Type **0** to disable the function entirely. Press ENTER after typing the interval.

Next the program prompts you for the disk or directory in which to place the backup file. This should probably be a disk or directory that is convenient for you to find and that will contain enough room for the backup file. Generally, you should store the backup in the same place that you normally store your documents. Therefore, on a floppy disk system, type **b:** and press ENTER. On a hard disk system, type **c:\wp\data** and press ENTER.

The program then asks whether you want to use the Original Backup option. Type **y** if you want to use the function, or type **n** if you do not. You will be returned to the Setup Menu screen.

Ending Setup and Entering WordPerfect

When you are finished setting the directories for the Speller and Thesaurus, changing the Initial Settings, and setting the backup options, type **0** for "End Set-up and enter WP." All of the changes that you made will be recorded, and you will enter WordPerfect.

WordPerfect is now fully configured for your system.

Appendix

B USING THE WORD SEARCH FUNCTION

The Word Search function on the List Files screen (see the "File Management" section of Chapter 1, "Basics Refresher") allows you to search through many files on disk to find a specific word or phrase.

For example, you might want to find all of your letters that mention a client named Roy Donovan. You would call up the List Files screen listing the files containing your letters (for example, by typing ***.ltr** if you used ".ltr" as a file extension), type **9** for "Word Search," type **roy donovan** at the "Word Pattern" prompt, and press ENTER (the program does not distinguish between uppercase and lowercase letters). The Word Search function then searches through all of the files displayed (and any others that you would see if you scrolled the List Files display down), looking for that phrase. When it is finished searching, you will see a new List Files display that shows only the files containing the specified phrase. You can then type **6** for "Look" to quickly scroll through each document, or you can type **1** for "Retrieve" and then press the <Search> key (F2) to find the specified phrase within a document.

You can type up to 20 characters at the "Word Pattern" prompt. The program will sometimes allow you to type more than this and will appear to be searching through the files on disk for the longer phrase, but no documents will be found.

To search for files that contain two or more specified words, type them at the "Word Pattern" prompt with a space between words. (You can also use a semicolon to separate the words.) Only files that contain all the words, not necessarily in succession or in the order you enter them, will be found. For example, if you type **drops murder weapon**, you are telling the Word Search function to locate all files that contain *drops* AND *murder* AND *weapon*. However, if you enclose the words in double quotes (for example, "drops murder weapon"), the Word Search function considers the words a *phrase* and will only find files that contain the entered words in succession.

Just as the space is used as a logical AND operator, a comma is used as a logical OR operator. To find all files that contain either *drops* or *murder* or *weapon*, you would type **drops,murder,weapon**.

You can also combine logical operators. For example, to find all files that contain either *drop* AND *dead* OR *take a hike,* you would type **drop dead,"take a hike"** at the "Word Pattern" prompt. The word pattern is always evaluated from left to right when the Word Search function combines operators.

You can also use wildcard characters in the word pattern, exactly as with DOS and the Spell function. The ? character replaces any single character, and the * character replaces one or more characters. For example, typing **r?t** would find files that contain *rat*, *rut*, and *rot*. Typing **gra*** would find files that contain *gracious*, *graft*, and *graphically*.

You can create word patterns that consist of any combination of phrases delineated with double quotes, logical operators, and wildcard characters.

C AUTOMATIC DOCUMENT RELOAD

You may frequently work on just one WordPerfect document for an extended period of time. Each time you sit down to edit the document, you have to repeat all the steps necessary to recall the file to the screen. However, you can automate these steps by creating an Automatic Document Reload procedure.

This procedure uses a combination of batch files and a simple BASIC program. (It was written primarily for hard disk systems, since normally a floppy disk system will automatically start WordPerfect when you boot the WordPerfect working copy disk.) The first batch file, called WPRUN.BAT, runs the BASIC program WPRUN.BAS. This program then prompts you for the name of a file to edit and then creates another batch file for you, called WPL.BAT. When the BASIC program is finished, the first batch file, WPRUN.BAT, picks up where it left off by executing the newly created WPL.BAT, which starts WordPerfect and automatically retrieves the specified document.

After you create these files, you can simply type WPL at the DOS prompt to run WordPerfect and load the document you specified in the first routine. When you want to change the document name to something else (for example, to the next chapter title of a book), simply rerun the WPRUN.BAT batch file. You will again be prompted for a file name.

In the listing that follows, line 80 asks for the name of the file to edit. Line 90 opens (creates) the batch file WPL.BAT. Lines 100 through 160 are the steps of the batch file. Note that line 140 will vary depending on the version of DOS you are running. Line 170 closes and saves WPL.BAT.

You can modify the steps of this program for your own purposes. For example, you may want the program to change to a subdirectory other than \WP\DATA. You might also want to add an option to line 140 (which starts WordPerfect) like /r to load the entire program into memory (see Appendix A, "Installation").

To create an Automatic Document Reload procedure, first enter the following program into BASIC, and save it in the *root directory* of your hard disk as WPRUN.BAS.

```
10 ' Program to allow WP to repeatedly enter last file edited.
20 ' Works along with batch file "WPRUN.BAT"
30 ' Creates batch file WPL.BAT
40 ' (c) 1986 Eric Alderman and Lawrence J. Magid
50 ' May be distributed and modified for non-commercial purposes
60 ' Not for resale
70 KEY OFF:CLS
80 INPUT "Enter name of File to Edit";FIL$
90 OPEN "wpl.bat" FOR OUTPUT AS #1
100 PRINT #1,"echo off"
110 PRINT #1,"cls"
120 PRINT #1,"ECHO Stand by for WordPerfect - ";FIL$
130 PRINT #1,"cd \wp\data"
140 PRINT #1,"wp ";FIL$
               For DOS 3.XX, line 140 should read:
               140 PRINT #1,"\wp\wp ";FIL$
150 PRINT #1,"cd \"
160 PRINT #1,"ECHO To edit  ";FIL$;",  type WPL from the DOS prompt"
170 CLOSE
180 SYSTEM
```

Then you must create the following batch file WPRUN.BAT, which runs the BASIC program.

```
echo off
basica wprun
wpl
```

The steps of this batch file are very simple. The first line turns off screen echo, so that you don't see all of the DOS prompts on the screen when the batch file is executed. The second line executes the BASIC program just listed. The third line executes the batch file that will be created by the WPRUN.BAS BASIC program.

To create this batch file, type it in WordPerfect, and then save it as WPRUN.BAT using the <Text In/Out> key (CTRL+F5) in the root directory of your hard disk.

D WORDPERFECT LIBRARY

WordPerfect Library is a set of useful programs for the WordPerfect user. The package, which is sold separately from WordPerfect itself, includes

- Shell, a hard disk menu program that lets you keep many WordPerfect Corporation products in memory at one time.

- M-Edit, a macro editing program.

- Notebook, a program that allows you to more easily manipulate WordPerfect secondary merge files.

- File Manager, a stand-alone program that resembles WordPerfect's List Files function.

- Calendar, a useful perpetual calendar and appointment-scheduling program.

- Calculator, a full-function financial, statistical, scientific, and programming calculator.

- Beast, an addictive game.

This appendix does not attempt to describe all of the programs in WordPerfect Library nor any of them in full detail. It will, however, provide some helpful comments on Shell, M-Edit, and Notebook—three of the most useful of these programs.

SHELL

Shell is a menu program for organizing the applications on a hard disk. It can also divide your RAM into sections so that more than one program can be loaded at a time.

Unlike general memory managers like DesqView (see Chapter 8, "Integration With Other Products"), Shell works best with programs that are specifically "Shell-aware." While currently limited to programs from WordPerfect Corporation, the list is expected to eventually include other programs.

You can leave Shell-aware programs (along with some other programs which have a "Drop to DOS" feature) *resident* in memory while other programs are executed. (Although any program can be installed on Shell's menu, not all can be left resident in memory.) With Shell, therefore, you can keep many WordPerfect Corporation programs instantly available, since they do not have to be reloaded from disk each time you use them. You can load as many programs as will fit into available RAM.

Each program on Shell's menu is identified by a letter. To start a program, simply press its letter. When you exit the program, you return to the Shell menu. With a WordPerfect Corporation program, you can use the program's "Go to Shell" command (via the CTRL+F1 key sequence) to return to the Shell menu while leaving the program resident. On the Shell menu, you will see the program you were running marked with an asterisk, indicating that it is currently resident. If you press the program's letter again, you are instantly returned to the program, right where you left off in your document.

Shell, like many other programs, can take advantage of expanded memory boards that follow the LIM (Lotus-Intel-Microsoft) standard. These boards provide you with memory above the usual 640K PC limit. With expanded memory in your system, you will be able to load even more WordPerfect Corporation programs into RAM at one time. You will also be able to leave a WordPerfect Corporation program resident while you run a Shell-unaware product, instead of having to exit the WordPerfect Corporation program first to free up memory.

Shell's Hot Keys

While you are running "under Shell"—that is, you start Shell first and then your application, such as WordPerfect—you can instantly switch to another program without actually returning to the Shell menu by using Shell's Hot Keys. First press SHFT+ALT, and then press the letter that designates the desired program on the Shell menu. If the program was already resident, it will appear instantly on the screen. If it was not resident, it will take some time to load.

For example, let's say you designate the letter W to execute WordPerfect and the letter M to execute M-Edit from the Shell menu. If, after starting Shell and entering WordPerfect by pressing W, you pressed SHFT+ALT+M, M-Edit would be executed. Pressing SHFT+ALT+W instantly returns you to WordPerfect. You can now shift back and forth between the two programs as needed.

This ability is tremendously useful for debugging a complex macro. Using Shell, you can quickly switch to a macro editing environment to modify the steps of a macro (M-Edit) and then switch to an environment to try out the macro (WordPerfect).

You can also execute any of Shell's numbered commands from within a Shell-aware application. For example, typing 1 from the Shell menu invokes the "Go to DOS" command, which allows you to use DOS temporarily while keeping all resident programs in memory. To go directly to DOS from within a Shell-aware program, press SHFT+ALT and type **1**. Type **exit** and press ENTER to return to the Shell menu, and then type the appropriate letter to reenter your application.

Shell's Clipboard

Shell's clipboard is a temporary buffer, very much like the buffer that holds deletions for WordPerfect's Undelete command or blocks for WordPerfect's Block Move and Copy commands. The difference is that the clipboard is maintained throughout the Shell environment, which means that any Shell-aware program can read from and write to the clipboard. This makes transfer of data among Shell-aware products very straightforward.

For example, you might want to incorporate some sales figures from a spreadsheet into a word processing document. To do this, you first mark as a block sales figures you have entered in MathPlan, a spreadsheet program from WordPerfect Corporation. Then use the <Shell> key (CTRL+F1) to save the cells to the clipboard and the "Go to Shell" command to return to the Shell menu. Next, choose WordPerfect from the Shell menu. From within WordPerfect, use the "Retrieve from Clipboard" command (also invoked via the CTRL+F1 key sequence). The sales figures are then inserted at the cursor position in your document.

To a limited extent, you can also use the clipboard with programs that are not Shell-aware. As part of the setup procedure, you can specify a "clipboard file name" when adding items to the Shell menu. Each time you exit a Shell-unaware program and return to the Shell menu, the file you specify will be retrieved and placed in the clipboard. It would therefore be up to the application you are running to create a file with the specified name containing text to be placed in the clipboard.

Using WordPerfect With Shell

When using WordPerfect with Shell, you can define a WordPerfect macro (such as ALT+Q) to perform the Go to Shell function. You can then quickly return to the Shell menu with just a few keystrokes. Note that WordPerfect macros are suspended while you are in Shell. When you return to WordPerfect, they pick up where they left off. (To create macros that continue operation within Shell—as well as within other Shell-aware programs—see the section "Shell Macros" that follows.)

When adding items to the Shell menu, you can specify a series of startup options that you would usually type after the name of the program when it is executed. For example, you could include here the /r option that causes WordPerfect to be loaded completely into memory (see Appendix A, "Installation").

When entering startup options, you can indicate that you want Shell to pause before starting a program to prompt you for one or more of the options. Use the following format to have the program prompt for a startup option:

```
?"prompt string"
```

where *prompt string* is what you want appearing at the bottom of the screen when you start the program. Here is an example of a startup options entry that pauses once for a file name and then again for a macro name:

```
?"Filename: " /m=?"Macro: "
```

The /m option tells WordPerfect to execute the specified macro after the program has been loaded.

Shell Macros

Shell has a macro function that is nearly identical to WordPerfect's macro function. Shell's macros, however, can be used with more than one program. In this way, you can use Shell macros to automate steps necessary for integrating various Shell-aware programs.

Starting Macro Definition

You can define a Shell macro anytime Shell is *active* (that is, you start Shell first and then select an application from the Shell menu). With Shell macros, you start the definition process by pressing SHFT+CTRL+F10 (instead of CTRL+F10 as with WordPerfect). The message "Define Shell macro:" will appear at the bottom of the screen.

There are two ways you can name Shell macros: by typing a macro name from 1 to 8 characters and pressing ENTER, or by pressing ALT+SHFT and any single letter. (You cannot define a temporary Shell macro by pressing ENTER by itself, as you can with WordPerfect.) Note that once you name a Shell macro with ALT+SHFT and a letter, you can no longer switch to a program that is designated by that letter on the Shell menu (as described in "Shell's Hot Keys").

After you enter a macro name, the message "∗ Starting Shell macro ∗" will appear momentarily at the bottom of the screen. You can now enter the steps of the Shell macro exactly as with a WordPerfect macro. All the steps that you enter in Shell or any of the Shell-aware programs (as well as DOS) are recorded in the macro.

Pause for Input

You can enter a Pause for Input into a Shell macro exactly as with a WordPerfect macro, except that the function is initiated with SHFT+CTRL+PGUP instead of with CTRL+PGUP. When you press the Pause for Input key sequence during macro definition, the message "∗ User input started ∗" appears. You then type an example of the user input and press ENTER to end the function, or just press ENTER if no example is needed. (See Chapter 2, "Macros," for a description of the Pause for Input function.)

You cannot enter a Timed Pause into a Shell macro, nor can you control Macro Visibility or Keystroke Delay — Shell macros are always visible. Unlike WordPerfect macros, however, you can have a Shell macro display a message and then wait for you to press any key. Use M-Edit to insert this function into a Shell macro.

Ending Macro Definition

When you are finished entering the steps of the Shell macro, press the SHFT+CTRL+F10 sequence a second time. The message "∗ Shell macro ended ∗" will appear at the bottom of the screen, and the macro will be stored on disk with the name you specified. If you named the macro with an ALT+SHFT key sequence, it will be stored on disk as ALTSHFT, the single letter you pressed, and the .SHM extension. For example, a macro named with ALT+SHFT+Q would be saved on disk (in the directory where the Shell program files are located) as ALTSHFTQ.SHM.

Executing Shell Macros

To execute a Shell macro named with ALT+SHFT, press that key sequence and the letter you used to name it. To execute a Shell macro with a longer name, press SHFT+ALT+F10, type the name of the macro, and press ENTER.

In general, all of the Shell macro key sequences are the same as WordPerfect macro key sequences only used in conjunction with the SHFT key. Table D-1 summarizes these key sequences.

Key Sequence	Purpose
SHFT+CTRL+F10	Define Shell macro
ALT+SHFT+F10	Invoke Longer Name Shell macro
ALT+SHFT+(letter)	Invoke Shell macro named with ALT+SHFT and (letter)
SHFT+CTRL+PGUP	Insert a Pause for Input into a Shell macro

Table D-1.   Shell Macro Key Sequences

M-EDIT

M-Edit is a program that allows you to edit macros created by any of WordPerfect Corporation's programs. The keystrokes in the macro are represented on screen by full word descriptions of each key, enclosed in brackets (similar to the style used in this book). You can also add comments to the macro steps to remind you of their purpose.

M-Edit, like most WordPerfect Corporation products, operates very much like WordPerfect. Most of the cursor controls are the same, and all WordPerfect functions duplicated in M-Edit are invoked with the same key sequences used in WordPerfect. Some examples are the <List Files> key (F5), the <Exit> key (F7), and the <Search> key (F2). This common user interface makes it easy to switch from one program to another.

As mentioned in the earlier section "Shell's Hot Keys," the most convenient way to use M-Edit with other WordPerfect Corporation programs like WordPerfect is with Shell. This way, you can quickly switch between editing a macro in M-Edit and trying it out in the application.

M-Edit Environments

When you retrieve a macro into M-Edit, the program looks at the macro's extension to determine which WordPerfect Corporation program created it. It then switches to the appropriate environment for that application. For example, WordPerfect macros end with .MAC. Therefore, when you retrieve a macro that ends with .MAC, M-Edit will know that it was created in WordPerfect. Shell macros end with .SHM. Look in the M-Edit manual for a list of macro extensions from other WordPerfect Corporation programs.

Once you retrieve a macro into M-Edit and the program has sensed its origin, the appropriate three-letter code (indicating the current macro environment) will appear in the lower left-hand corner of the screen. If you wish to *create* a macro in a particular environment, you can press the <Interpret> key (CTRL+F5) and choose an environment from a list at the bottom of the screen.

Knowing the appropriate environment allows M-Edit to *interpret* the codes in the macro file so that it can display on the screen the correct key names for the various functions. Since the WordPerfect Corporation programs differ from each other in the way they store keystrokes in a macro, as well as in the functions some of the keys perform, it is important for M-Edit to know which application created (or will be using) the macro.

Inserting Functions

When you edit a macro in M-Edit, pressing a function or cursor control key performs an editing function, as in WordPerfect. In M-Edit, however, you can also choose to insert *codes* into a macro that *represent* the functions for the current macro environment by turning on Functions mode. This allows you to add functions to an existing macro or to create a complete macro from scratch.

To turn on Functions mode, press the <Functions> key (CTRL+F10); the message "Functions" will appear at the bottom of the screen.

Let's say that you are currently editing a WordPerfect macro ("MAC" appears at the lower left-hand corner of the screen) and that you have turned on the Functions mode. If you were to press the F5 key, the string "<List Files>" would be inserted into the macro at the cursor location, since this is the function that pressing the F5 key would perform in WordPerfect. If you pressed BACKSPACE, the string "<Backspace>" would be inserted. All of these keystrokes would become steps in the macro you are editing.

To turn off Functions mode (to resume normal M-Edit functions), press the <Functions> key again. If you are editing a Shell macro, you will be given the opportunity to insert a Pause or User Input code into the macro instead of turning off Functions mode.

To use M-Edit to insert one of the Pause/Delay functions into a WordPerfect macro (as described in the section "The Pause That Refreshes" in Chapter 2, "Macros"), you must first be in Functions mode. Then press the WordPerfect <Pause> key (CTRL+PGUP). The message "Key:" will appear at the bottom of the screen. If you press ENTER, you will create a Pause for Input, and the string "<Pause>" will appear in the macro at the cursor location. If you type a number (for tenths of a second) and press ENTER, you will create a Keystroke Delay (which also affects Macro Visibility and can be used to create a Timed Pause). The string "<Delay *n*>" will appear in the macro at the cursor location (where *n* is the number you entered).

Macro Comments

Every good programmer knows that programs should be self-documenting whenever possible. That is, each step of the program should be accompanied by a text description that explains its purpose. With M-Edit, you can add such comments to your macros.

The advantage of adding comments to your macros is twofold. First, it is not typically a simple task to look at a macro you created sometime earlier and decipher the *intent* of the various steps. If you want to modify the macro in any way, however, you will need to know what you were thinking when you created the macro in the first place. By adding a comment to each step, you can remind yourself of what the macro is actually doing at each step.

Second, adding comments to a macro makes it more readable and understandable to others. If you think *you* might have problems understanding what your intent was when you created a macro, you can imagine the difficulties *someone else* would have if he or she had to infer your intentions from the macro listing.

Figure D-1 shows the macro STRIP.MAC from Chapter 10, "Macro Library," as seen on the screen in M-Edit, with comments added for each

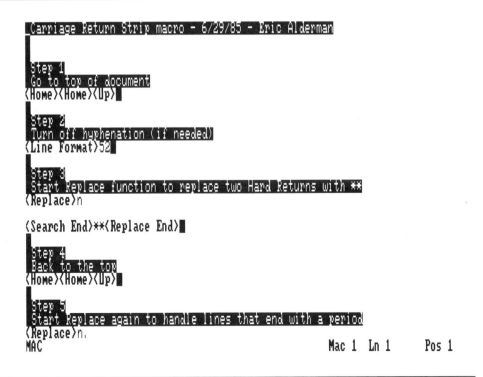

Figure D-1. Macro with comments—STRIP.MAC

step. You can add a comment anywhere within a macro, even in the middle of a line. However, generally it is best to place a comment on its own line since this gives you more room. (Comments can be only one line long so you may need to insert several comments for long descriptions.)

To insert a comment into a macro, first move the cursor to the location in your macro where you want the comment to appear. Then press the <Comment> key (SHFT+F1); a *comment marker* (a small square) will be placed at the cursor location. Type the comment. Notice that a Hard Return has been inserted after the cursor, ensuring that any macro keystrokes after the comment will begin on the next line. Do *not* press ENTER after you type the comment since this would insert an additional, unwanted Hard Return in your macro. When you are finished, simply reposition the cursor using the cursor control keys.

Everything that appears on the comment line *after* the comment marker will be ignored by the application when the macro is later executed, including the Hard Return at the end of the line. Therefore, you can use the Comment function to insert blank lines in a macro listing to make it more readable. Simply press the <Comment> key where you want the blank line to appear, without typing additional text. You can also use the Comment function to break a line of text and commands into several smaller, more logical lines.

The Wrap Function

The Wrap function searches through the steps of a macro and inserts comment markers in lines that extend beyond the right edge of the screen. This breaks the line at the location of the comment marker. If you like, you can also have the function ask for confirmation before it breaks the line. Before confirming, you will also have the opportunity to alter the wrap location.

To initiate the Wrap function, first move the cursor above the macro steps you want to wrap. Then press the <Wrap> key (CTRL+F2). The program will ask you "Wrap With Confirm?" Type **y** if you want the program to confirm each wrap location, or type **n** if you do not. If you type **y**, the program will move the cursor to the first location in the macro where it thinks a line should be wrapped; it will also insert a comment marker. The message "Wrap Here?" appears at the bottom of the screen. At this point, you can use the LEFT ARROW and RIGHT ARROW keys to reposition the comment marker to an appropriate location. When you are satisfied with the position of the comment marker, type **y**, and the function will continue with the next line to be wrapped.

NOTEBOOK

Notebook allows you to manage WordPerfect secondary merge files easily (see the section "Secondary Merge Files" in Chapter 3, "Merge"). With Notebook, you can view records from your secondary merge file either in a row-and-column format (as in a spreadsheet program) or in a record layout, where you can use a custom-designed screen to view each record (as in a database program).

A secondary merge file saved from Notebook can be used immediately by WordPerfect in a merge operation, without prior translation. Notebook inserts a header record containing special information, such as the record layout, field sizes, and field names. During the merge operation, this header record is ignored. A section in Chapter 8, "Integration With Other Products," describes this header record and how to edit it with WordPerfect.

The Dial Function

One nice feature of Notebook is its ability to dial phone numbers using a telephone modem and data from a secondary merge file. To use this feature, first configure Notebook for dialing by telling it which field in the merge file contains the phone number.

To do this, first retrieve the file into Notebook. Then press the <Setup> key (SHFT+F8) and type **3** for "Dialing." The Telephone Dialing Instructions screen will appear, as shown in Figure D-2.

You can configure the sequences shown on the screen for common dialing sequences that you may need. For example, you may have to dial a long distance access number and then an account number before dialing the actual phone number, or you may have to dial a number to get an outside line. To change one of the sequences, first press its letter; then type the sequence and press ENTER. (For details on sequence contents, see the WordPerfect Library manual.)

To tell Notebook which field contains a phone number, use the UP ARROW and DOWN ARROW keys to scroll through the fields in your file until the correct field name appears (the field name will appear next to

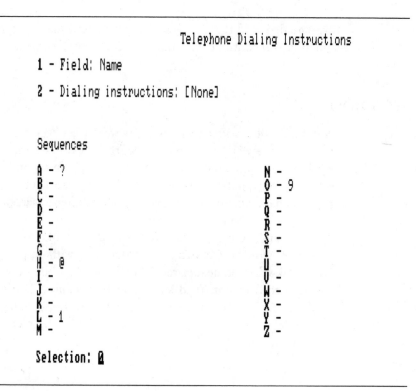

Figure D-2.   Telephone Dialing Instructions screen

"1 - Field:" at the top of the screen). Then type **2** for "Dialing Instructions." If you need to use one or more of the sequences, type the appropriate letter(s). (If you want the program to prompt you for a sequence letter before dialing each number, type **?**.) Then type **@** (which indicates the phone number field contents) and press ENTER. You have now specified appropriate dialing instructions for this field. You can repeat the process for other phone number fields in your file. When you are finished, press the <Exit> key (F7).

To call someone, you first highlight the person's record on screen, and then you press the <Dial> key (F4). If you configured more than one field with dialing instructions, the program will prompt you to point to the correct field. When you have done so, press ENTER. You will hear the dial tone through the modem's speaker, and the number being dialed. When you hear someone answer the phone, you pick up the handset and strike any key to disengage the modem.

E OFFICE AND LEGAL FEATURES

WordPerfect has several functions that are intended for use in general office environments, and some intended specifically for use in a law office. These are

- Document Summary

- Comments

- Line Numbering

- Table of Authorities generation.

The first three features can be used in any type of office environment. The Document Summary function allows you to specify some summary information about each document, such as the author, typist, and a general description of the document. The Comments function allows you to insert comments in the body of your text that will not print, and will not affect the layout of your document. The Line Numbering function will place line numbers along the left edge of the paper when the document is printed. It is useful both for legal documents which must be printed in this format, and for any document where line numbers would provide a useful reference to the material, such as for a draft.

The Table of Authorities function is designed specifically for use in the law office. It provides the ability to compile up to 16 separate collections of authorities that are marked in the text.

This appendix will discuss each of these features.

DOCUMENT SUMMARY AND COMMENTS

WordPerfect has the ability to place both a document summary and comments into the body of your text. These do not appear when you print the document; they only appear on the screen. If you wish, you can choose to suppress the display of one or both on the screen as well. This is useful when you want to edit the document without the distractions of the summary or comments. In this case, the only way you will know these features have been used in a document is by using the Reveal Codes function.

Document Summary

You can use the Document Summary function in two ways. You can choose which documents should have a Document Summary, and then manually insert one into each. Or you can choose to have WordPerfect automatically prompt you for the Document Summary information the first time any file is saved. In either case, you will be able to edit the document summary information at any time.

Automatic Operation

To invoke the automatic feature of the Document Summary function, you first need to get to the Setup menu (see "Using the Setup Menu" in Appendix A). Then, type **2** for "Set Initial Settings," press the <Text In/Out> key (CTRL+F5), and type **Y** at the prompt "Enter Document Summary on Save/Exit?" Press ENTER to return to the Set-up menu, and type **0** to enter WordPerfect. From that point on, each time you press the <Save> key, or press the <Exit> key and type **Y** for "Save Document?", the Document Summary screen will automatically appear.

Manual Operation

To manually insert Document Summary information, the cursor can be positioned anywhere within the document. Press the <Text In/Out> key (CTRL+F5), and type **A** for "Create/Edit Summary". The Document Summary screen will appear.

Document Summary Contents

If you have previously named the current document (that is, you retrieved a file, or you created a file and subsequently saved it), its filename along with its full pathname appears as the first entry on the Document Summary screen. This information is not actually stored with the Document Summary in the document. For example, if the file is copied to another directory on your hard disk, or saved with a different name, the information on the Document Summary screen will change appropriately.

The second item on the Document Summary screen is Date of Creation. This date is automatically inserted for you, based on the current date stored in the computer's memory. In order for this to be accurate, you must be sure the date is correctly set whenever you start your computer.

The next items on the screen are the names of the Author and the Typist of the document. These items are commonly used in an office environment where the person entering the document is typically not the same person who wrote the text. Type the name of the author of the document and press ENTER, then type the name of the typist and press ENTER. You can enter up to 40 characters in each of these fields.

The last item on the screen is a box for any comments about the document. This is a useful way to remind yourself about the contents of a file. For example, you may have several versions of the same document. While these might be difficult to tell apart by simply scrolling through them, the Document Summary could be used to describe the differences.

As you enter Comment text, the words will automatically wrap to the next line when you reach the end of each line. You can use the ENTER key to end a line, or to make blank lines, and you can use most of WordPerfect's cursor controls. You can also use bold and underline to spruce up the text. You can enter up to 880 characters of Comments text.

When you are finished entering Comments, press the <Exit> key (F7). You will be returned to the document, and a [Smry/Cmnt] hidden code will be inserted at the beginning of the document. (You may notice a delay before the screen appears. This is because WordPerfect must position itself at the beginning of the document, insert the hidden code, and then reposition back to where you were when you entered the Document Summary.)

If you have set WordPerfect to display the Document Summary on screen (see the next section), you can position the cursor at the beginning of the document and you will see the Document Summary information you entered surrounded by a double-line box.

Displaying and Hiding Document Summary and Comments

You can choose whether or not the Document Summary box will be visible on the screen. To do this, press the <Text In/Out> key (CTRL+F5), type **D** for "Display Summary and Comments," and then type **Y** to display the Summary, or type **N** to hide the Summary. You will then be asked whether WordPerfect should display Comments. Type **Y** to display Comments, or type **N** to hide them.

The Document Summary Hidden Code

The [Smry/Cmnt] code that is generated when you exit the Document Summary screen is placed at the very beginning of the current document. The code must remain in this location—in other words, you should be careful not to insert any text in front of the Summary code. You can, however, insert formatting codes before the Summary code.

The cursor control key sequence HOME, HOME, UP ARROW will position the cursor in front of the Summary code, making it easier to accidentally insert text before it. If this happens, WordPerfect will not recognize the Summary, and will not allow you to edit its contents. Simply delete any inserted text in front of the code (or be sure the code is at the beginning of the document using any other method) and WordPerfect will again recognize the code.

Only the first 100 characters of the Document Summary information appear within the code on the Reveal Codes screen.

One of the most useful aspects of the Document Summary function is that it can help you when you're looking for a particular document. When you use the Look function from the List Files display, the full contents of the summary information are displayed at the top of the document.

Editing the Document Summary

To edit the contents of the Document Summary, press the <Text In/Out> key, and type **A** for "Create/Edit Summary." The previously created Summary will appear on the screen. Enter the appropriate number of the section you wish to edit. Press the <Exit> key when you are finished editing.

Comments

The Comments function is closely related to the Document Summary function. With it, you can place nonprinting comments anywhere in a document, even in the middle of a line. A comment can be useful to remind yourself to rewrite some text, or to mark the location of a sequence of hidden codes.

Inserting Comments

To insert a comment into the text, position the cursor where you want the comment to appear. Then, press the <Text In/Out> key (CTRL+F5), type **B** for "Create Comment," and type the text of the comment. When you reach the end of a line, the text will automatically wrap to the next line. Use the ENTER key to end a line, or generate blank lines. You can use most of WordPerfect's cursor controls, as well as bold and underline. You can enter up to 1024 characters in a single comment. When you are finished entering text, press the <Exit> key (F7). A [Smry/Cmnt] hidden code will be inserted in your text.

If you have set WordPerfect to display Comments (see the section "Displaying and Hiding Document Summary and Comments" presented earlier in this appendix), the comment text you entered will appear at the cursor position, surrounded by a double-line box. If you inserted the comment when the cursor was in the middle of a line, you will notice that the cursor is now located in the correct column, underneath the comment. Although the Comment breaks up the text on the line, Word-Perfect keeps track of the column and line position, and simply picks up where it left off after the comment. You can continue to use the RIGHT ARROW and LEFT ARROW keys, as well as the <Word Right> and <Word Left> keys to position the cursor on the line.

Editing Comments

To edit the contents of a comment, position the cursor anywhere after the comment you wish to edit, press the <Text In/Out> key, and type **C** for "Edit Comment." The Comment text will appear on the screen. Edit the text and press the <Exit> key when you are finished. Your cursor will be positioned directly after the Comment you edited.

If there is no comment before the cursor when you issue the Edit Comment command, you will edit the first comment in the document. If there are no comments in the document, WordPerfect will respond "* Not Found *."

To display or hide comments in your document, refer to the section entitled "Displaying and Hiding Document Summary and Contents" presented earlier in this appendix.

LINE NUMBERING

WordPerfect has a function that will place line numbers along the left edge of the text when a document is printed. This is a common need for many legal documents. In addition, it is a useful feature anytime you want to number the lines in a document. For example, if a document is being reviewed by several people, or is being edited on paper by one person and on screen by another, line numbers provide an easy way to locate specific text.

Using Line Numbering

First, position the cursor at the place in your document where you want line numbering to begin. Be sure the cursor is at the beginning of a line—otherwise, line numbering will begin with the following line. Press the <Print Format> key (CTRL+F8) and type **B** for "Line Numbering." You will see the Line Numbering screen. Type **2** to turn on line numbering. Before returning to the document, you can also change any of the other parameters on this screen from their initial values.

One option is whether or not WordPerfect will include blank lines when counting the lines in the document. Another is the increment with which the program will place the numbers. For example, a common incremental setting of 5 would cause WordPerfect to place a number every five lines.

You can also specify how far from the left edge of the paper the line numbers should appear. You specify this in increments of 1/10 of an inch, or number of characters at 10 pitch—just as with the Binding Width function. The initial value for this is 6/10 of an inch, or six 10-pitch characters.

Lastly, you can specify whether or not line numbering should restart at the beginning of each page. If you choose not to, line numbering will continue through the entire numbered area. You may need to adjust the position of the line numbers to allow enough room for larger numbers.

When you are finished changing the parameters, press the <Exit> key to return to the Print Format menu, and then the <Exit> key again to return to the document. A [LnNum:On] hidden code will be inserted into the text at the cursor position.

You can use the Print Preview function (see Chapter 1, "Basics Refresher") to see how the line numbers will appear when the document is printed.

Text within footnotes and endnotes are included in the line numbering, but not text within headers and footers.

Ending Line Numbering

If you want line numbering to end before the end of the document, first position the cursor at the place where you want numbering to end. Be sure you position the cursor at the beginning of a line—otherwise, line numbering will end on the following line. Press the <Print Format> key (CTRL+F5), type **B** for "Line Numbering," and type **1** to turn off line numbering. Press the <Exit> key twice to return to the document. A [LnNum:Off] hidden code will be inserted in the text.

TABLE OF AUTHORITIES

The Table of Authorities function allows you to compile up to 16 separate tables of cases and other authorities cited in a legal brief. For example, you might want to maintain one table for cases, another for legislative material, and another for statutes. You can specify a different format for each table.

The three steps to compiling a table of authorities are

- Mark the authorities
- Define and position the table
- Generate the table.

Marking Authorities

There are two distinctly different methods for marking an authority in the text. The first is for marking the first occurrence of an authority and the second is for marking subsequent occurrences. When you mark the first occurrence, you enter the text of the authority exactly as you want it to look in the finished table, and you give the authority a *short form*, or nickname. Then, you use the short form to mark subsequent occurrences of the authority.

Marking the Full Text of an Authority

To mark the full text of an authority, first mark the authority as a block. The text of the authority may appear in the body of the text, or in a footnote. Then, press the <Mark Text> key (ALT+F5) and type **6** for "ToA." Type the section number in which the authority should appear, and press ENTER. For example, if this authority is a statute, and your table of statutes corresponds to Section 2, type **2** and press ENTER. The Table of Authorities Full Form screen will appear.

At the top of the screen, you will see the text of the authority you marked as a block. Edit the authority to look exactly as you want it to appear when the table is actually compiled, by adding or deleting text as necessary. You can use many of WordPerfect's cursor controls, and you can shorten lines or add blank lines by pressing ENTER. You can also embellish the text with the bold or underline functions, or by inserting Font codes. The text can be up to 30 lines long. When you are finished editing the text, press the <Exit> key (F7).

If the full text of the authority will not closely resemble any text in the document, you can choose to start with a blank screen when entering the Full Form. To do this, simply position the cursor at the place in the document where the authority should be referenced, press the <Block> key, the <Mark Text> key, and then proceed as previously explained. When you see the blank Full Form screen, type the full form of the authority, and then press the <Exit> key.

After you have entered the text for the full form, you will see the prompt "Enter Short Form:" at the bottom of the screen. WordPerfect suggests the first 40 characters of the full form. You can either accept the suggested short form by pressing ENTER, type a new short form and press ENTER, or edit the existing short form using the cursor control keys and press ENTER. The short form will be used to mark subsequent occurrences of the same authority. It should be short enough to be easily typed, yet long and unique enough to describe the authority. Typically, the first word or two of the full form makes an appropriate short form.

After you have entered a short form for the authority, you are returned to the document. A [ToA:n] hidden code is placed in the text at the cursor position, where n is the section number you specified.

Using the Short Form

For subsequent occurrences of the same authority, you use the short form you specified when you marked the first occurrence. To do this, first position the cursor near the authority you wish to mark. Then, press the <Mark Text> key (ALT+F5), and type **4** for "Short Form." WordPerfect suggests the most recently entered short form name. If this is the correct short form, you can simply press ENTER. Otherwise, type a new short form or edit the suggested one, and press ENTER.

WordPerfect will not check to make sure that you have entered a valid short form name at this time. When the table is compiled, short forms that were not matched with a full form will appear with a leading asterisk. If this happens, you should go to the indicated page and search for the [ToA] code using Reveal Codes. Delete the code, and enter another with an accurate short form.

A short form hidden code can appear before its full form. This might happen, for example, if you move text around in your document. When the table is compiled, WordPerfect will sort through all of the short forms and full forms, regardless of their respective positions in the document.

Editing the Full Form

To edit the text of a full form you have entered, or to change its section number, first position the cursor directly after the full form hidden code that you wish to edit. You may want to use Reveal Codes to help you with this. You can also use the Search function to locate the [ToA] hidden codes. (If there is no full form hidden code before the cursor position when you give the command to edit the reference, the first one in the document will be used instead.)

Press the <Mark Text> key (ALT+F5), type **6** for "Other Options," and type **7** for "Edit Table of Authorities Full Form." The Table of Authorities Full Form screen will appear, with the text of the appropriate authority. Edit the text as desired, and press the <Exit> key. You will be prompted for a section number for the full form, and WordPerfect will be suggesting the reference's previously entered section number. Press ENTER to leave the section number unchanged, or type a new section number and press ENTER.

Defining and Positioning The Table

The next step is to define and position the table in the document. First, position the cursor at the place in the document where you want the table to appear, normally at the top of the document. You may want to type any heading information that you want to appear before the table when it is generated. For example, if this will be a Table of Cases Cited, you may want to type that title, centered and bolded, and then press ENTER several times to leave some blank space.

When you are ready to position and define the table, press the <Mark Text> key (ALT+F5), type **6** for "Other Options," and type **4** for "Define Table of Authorities." Type the section number you wish to define, and press ENTER. The Table of Authorities definition screen will appear. At this point, you can type an appropriate number to change one of the settings, and then type **Y** if you want the option, or type **N** if you do not.

The first option is whether or not you wish to have dot leaders inserted before the page references, or whether they should be flush right without dot leaders. The second option is whether to allow underlining in the compiled table. Often you will use underlining in an authority in the body of your text, but you do not want it to appear in the finished table. When you type **N** for this option, WordPerfect will automatically delete all underlining codes from the table. The last option is whether or not the authorities in the table will be separated by a blank line.

You can change any of the options, or simply leave them all at their initial settings. (You can change these initial settings at the Change Initial Settings screen. See the section "Using the Setup Menu" in Appendix A, "Installation.") When you are finished changing the options, press the <Exit> key. A [DefMark:ToA] hidden code will be inserted in the text at the cursor position.

After you have defined the format and position of the table, you may want to enter a Hard Page Break so that subsequent text will begin on a new page. Also, you should enter a New Page Number code on the first page of actual text, so that the page numbers that appear in the table are accurate.

Generating the Table of Authorities

When you are ready to generate your tables of authority, press the <Mark Text> key (ALT+F5), type **6** for "Other Options," and type **8** for "Generate Tables and Index." (Your cursor can be positioned anywhere in the document.) WordPerfect displays a reminder that the generation process will replace any previously generated tables. If you want to retain these tables, type **N** and the generation process will be aborted. Otherwise, type **Y** to proceed with the generation.

During the generation, a counter at the bottom of the screen indicates WordPerfect's progress. This counter, however, has no known relevance to anything within the document. A message may appear that indicates you do not have sufficient memory to complete the generation. If this happens, clear the screen in Document 2, and try to generate again.

When generation is complete, you will be returned to the document, and the new Table of Authorities will appear in the location where you placed the definition code.

F WORDPERFECT RESOURCES

CONTACTING WORDPERFECT CORPORATION

You can use several phone numbers to contact WordPerfect Corporation. To receive technical support, you can call (800) 321-5906. Since toll-free lines tend to be busy and cannot be used outside of the U.S., the company also maintains a non-toll-free phone number, which is (801) 226-6800. Support is available from 7:00 a.m. to 6:00 p.m. Mountain Standard Time, Monday through Friday, and 8:00 a.m. to 12:00 p.m. on Saturday.

To get information about updates to WordPerfect, information about any current or future WordPerfect Corporation product, or for any other questions, call Information Services at (801) 225-5000. This office is open from 7:30 a.m. to 5:30 p.m. Mountain Standard Time, Monday through Friday.

The company's address is

WordPerfect Corporation
288 West Center Street
Orem, Utah 84057

Be sure to specify the department you wish to address, such as Technical Support.

THE WORDPERFECT SUPPORT GROUP

The WordPerfect Support Group is an independent organization that provides support for WordPerfect Corporation products. With more than 10,000 members, it is the largest WordPerfect-oriented user group in the country. The group's newsletter, "The WordPerfectionist," contains tips, tricks, and articles that discuss various topics relating to the use of WordPerfect. You can contact the group by writing to

The WordPerfect Support Group
P.O. Box 1577
Baltimore, MD 21203

TRADEMARKS

dBASE III®	Ashton-Tate
DESQview™	Quarterdeck Office Systems
IBM®	International Business Machines Corporation
Keyworks™	Alpha Software Corporation
Lotus®	Lotus Development Corporation
MultiMate®	Multimate International
1-2-3®	Lotus Development Corporation
PC-Talk®	Headlands Press, Inc.
ProKey™	RoseSoft, Inc.
RoseSoft™	RoseSoft, Inc.
SideKick®	Borland International, Inc.
System 55®	Systems Integrators, Inc.
VisiCalc®	VisiCorp
WordPerfect®	WordPerfect Corporation (formerly Satellite Software International)
WordStar®	MicroPro International Corporation

Corvus Omninet®	Corvus Systems Inc.
dBASE®	Ashton-Tate
dBASE II®	Ashton-Tate
dBASE III® PLUS™	Ashton-Tate
Jazz™	Lotus Development Corporation
MS-DOS®	Microsoft Corp.

INDEX

< Search >	F2
↓ Search >	SHFT+F2
← Indent >	F4
← ↑ Indent ↓ >	SHFT+F4
Block>	ALT+F4
Bold>	F6
Cancel/Undelete>	F1
Center>	SHFT+F6
Date>	SHFT+F5
Exit>	F7
Flush Right>	ALT+F6
Footnote>	CTRL+F7
Help>	F3
Line Format>	SHFT+F8
List Files>	F5
Macro Def>	CTRL+F10
Macro>	ALT+F10
Mark Text>	ALT+F5
Math/Columns>	ALT+F7
Merge Codes>	ALT+F9
Merge End-of-Field>	F9
Merge End-of-Record>	SHFT+F9
Merge/Sort>	CTRL+F9
Move>	CTRL+F4
Page Format>	ALT+F8
Print>	SHFT+F7
Replace>	ALT+F2
Retrieve Text>	SHFT+F10
Reveal Codes>	ALT+F3
Save Text>	F10
Screen>	CTRL+F3
Shell>	CTRL+F1
Spell>	CTRL+F2
Super/Subscript>	SHFT+F1
Switch>	SHFT+F3
Text In/Out>	CTRL+F5
Thesaurus>	ALT+F1
Underline>	F8

Macro Controls

Pause

CTRL+PGUP, ENTER *example text* ENTER

example text is optional

Macro Visiblity

CTRL+PGUP *n* ENTER

(where *n* = 0- to 255-tenths-of-a-second delay between keystrokes)

0 = Top speed visibility

10 = 1-second delay

255 = Invisible

Timed Pause

CTRL+PGUP *n* ENTER

(where *n* = tenths of a second to pause)

CTRL+PGUP 0 ENTER

(to return to top speed)

Merge Code Summary

^C	Request input from Console (keyboard).
^D	Insert Date.
^E	Mark the End of a record in a secondary file.
^Fn^	Merge Field n from the secondary file into the current primary file at the position of the code.
^Gmacroname^G	Goto (start) a macro from within a merge. The macro will begin after the merge is completed.
^N	Use the Next record in the secondary file.
^Omessage^O	Output a message to the screen.
^Pfilename^P	Change to a new Primary file.
^Q	Quit the merge.

Merge Code Summary *(continued)*

^R	Mark the Return (end) of a field in a secondary file.
^Sfilename^S	Change to a new Secondary file.
^T	Type (print) and delete the text merged to that point.
^U	Update (rewrite) the screen wherever it is encountered in the merge.
^Vmerge code^V	Inserts the merge code(s) into the merged document without executing them. These codes can then be used for a dual merge.

Merge Code Sequences

Suppress page break *(for reports)*

^N^P^P

Merge to the Printer

^T^N^P^P

Prompt for input

^OEnter client's name^O^C

Prompt for macro name

^OEnter name of macro to execute: ^G^C^G^O

WordPerfect Startup Options

WP	No action
WP/B-*n*	Backup every *n* minutes
WP/D-*path*	Store temporary files in *path*
WP *filename*	Load *filename* after starting WP
WP/I	Install WP with current path
WP/M-*macroname*	Execute *macroname* after starting WP
WP/NF	Non-flash—used with some windowing programs
WP/NS	Non-Sync—used with Hyperion computers
WP/R	Load all of WP into RAM
WP/S	Bring up WP Setup menu

All options can be combined except /S.

Advanced WordPerfect®: Features & Techniques

The following is a list of all the WordPerfect codes that may appear on the Reveal Codes screen ("n" represents numbers that may appear in the code).

Code	Description
[^/(blinking)]	Cursor Position
[ ]	Hard Space
[-]	Hyphen
- (blinking)	Soft Hyphen
/ (blinking)	Cancel Hyphenation
[A][a]	Tab Align or Flush Right (begin and end)
[Adv ▲]	Advance Up 1/2 Line
[Adv ▼]	Advance Down 1/2 Line
[AdvLn:n]	Advance to Specific Line Number
[Align Char:]	Alignment Character
[B][b]	Bold (begin and end)
[Bin#:n]	Sheet Feeder Bin Number
[Block]	Beginning of block
[Block]	Beginning of block
[BlockPro:Off]	Block Protection off
[BlockPro:On]	Block Protection on
[C][c]	Centering (begin and end)
[Center Pg]	Center Current Page Top to Bottom
[Cmnd:]	Embedded Printer Command
[CndlEOP:n]	Conditional End of Page (n = number of lines)
[ColDef:]	Column Definition
[ColOff]	End of Text Columns
[ColOn]	Beginning of Text Columns
[Date:n]	Date/Time function (n = format)
[DefMark:Index,n]	Index Definition (n = format)
[DefMark:List,n]	List Definition (n = List Number)
[DefMark:ToA,n]	Table of Authorities Definition (n = section number)
[DefMark:ToC,n]	Table of Contents Definition (n = ToC Level)
[EInd]	End of ▼ Indent or ▼ Indent ▲
[EndDef]	End of Index, List, or Table of Contents
[EndMark:List,n]	End Marked Text (n = List Number)
[EndMark:ToC,n]	End Marked Text (n = ToC Level)
[Font Change:n,n]	Specify New Font or Print Wheel (n = pitch, font)
[FtnOpt]	Footnote/Endnote Options
[Hdr/Ftr:n,n:text]	Header or Footer Definition (n = type, occurrence)
[HPg]	Hard Page
[HRt]	Hard Return
[Hyph on]	Hyphenation on
[Hyph off]	Hyphenation off
[HZone Set:n,n]	Reset Size of Hyphenation Zone (n = left,right)
[▼ Indent]	Beginning of Indent
[▼ Indent ▲]	Beginning of Left/Right Indent
[Index:heading; subheading]	Index mark
[LPI:n]	Lines per Inch
[← Mar Rel:n]	Left Margin Release (n = positons moved)
[Margin Set:n,n]	Left and Right Margin Reset
[Mark:List,n]	Begin Marked Text for List (n = List Number)
[Mark:ToC,n]	Begin Marked Text for ToC (n = ToC Level)
[Math Def]	Definition of Math Columns
[Math Off]	End of Math
[Math On]	Beginning of Math
!(bold)	Formula Calculation
t(bold)	Subtotal Entry
+ (bold)	Do Subtotal
T (bold)	Total Entry
= (bold)	Do Total
*(bold)	Do Grand Total
N(bold)	Negative Entry
[note#][text]	Endnote (n = Endnote Number)
[Note:Foot,n; [note#][text]	Footnote (n = Footnote Number)
[Ovrstk]	Overstrike preceding Character
[Par#:Auto]	Automatic Paragraph/Outline Number
[Par#:n]	Permanent Paragraph Number (n = level number)
[Par# Def]	Paragraph Numbering Definition
[Pg#:n]	New Page Number
[Pg#Col:n,n,n]	Column Position for Page Numbers (n = left, center, right)
[PgLnth:n,n]	Set Page Length (n = form lines, text lines)
[PosPg#:n]	Set Position for Page Numbers
[RedLn][r]	Redline (begin and end)
[Rt Just Off]	Right Justification off
[Rt Just On]	Right Justification on
[Set Ftn#:n]	New Footnote Number
[Smry/Cmnt:text]	Document Summary or Comment
[Spacing Set:n]	Spacing Set
[SPg]	Soft New Page
[SRt]	Soft Return
[StrkOut][s]	Strikeout (begin and end)
[SubScrpt]	Subscript
[SuprScrpt]	Superscript
[Suppress:n]	Supress Page Format Options (n = format(s))
[TAB]	Move to Next Tab Stop
[Tab Set:]	Tab Reset
[ToA:n:text]	Table of Authorities mark (n = section number)
[Top Mar:n]	Set Top Margin in Half-Lines
[U][u]	Underlining (begin and end)
[Undrl Style:n]	Underline Style
[W/O Off]	Widow/Orphan Off
[W/O On]	Widow/Orphan On

IF YOU ENJOYED THIS BOOK...

help us stay in touch with your needs and interests by filling out and returning the survey card below. Your opinions are important, and will help us to continue to publish the kinds of books you need, when you need them.

What brand of computer(s) do you own or use? _____

Where do you use your computer the most? ☐ At work ☐ At school ☐ At home

What topics would you like to see covered in future books by Osborne/McGraw-Hill? _____

How many other computer books do you own? _____

Why did you choose this book?

☐ Best coverage of the subject.
☐ Recognized the author from previous work.
☐ Liked the price.
☐ Other

Where did you hear about this book?

☐ Book review.
☐ Osborne catalog.
☐ Advertisement in: _____
☐ Found by browsing in store.
☐ Found/recommended in library
☐ Other

Where did you find this book?

☐ Bookstore
☐ Computer/software store
☐ Department store
☐ Advertisement
☐ Catalog

☐ Required textbook
☐ Library
☐ Gift
☐ Other

Where should we send your FREE catalog?

NAME _____

ADDRESS _____

271-2 CITY _____ STATE _____ ZIP _____

BUSINESS REPLY MAIL
FIRST CLASS   PERMIT NO. 3111   Berkeley, CA

Postage will be paid by addressee

Osborne **McGraw-Hill**
2600 Tenth Street
Berkeley, California 94710

No Postage
Necessary
If Mailed
in the
United States